Crash Blossoms, Eggcorns, Mondegreens & Mountweazels

101 Terms About Language You Didn't Know You Needed

Mike Pope

Contents

Introduction

You've probably heard someone say "for all intensive purposes" instead of "for all intents and purposes." Or they say "old-timer's disease" instead of "Alzheimer's disease." It turns out there's a name for this type of mistake: these are *eggcorns*.

Maybe you've heard someone say *asterisk* as "asterix." When people swap letters like this (saying *ks* for *sk*), there's a word for that, too: *metathesis*. What's it called when people say "flim-flam" or "fancy-schmancy"? *Reduplication*. Have you ever misheard song lyrics? Those mishearings are *mondegreens*.

I am delighted every time I discover another one of these names for a word thing or language thing. So at some point I started a collection.

Over time I've collected many dozens of these terms, which I share here with you. I can pretty much guarantee that as you read, you'll recognize the language situations that you'll read about. (Consider the examples that I started this introduction with and how they might seem familiar to you.)

What you'll get from this book, then, is a catalog of language terminology: words that people use when they observe language. As the linguist Brianne Hughes says about her own *Encyclopedia Briannica*,[1] what I'm doing here "aims to expand and shift the public language conversation away from apostrophe fights and dictionary gatekeeping to focus on everyday speech acts you already perform and understand but never had a name for."

For me, I've found that learning terms like those in the book has altered my relationship to what I hear and read (and occasionally to what I write or say). Sure, when people say *ATM machine*, that's redundant. But simply having a word for this phenomenon—it's a *pleonasm*—helps me understand that this is a common practice, and I've learned that there are good reasons why people say this. These days, when I encounter some curious language construction, I often wonder "Is there a name for this thing?"

How did I pick these words? The terms here represent a combination of the following criteria:

---

[1] http://www.encyclopediabriannica.com/?page_id=2

- Terms that language people use frequently for language situations: *anthimeria, infixation, rhotic.*
- Whimsical terms that are common in the language community: *eggcorn, snowclone, zombie rule.*
- Words that describe phenomena that made me laugh to learn about: *Scunthorpe problem, squinting modifier.*
- Terms that come up in discussions of language issues in the popular media: *greengrocer's apostrophe, singular they, uptalk.*

I don't have entries for the technical vocabulary of linguistics. You won't find information here that, for example, helps you understand the difference between a *phoneme* and an *allophone*. (For that there are linguistics textbooks.) I do occasionally use some basic language terms, like *syntax* (how sentences are put together), *morphology* (how words are put together), and *phonology* (the sounds of language). Just in case these aren't familiar to you, I included a brief glossary of terms later in this intro.

I think that even if terms like *morphology* are not terms you throw around every day, you won't have trouble understanding anything I've written.

§

This book isn't intended to be a scholarly work, so I didn't add formal bibliographic citations, although I do link to sources when they're available. However, I did my best not to say anything that I can't attribute to someone more knowledgeable than me. I tried particularly hard *not* to pass along myths or folk tales about language, of which there are already far too many.

§

I'm an editor by profession, meaning I do a lot of language policing in my job. However, this is not a usage manual—my goal is not to tell you how to use words, or what words to avoid, or how You're Doing It Wrong.

Even so, you might occasionally find my biases peeking out. I think what you'll find, though, is that such bias as I have is against being uninformed about language.

Terminology

Throughout the book, I use a few terms that you might not be familiar with. Since this isn't the type of book you read from front to back, it doesn't seem useful for me to define the terms on first mention, as per the usual editorial convention. Instead, I'll just list them here. (It does not escape my notice that I'm providing a glossary for a glossary.) Note that I'm trying to keep the definitions simple here, so be aware that linguists would have a lot more to say about each term.

Anglo-Saxon, also known as ***Old English***. This is the ancestor language of modern English. Germanic tribes like the Angles, the Saxons, and the Jutes started invading the British Isles about 450 AD, bringing their dialects with them and settling on land that they took from the existing inhabitants, including the Celtic-speaking Britons. Anglo-Saxon thrived in its new home until French-speaking Normans invaded in 1066 and conquered England. Over the next few centuries, the overlay of French had a profound influence on Anglo-Saxon, which morphed into a different language that we now know as Middle English. Most people can't read texts in Old English or in Middle English; these are effectively foreign languages to us today. Middle English lasted from about 1100 till about 1500, after which it morphed *again* into Modern English starting at about 1500. That's when English became what we'd now recognize—we can read Shakespeare, even if it still seems antiquated. (Obviously, many details are omitted here, and language change is continuous, so the dates are general.) If you'd like a little more detail, Tom Freeman, a.k.a. Stroppy Editor, has what he calls "A ridiculously brief, outrageously selective and painfully simplified history of Standard English" on his blog.[2]

etymology. The origin and history of a word. Some etymologies are pretty clear, like *dugout* or *telescope*. (Well, for the latter you have to know your classical roots.) Others can be less obvious, like the origins of *praline* or *marmalade*. It can be particularly interesting when a word's current usage is quite different from its etymology, as with *broadcast* (originally a technique for sowing seeds) and *silly* (which once meant "blessed").

---

[2] https://stroppyeditor.wordpress.com/2015/02/06/a-ridiculously-brief-outrageously-selective-and-painfully-simplified-history-of-standard-english/

lexicography. The writing of dictionaries, including definitions, pronunciation guides, and etymologies. A *lexicographer* is a person who does this researching and writing.

morpheme, *morphology*. A *morpheme* is an individual word part that contains meaning—for example, the word *doghouses* contains three morphemes: *dog*, *house*, and the *s* suffix to indicate plural. (The word *morpheme* comes from roots that mean "form" + "unit.") *Morphology* is the study of how words are put together. Morphology studies things like how we form the plural of a noun (add *s*, mostly), how we form the past tense of a verb (add *ed*, mostly), and what sorts of endings you can use to make a verb out of a noun (like *ize*).

OED. The *Oxford English Dictionary*, a dictionary whose ambitious aim is to catalog every meaning that every word in the "literature of English" has ever had. The OED has been in the making for over 150 years and basically will never be finished. It's an incredible resource for researching the historical meanings and roots of our vast lexicon. The OED is a historical dictionary, so it wouldn't be your first choice for looking up words like *selfie* or whether *e-book* has a hyphen in it. But if you want to know how the word *nice* was used in the 1300s, the OED is a great resource. Many libraries provide online access to the OED; ask your local librarian.

phonology. The study of language sounds. For example, phonology describes how we form vowels and consonants in our mouths.

semantics. The study of the meaning of words.

syntax. The study of how sentences and their constituent pieces are put together. When you think about "grammar" as you studied it in school, this is probably the closest thing in linguistics.

A note about references, footnotes, and formatting

This book was originally conceived as an e-book, with numerous links to external sources and with links between entries. Those don't work in a print book, obviously, so I've made a couple of adjustments.

For the links to external sources, I've mostly used footnotes. I thought this was preferable to including the URLs inline with the text and to dropping the reference information altogether.

To indicate that a term is covered as an entry in the book, I've marked it by using a contrasting typeface. For example, if you see "The word *nonplussed* is a skunked term," the contrasting typeface for skunked term tells you that there's an entry for that term in the book.

I hope that this approach to references and cross-references and my use of footnotes don't prove distracting to you.

With this preface out of the way, on to the words!

Crash Blossoms, Eggcorns, Mondegreens & Mountweazels

absolute adjective (non-gradable adjective)

One thing about being dead is that it's not really something that you can do halfway. You're either alive or you're dead—you can't be *sort of* dead. (This could be confusing for a funeral director, for example.) That's true also of being pregnant. I mean, either you're pregnant or you're not, right?

These conditions are *absolute*: they don't lend themselves to grades or degrees, like a "a little bit" or "a lot." They're on-or-off, yes-or-no states. As with states, so with adjectives: an *absolute adjective* or *non-gradable adjective* is one that doesn't have a comparative form (*-er* or *more*) or a superlative form (*-est* or *most*). A line you'll never hear on *Star Trek* is "He's deader, Jim."

Strictly speaking, all sorts of adjectives could be considered absolute: *round, square, full, empty, supreme, impossible, favorite, complete, black, white, boiling, freezing, first, last, fatal, infinite, married, perfect.* Can someone run a race and come in firster or laster than someone else? Can one couple be the most married couple? Is there a Supremer Being? Is this disease fataler than that one? (Does one disease make you more dead than the other?)

Not all absolute adjectives describe extreme ends of a scale. For example, the word *okay* doesn't describe an extreme—on the contrary, it's sort of medium-ish. I looked in several dictionaries, but although they all listed the word *okay* as an adjective, none of them listed a comparative form (*okay-er*, with or without a hyphen) or superlative form (*okay-est*).

Compare the opposite of an absolute adjective, namely a *gradable adjective*. For example, the adjective *rich* is plenty gradable—you can be *rich*, or *very rich*, or be *more rich* or *less rich*, or *richer*, or even the *richest*.

Yet we do use absolute adjectives in graded ways. In everyday use, we might say that one glass is fuller than another, even though the Merriam-Webster definition for *full* is "containing as much or as many as is possible or normal." Although the word *complete* means "done," you might nonetheless consider one of the projects you're working on to be more complete than one that you just started. In a mathematical sense, *round* is an absolute condition: a shape is either round or it isn't. But we non-

1

geometricians might still talk about something being *rounder*, with the sense of "more approximately round," than some other thing.

A theoretically absolute adjective that people particularly take note of is *unique*. In a narrow sense, *unique* means "one of a kind"; *uni* refers to "one." It should theoretically not make sense to say "very unique"—how could something be *more* one of a kind? Similarly, if *perfect* means something is as good as it can be, does it make sense to talk about something being "more perfect," as it says in the Preamble to the United States Constitution? ("… in Order to form a more perfect Union …") Not long ago I heard someone say "most optimal," which is a lot like *more perfect*.

The Snopes.com site rates the veracity of different stories, and on their scale, something can be "mostly true." In logic, a proposition is either true or false; there's no "Therefore, Socrates is mostly mortal." Yet we can understand what the Snopes people mean when they use *true* in a graded way.

People sometimes object to these types of graded uses of absolute adjectives. But in those cases they're focusing too much on a narrow meaning of the word in question. When someone says that a friend is "very pregnant," they appear to be talking about an absolute state—pregnancy—in a graded way. But they're not addressing the yes/no state of whether the friend is pregnant. Instead, they might be referring to the outward manifestation of the pregnancy—the *baby bump*, as people sometimes call it—which does have a gradable quality. Or they might be referring to how far along the pregnancy is, where *very pregnant* means getting close to the birth date.

With *unique*, the term simply has more than one meaning. When someone refers to a piece on Etsy as "very unique," they're not using the word to refer to the singular state of a thing. Instead, they're using *unique* to mean *unusual*, which, etymology notwithstanding, is an attested meaning of that word. It's true, then, that some adjectives describe absolute states. But we can be flexible in how we use or interpret those adjectives, which can result in usages that *seem*—but aren't really—sort of illogical.

Related terms: etymological fallacy, flat adverb

antedating

In 2010, then-governor Sarah Palin was on TV talking about the Obamas when she said, "They could refudiate what it is that this group is saying." Word people took note at the neologism *refudiate*, and the Oxford Dictionary people even named *refudiate* their word of the year for 2010. But if you did a little digging, you'd find that *refudiate* had been used in 2006, and in 1984. And you even find a headline from 1925 that uses *refudiated*. Congratulations, you're *antedating* the word *refudiate*, meaning that you're finding earlier examples of the use of a word. (The lexicographer Ben Zimmer did exactly this research about *refudiate*.[3])

Part of the craft of dictionary making—lexicography—is determining when a word was first used in the language. For example, the Merriam-Webster definition for *blog* says that the first known use of that word was in 1999. If someone finds an example of *blog* that's earlier than 1999—well, that would be antedating the word.

As with the example of *refudiate*, words that seem recent often turn out to be older than we think. Many people think that the abbreviation *Ms.* as an alternative for *Mrs.* or *Miss* was coined in the 1960s or 1970s, when *Ms.* magazine was launched. But no; Ben Zimmer also antedated instances of the title *Ms.* to as early as 1901.

The lexicographer Kory Stamper provides an example on her blog of the usefulness of antedating. Someone wrote to Merriam-Webster, where Stamper used to work, to suggest that the term *Nosy Parker* originated from a busybody character named Mrs. Parker in a series of Lionel Barrymore movies. But Stamper writes:

> That would be a wonderful etymology for "Nosy Parker," but alas, time is not on your side. "Nosy Parker" first showed up in print in the late 1800s; Lionel Barrymore's movies date to the 1940s.[4]

The availability of online databases of historical texts (see corpus) has helped with antedating because people can perform computer searches through hundreds or thousands of texts to find terms. In fact, as the lexi-

---

[3] http://languagelog.ldc.upenn.edu/nll/?p=2490
[4] https://korystamper.wordpress.com/2014/12/19/answers-i-wish-i-could-send-etymology-edition

cographer Erin McKean has written,[5] people have come to treat antedating as a competitive sport—when you see a "first recorded" date in a dictionary, you can wield your search skills in the corpora and see if you can find an earlier citation.

In May 2020, the folks at the *Oxford English Dictionary* (OED) posted a page on their website[6] inviting people—anyone, which can include you and me—to help them antedate entries. As they explain, many databases (corpora) have come online that will let people research the history of English words. And the OED is happy to have you submit your updates to the first known dates for words in that august dictionary.

Related terms: corpus

anthimeria (functional shift)

> ***Adulting*** is hard.
>
> What are the key ***learnings***?
>
> Last week's party was ***funner***.
>
> The future of ***awesome*** (Xfinity slogan)

You probably recognize that in each of these examples, the marked word is being used in an unusual way:

- *Adult* is a noun, but in the first example it's being used as a verb (*adulting*).
- *Learning* is one form of a verb, but not only is it being used as a noun, it's being used as a count noun—one that can take a plural (*learnings*).
- *Fun* is a noun ("we had fun"), but *funner* is being used as a comparative adjective.
- *Awesome*—normally an adjective—is being used as a noun.

---

[5] http://www.boston.com/news/globe/ideas/articles/2007/10/14/what_came_first/
[6] https://public.oed.com/appeals/oed-antedatings/

This process of using a word as a different part of speech than normal is called *anthimeria*. The term comes from the Greek for "against" + "part." Other terms for this phenomenon are *functional shift* and *conversion*.

There are even terms for each type of change. Converting a word into a verb is known as *verbalization* or *verbing*. Verbs created from nouns are called *denominal* verbs. Turning a word into a noun is called *nominalization* or *nouning*. (*Verbing* and *nouning* are themselves examples of anthimeria.)

In anthimeria, words change categories without changing their form. Compare a word like *accessory*, which is a noun. We have a corresponding verb, namely *accessorize*, which was formed with the *ize* ending that we see on a lot of verbs. That's not anthimeria. But look at the example of *adulting*. Someone took the noun *adult* and didn't add something like *ize*; instead, they just verbed the noun *adult*. In linguistics, this type of category change without a change in form is called *zero derivation*.

Some people object when they run across anthimeria that's new to them (*an ask* as a noun, *to adult* as a verb, *a fail*). But the history of English is littered with words that made a functional shift that's unremarkable today. In the book *The Language Instinct*, Steven Pinker writes, "[E]asy conversion of nouns to verbs has been part of English grammar for centuries; it is one of the processes that make English English. I have estimated that about a fifth of all English verbs were originally nouns."

For example, we routinely use the nouns *contact*, *address*, *email*, *blog*, and *phone* (*telephone*) as verbs today. Some of these, maybe to your surprise, were controversial usages when they were new. For the word *test*, which do you think came first, the noun or the verb? What about *chill*? (Answer: both started as nouns.)

Creating verbs from nouns is easy and has been a productive way to form new words over the centuries. But we perform other functional shifts just as easily:

- A *tell* and a *deal* (both from poker), a *kick*, a *win*, a *ride*, and a *drive* are nominalized verbs.
- The expression *Don't talk the talk if you can't walk the walk* neatly incorporates words that act as both nouns and verbs.
- We use the nouns *fun*, *genius*, and *giant* as adjectives today without much controversy, although they started as nouns.

- In the expression *no ifs or buts*, two conjunctions have shifted to become nouns.
- When you talk about life's *ups and downs*, you're using adverbs as nouns.
- The Biblical reference to *the poor, and the maimed, and the halt, and the blind* (Luke 14:21 in the King James Version) are all examples of adjectives shifted to nouns. Or to use a more contemporary experience, *the fast and the furious* shifts two adjectives to nouns.

People do this constantly in informal contexts, creating nonce words as anthimeria—imagine an angry mother scolding a child with something like "Don't you 'not my fault!' me, young man! In that case, the mother shifts an entire phrase (*not my fault*) to function as a verb.

Advertisers love anthimeria, and product slogans are a rich source of functional shifts: *Find your festive* (Dunkin' Donuts), *Let's Burger* (Red Robin), *Change how you grocery* (Walmart). The theory in advertising is that using anthimeria grabs people's attention in a way that normal slogans might not. (Presumably the advertisers believe that you won't boycott them because you hate their examples of anthimeria, which some people claim to do.)

Trademarks sometimes experience anthimeria, and brands get themselves verbed: *to hoover the floor, to xerox a document, to google a question, to uber to the party*. Companies take pains to avoid having their brand genericized, thus losing the trademark.

Cartoonists have had fun with anthimeria. In what's become a kind of slogan for anthimeria, a 1993 panel from the comic strip *Calvin and Hobbes* introduced the phrase[7] "verbing weirds language," which exhibits noun-to-verb anthimeria (*verbing*) and adjective-to-verb anthimeria (*weirds*).

Related terms: back-formation, genericization, nonce word

---

[7] http://www.gocomics.com/calvinandhobbes/1993/01/25

aposiopesis

Sometimes you get so emotional about something that it affects your speech. Someone says something to you that makes you so mad that the best you can manage is, "Why, you ..." or maybe "Listen, pal ...." Or you hear your kids squabbling, and one of them says, "You better stop, or else!" Or a friend of yours is so overwhelmed that they tell you "I can't even."

This device—speech that breaks off because the speaker can't or won't continue—is known as *aposiopesis*. (It's another term from Greek, which means "becoming silent.") It's used for various purposes; a common one is "emotive aposiopesis," where the speaker stops because, well, they can't even. The linguist Gretchen McCulloch has a great description of emotive aposiopesis: "stylized verbal incoherence mirroring emotional incoherence."[8]

As a rhetorical device, aposiopesis is old. Shakespeare used aposiopesis; there's a good example in *King Lear* (Act II, scene 4):

> I will have such revenges on you both
> That all the world shall— I will do such things—
> What they are yet, I know not; but they shall be
> The terrors of the earth!

And it goes back to the ancients, showing up in Latin texts.

The last example (*I can't even*) is a relatively new construct, but you can see that it has the same "stylized verbal incoherence" of the other examples. A post from Tumblr user "just-shower-thoughts" makes the sage observation that "Teenage girls saying 'I can't even' is basically the same as old ladies saying 'Well, I never!'"[9]

Related terms: minced oath

---

[8] http://allthingslinguistic.com/post/68609127446/because-internet
[9] https://just-shower-thoughts.tumblr.com/post/121840862064/teenage-girls-saying-i-cant-even-is-basically

aptronym, charactonym

It seems too pat to be true, but a man who developed several casinos in Las Vegas is named Steve *Wynn*. A beloved English Romantic poet was William *Wordsworth*. One of the most successful Olympic sprinters ever is Usain *Bolt*. A well-known saxophone player is named Jim *Horn*. The book *Reading Like a Writer*, a writing guide, was written by Francine *Prose*. In March 2021, this amazing headline in the *Independent* (UK) announced that Terry Boot would be replacing Peter Foot as the CFO of the UK-based company Shoe Zone:

News > Business > Business News

Off to the laces: Terry Boot replaces Peter Foot as Shoe Zone finance boss

He'll tackle role following tough period for retailer which has been hit hard by Covid-19

These types of cannily appropriate names are known as *aptronyms*. This term was invented in the 1930s by the newspaper columnist Franklin P. Adams as an anagram of patronym. (This explains why there's an *R* in the term, although the variant *aptonym* is also sometimes used.) Other names are *euonym* (Greek for "good name") and *namephreak*.

There are a surprising number of examples. In addition to the names listed earlier, there's an Australian surfer named Layne Beachley, a doctor named Atchoo, a meteorologist named Amy Freeze, and an Australian tennis player named Margaret Court. Not to mention the American politician Anthony Weiner, who was disgraced for his sexting.

Many people have names that reflect the trade of an ancestor—Baker, Cooper, Draper, Miller, Smith, Taylor, Weaver, and so on. For those ancestors, and for anyone who followed in the family vocation, these names would of course been aptronyms. In our day, having a name that directly reflects your vocation is rare enough that we take notice.

When you investigate aptronyms, you'll run across the idea of *nominal determinism*. This theory suggests that people are actually drawn to professions that are appropriate for their names. As noted, people historically had names that reflected their work. And when you review aptronyms for real people, you have to sometimes wonder.

In the realm of fiction, writers have assigned aptronymic names to their characters for a long time. (An aptronymic name for a literary character is sometimes referred to as a *charactonym*.) In *Pilgrim's Progress* (1677), John Bunyan unsubtly used names like Christian, Evangelist, Superstition, Little-faith, and Mr. Great-heart. Shakespeare used them as well, albeit not quite so obviously, with names like Mistress Quickly. In *The Threepenny Opera*, a play about underworld characters, one of the characters is named Filch. The comic strip *Little Orphan Annie* featured a character named Daddy Warbucks.

A running gag on the old NPR radio show "Car Talk" was the list of credits—ironic charactonyms—that were listed at the end of the show, like "Complaint-Line Operator Levon Hold" and "Staff Drycleaner Preston Creases."[10]

Just as there are aptronyms, there's also the opposite: *inaptronyms*. An example is Lance Armstrong, the bicyclist. Although the name suggests he's got huge biceps, Armstrong is well known for the strength of his legs. An older example is the Catholic cleric names Jaime Sin. And there is—hard to believe, but apparently true—a police constable in Britain named Rob Banks.[11]

Related terms: eponym, hypocorism, mononym, onomastics

attachment ambiguity (syntactic ambiguity)

There's a classic Groucho Marx joke from the movie *Animal Crackers* that goes like this:

> One morning, I shot an elephant in my pajamas. How he got in my pajamas, I don't know.[12]

There's always some risk in analyzing humor, but I'm sure this joke will survive even if we break down what's happening. Why is this joke funny? Because of something called *attachment ambiguity* or *syntactic am-*

---

[10] https://www.cartalk.com/content/staff-credits
[11] https://tinyurl.com/mryuwb25
[12] Video: https://youtu.be/NfN_gcjGoJo

biguity—ambiguity based on how the sentence is constructed. (This contrasts with *lexical* ambiguity, where the ambiguity pertains to what a word means.)

The term *attachment* here comes from the tree diagrams—*phrase-structure trees*—that linguists use to show the structure of a sentence. (These are different from the type of sentence diagram that you might have learned in school.) Here's a simplified tree diagram for "The dog bit the man":

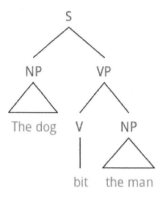

In the diagram, *S* means "sentence," *NP* means "noun phrase," and *VP* means "verb phrase."

For the joke "I shot an elephant in my pajamas," the following tree diagram illustrates a reasonable interpretation of the sentence:

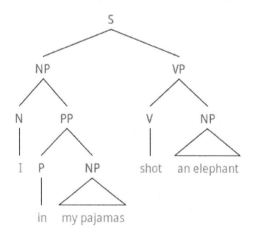

In this interpretation, *in my pajamas* is attached to the noun phrase that contains the subject (*I*). The meaning is unremarkable: I was in my pajamas during the purported shooting.

But the joke's punchline ("How he got in my pajamas I don't know") forces you to reinterpret the sentence in a funny way: in the new interpretation, *in my pajamas* modifies the noun phrase that contains *elephant*. Here's the tree for the funny interpretation:

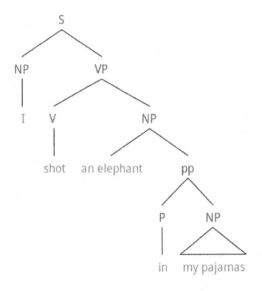

All of which is to say that in the sentence *I shot an elephant in my pajamas*, the phrase *in my pajamas* shows attachment ambiguity. And Groucho Marx (or his joke writer) took advantage of this for a laugh.

In his book *The Sense of Style*, Steven Pinker discusses another great example of attachment ambiguity:

> Among the sessions will be a faculty panel on sex in college with four professors.

Pinker includes tree diagrams to show where *with four professors* is attached—namely, either to *panel* (intended interpretation) or to *sex* (amusing interpretation).

Newspaper and magazine headlines are often written to meet space constraints. To do this, they tend to leave out function words that help us understand attachments. As a result, headlines often exhibit attachment ambiguity. In fact, there's a special name for the ambiguity found in headlines: crash blossoms, which I address elsewhere.

Related terms: crash blossom, garden-path sentence, squinting modifier

autological word (homological word), heterological word

The word *noun* refers to a noun. The word *word* refers to a word. The word *unhyphenated* has no hyphen in it. The word *polysyllabic* has many syllables. The word *English* is in English. These are all examples of *autological* or *homological* words. Autological words illustrate what they mean, or "describe themselves."

You'd think that there would be a lot of autological words, but there aren't. Most words don't have anything to say about themselves (*dog, jump, early*). Or in some cases they're the opposite: *heterological*, meaning that a word that explicitly contradicts itself (so to speak). Examples of heterological words are *monosyllabic* (which is not monosyllabic), *long* (which is not long), and *verb* (which is a noun, not a verb).

If you allow the idea of autological words to include spelling, you can expand your list. Consider *CAPITALIZED* and *lowercase*. I saw someone propose the word *olde*, as in Ye Olde Shoppe, as an autological word, and I can't argue with that.

There are some cases of autological or heterological words that depend on how they're used. If you say the word *loud* loudly, it's autological. But if you whisper it, it's heterological. The opposite, of course, applies to the word *quiet*—if you shout it, it's heterological, but if you whisper it, it's autological.

And if you like logic puzzles and paradoxes, consider whether the word *heterological* itself is heterological. If *heterological* is heterological, then it doesn't describe itself, per the definition of the word *heterological*. But then *heterological* is actually autological, not heterological, which is a logical contradiction. If this seems confusing, you're not alone; these head-scratchers are examples of the Grelling–Nelson paradox.

In spite of all this fun, there's no linguistic significance to these characteristics. With the possible exception of a relatively few cases of phonesthemics, words are arbitrary. So *homological* and *heterological* words are just a novelty that's sure to liven up your dinner party or work meeting. Although that might depend on who you hang out or work with.

Related terms: phonesthemics

avoidance character

What do you do when you're writing (a) an email or a social media post and (b) you're quoting something offensive and (c) you worry that some people will be offended by some of the words? Well, one approach is to use *avoidance characters* for parts of the offensive word, like this:

Oh, sh**!

Your strategy pretty much *****

Out, d—d spot!

Typical avoidance characters are asterisks (*) and hyphens or dashes (-), and the occasional at-sign (@). But the range of avoidance characters can be wide; people also use character substitutions from leetspeak, like *a55* for "ass." As an article in *Fast Company* reports,[13] when some researchers were investigating the nature of cursing on social media, they had to expand the list of terms they were looking for to include spellings like "a55, @$$, $h1t, b!tch, bi+ch, c0ck, f*ck, l3itch, p*ssy, and dik."

At the *Wall Street Journal*, at least according to the editor Bill Power, using a dash as an avoidance character became known as a *Barney dash*.[14] This was named for the editor Barney Calame at that publication.

---

[13] https://www.fastcompany.com/3026596/140-characters-of-fck-sht-and-ss-how-we-swear-on-twitter

[14] https://www.wsj.com/articles/BL-STYLEANDSUBSTANCEB-506 (paywall)

The linguist Mark Liberman has also referred to the use of these characters as *typographical bleeping*.

When avoidance characters are used to convey a taboo word, enough of the word has to remain for the reader to understand what's being censored. This can occasionally be a problem. In the *Guardian*, a British newspaper, a sympathetic writer asked, "How is the poor reader expected to differentiate between b******* and b*******?" (As he explains, the former is *bastards* and the latter is *bollocks*.) One of the examples earlier says, "Your strategy pretty much *****." You can make a pretty good guess about the writer's intent from context (I'm guessing that the bleeped word is *sucks*), but the reader can't be certain in this case.

Avoidance characters have other uses as well. For example, in some religious contexts, writers use avoidance characters when writing the name of the deity; they might write *God* as "G-d." In the Jewish tradition, this might be done to avoid a problem of erasing or destroying a document that mentions God, which would be a form of disrespect.

A special flavor of avoidance characters are grawlix, a.k.a. *obscenicons*, which use a kind of vocabulary of characters for swearing, like *$#*!*. You see this type of avoidance character in comics and other places where the goal is not just avoidance but emphasis or humor.

As mainstream print media has gotten less squeamish about printing swear words, the use of avoidance characters has gone down. Many newspapers and magazines will print swear words in full if they're quoting someone. Others, such as the *New Yorker,* have stopped using these characters at all and print the words in full.

Filters for online content such as forums are sometimes programmed to substitute avoidance characters in certain words. For example, the iTunes library will use asterisks in potentially offensive song titles. This strategy can sometimes go awry; for details, see Scunthorpe problem.

Related terms: grawlix, minced oath, Scunthorpe problem

back-formation

The thing that a burglar does is to ... *burgle*? If you use a Taser weapon on someone, you've ... *tased* them? People who engage in a conversation are ... *conversating*?

Each of these words—*to burgle, to tase, to conversate*—was created by taking an existing word, chopping off the end, and then using it as new parts of speech—*to burgle* is a verb based on the noun *burglar*; *to tase* is a verb formed from the noun *Taser*; *to conversate* was created by chopping off part of *conversation* and then using the new word as a verb.

The formal term for this type of word is *back-formation*, meaning they were formed by working backward from an existing word. We English speakers create back-formations readily. A fair number of existing words in English are back-formations, and we create new ones all the time.

The examples above might not sit well with you; people sometimes object to back-forming terms like *to burgle* or (especially) *to conversate*. As it turns out, the back-formation *to burgle* has been around since at least 1872 and *to conversate* since 1811. But there are other examples that not only are more familiar words, but that you might be surprised to hear are back-formations:

- *to bartend* is a back-formation from *bartender*
- *to diagnose* is a back-formation from *diagnosis*
- *to demarcate* is from *demarcation*
- *to edit* is from *editor*
- *to eavesdrop* is (probably) from *eavesdropper*
- *to injure* is from *injury*
- *to jell* is from *jelly*
- *to laze* is from *lazy*
- *to liaise* is from *liaison*
- *to legislate* is from *legislation*
- *to spectate* is from *spectator*
- *to televise* is from *television*
- *to troubleshoot* is from *troubleshooter*
- *to tweeze* is from *tweezers*

You probably noticed that these are all verbs. It's particularly easy to form verbs from nouns, but there are some back-formations that involve other parts of speech. We also have back-formations that created nouns out of adjectives:

- *ditz* comes from *ditzy*
- *exurb* is from *exurban*
- *greed* is from *greedy*
- *sleaze* is from *sleazy*
- *sophisticate* is from *sophisticated*

An interesting historical example of a back-formation is *pea*, which came from *pease*, as in "pease porridge hot." The original *pease* was the name of the plant (Latin: *Pisum sativum*). Because the term ended in *s*, speakers thought it was the plural, and they created singular form *pea*. A similar process derived *cherry* as a singular noun from the original Old English *ciris* (compare *Kirsch* in German). These back-formations to create singular forms like *pea* and *cherry* are examples of *inferred singular forms*.

A more recent version of this story is the term *kudo*, a back-formation from *kudos*, a Greek word meaning "honor" or "glory." Because the Greek term ends in *s*, English speakers have sometimes interpreted it as a plural and back-formed the invented singular *kudo*. Or if that doesn't ring any bells, there's the words *biceps*, which is singular in Latin and meant "two-headed." But we English speakers have back-formed *bicep* to create a singular version more in keeping with our intuitions about the language.

We sometimes do this consciously. A linguist I know made up the term *Netflick* to refer to a single movie on Netflix, fully aware that she was creating a back-formation.

Words like *kudo* and *bicep* create new nouns out of existing nouns. A more athletic back-formation is the term *to verse*, meaning "to fight, face off against." The verb *to verse* came about when people (mostly kids, it seems) interpreted the preposition *versus* as a verb, hearing *Godzilla versus King Kong* as "Godzilla faces off against King Kong." Many people dislike this usage, and it's not listed in most dictionaries, but kids who use it eventually grow up, so check back in a generation or two.

It's particularly useful to create back-formations when we need a verb for an activity that's described using multiple words. For example, if it gets hot while you're driving around, you might flip the switch in your car to *air-condition* it, a back-formation from *air conditioning*. Maybe you're driving to your favorite spot *to fly-fish*, a verb we made out of *fly-fishing*.

There are lots of these back-formations from compounds, which the linguist Arnold Zwicky has termed *two-part back-formed verbs*, or *2pbfvs* for short. An interesting aspect of these verbs is how the constituent parts are related. The second part is always the verb. But the first part can have different roles:

- The first part describes "by means of, using": *to fly-fish, to spear-fish, to bow-hunt.*
- The first part describes "how": *to crash-land, to freeze-dry, to hen-peck, to spray-paint, to sleepwalk, to dry-clean, to social-distance* (?), *to gay-marry.*
- The first part describes "why": *to Christmas-shop, to Halloween-party, to future-proof.*
- The first part describes "what": *to air-condition, to back-stab, to rabble-rouse, to house-sit, to role-play.*

Some of these seem more natural than others, but part of the reason might just be familiarity. When Zwicky wrote about two-part back-formed verbs, he wondered whether there are certain back-formations that English speakers would reject. His conclusion:

> As I have more and more experience with two-part back-formed verbs, I am less and less willing to label candidates as unacceptable or impossible. I keep finding surprises. I'm inclined to think that so long as the back-formed verb would be useful to speakers, sooner or later someone will come up with it.[15]

Here's some linguistics humor for you: a good example of a back-formation is the verb *to back-formate*.

Related terms: anthimeria, cutthroat compound, rebracketing, retronym

---

[15] https://arnoldzwicky.org/2009/06/09/back-formings/

backronym

In 1980, a mother who had lost a child to a drunk driver founded an organization named Mothers Against Drunk Driving, which works to reduce traffic accidents caused by impaired drivers. The acronym for the organization is MADD, which captured the sentiment that the founder and others had about these tragic deaths.

The fact that the acronym spelled out a relevant word was of course not a coincidence. That's because MADD is a *backronym*—an acronym specifically designed so that its letters spell out a message.

You might also be familiar with the medical condition known as SAD, which stands for Seasonal Affective Disorder. The condition was named in 1984 by a researcher who noticed that his mood went down in months when there was less light. He thought it would be a good idea to give the newly named malady a memorable acronym, so he came up with the backronym SAD.

Creating a memorable acronym isn't a bad idea. We remember MADD and SAD better *because* they have names that remind us of what they stand for.

Legislators are fond of using backronyms for naming bills, for the same reason—to make the names more memorable. Some well-known backronymic legislative acts are:

- DREAM Act (Development, Relief, and Education for Alien Minors). This bill proposes a path to permanent residency for children who arrived in the US as undocumented minors. An interesting development from this backronym is that those who would be eligible for residency as a result of this bill are known as *dreamers*—a kind of full circle from word to backronym back to word.
- CARES Act (Coronavirus Aid, Relief, and Economic Security). A bill introduced in 2020 to help people who were displaced by measures that were designed to slow the spread of COVID-19.
- STALKERS Act (Simplifying the Ambiguous Law, Keeping Everyone Reliably Safe). A bill introduced in 2010 to strengthen the laws about stalking.

- USA PATRIOT Act (Uniting and Strengthening America by Providing Appropriate Tools Required to Intercept and Obstruct Terrorism). Certainly among the most unashamed examples of legislative backronyming, this legislation expanded the powers of the US government to perform surveillance and investigate suspects.

Backronyms aren't limited to advocacy or medicine or legislation. The first programming language I ever used was called BASIC. This language was invented in the 1960s at Dartmouth College as an easy-to-use (that is, basic) programming language. Not surprisingly, the name is a backronym: Beginner's All-purpose Symbolic Instruction Code. (They even cheated a little with "All-purpose.") The language still exists, much evolved, but has long since been spelled as just "Basic," the backronymic origin of the name no longer obvious.

In late 2018, NASA landed a probe on Mars as part of the InSight mission. If you go to the NASA site, you learn that *InSight* actually stands for Interior Exploration using Seismic Investigations, Geodesy and Heat Transport. I bet it took more than one meeting to come up with that backronym.

As with BASIC/Basic, sometimes people don't even know that a term is supposed to be a backronym. For example, in the US we have AMBER Alerts, a system for using public media to report on missing children. The name nominally stands for "America's Missing: Broadcast Emergency Response," but really was named after a young girl named Amber who was abducted in 1996. The term *AMBER Alert* is widely understood; many people in the US even get AMBER alerts on their cellphones. But few people probably know that AMBER is a backronym, let alone what the letters in AMBER stand for or why.

Related terms: etymythology, numeronym, retronym, syllable acronym

biscuit conditional (relevance conditional)

We think of sentences that involve the word *if* as being logical statements: there's a condition (*if*). If the condition is true, there's a result (*then*). That's how it works in these examples:

> If it snows tonight, [then] they'll close the schools. (But if it doesn't snow, they won't.)

> If she's at home, [then] she can sign for the package. (But if she's not at home, she can't sign for the package.)

> If you're going to the store, [then] please pick up some milk. (But if you're not going, never mind.)

As you can see, in each case, if the condition isn't true, the result isn't true either.

However, we can also make perfectly normal *if* statements that aren't logical in this sense. Think about this example:

> If you're thirsty, there's beer in the fridge.

What if you're *not* thirsty? The beer is still in the fridge; the existence of beer in the fridge doesn't depend on whether you're thirsty. In a sense, there's no *then* part for this *if* statement.

That's because this type of *if* statement isn't a true/false conditional statement. Instead, it's something called a *biscuit conditional*. The term got its name from a well-known example: *There are biscuits on the sidebar if you want some.* This sentence was used as a sample sentence by the language philosopher J. L. Austin in a paper where he examined this construction in detail.

In cases like these, the *if* statement is really about relevance—the *if* clause tells the listener something relevant about the main statement. There's beer in the fridge. Why are you telling me this? Well, it might be relevant if you're thirsty. This type of *if* statement is therefore also sometimes referred to as a *relevance conditional*. But really, why would you use *relevance conditional* when you can use the excellent term *biscuit conditional*?

There's a real-life example I've heard many times while listening to the NPR program *Fresh Air*, which you might have heard too. Every time the host, Terry Gross, returns after a station break, she says "If you're just joining us, my guest today is [name]." Obviously, her guest is the same whether you're just joining her or you've been listening all along. In that case, the *if* clause again doesn't state a true/false condition, but instead provides relevance for the listener. Instead of just saying "My guest is [name]," which could come across as unnecessary for the people who've been listening ("yes, we know"), she adds an *if* clause to describe why her announcement is relevant ("If you're just joining us ...").

We also use relevance conditionals like this as a form of politeness. Imagine that you want to send your work colleagues a link to an interesting article. But they're well-informed people, so maybe they already know about it, and you don't want to suggest otherwise. To hedge against this possibility, you start your email with "If you haven't already seen this, here's an interesting article." The link is in the email whether they've seen the article before or not, so clearly the *if* clause is about relevance. The expression *in case you missed it*—abbreviated as *ICYMI* in online discourse—is just a different, non-*if* version of a biscuit conditional.

Once you know about biscuit conditionals, you hear them everywhere. You can get a limited amount of mileage out of pretending the biscuit conditionals are real conditions, and yell at the radio ("And who's your guest if I'm *not* just joining you, Terry?"). But I can tell you from personal experience that your spouse could well grow weary of this particular form of amusement.

Related terms: tag question

bounding asterisks (bounding brackets)

Suppose it's Sunday night and you're reading a social media post from one of your friends who has kids in school. She writes something like this (an invented example, but hey, I've been a parent):

> Youngest child just now remembered that he needs a tri-fold story board for his book report. The office supply store closed ten minutes ago. *tears hair out*

21

This is a sad (though not unfamiliar) story, which also has an interesting element: the asterisks around "tears hair out." The writer needs *some* way to indicate that "tears hair out" is not part of the story; instead, it's a kind of stage direction. Quotation marks don't work, so the writer uses *bounding asterisks* around this meta element.

In this case, the meta element refers to a gesture. But they're also used to indicate a non-verbal sound like *cough*, *sigh*, or *squee*—really, anything that's not supposed to be read as a literal part of the current text.

Asterisks are popular for this, but writers also use *bounding brackets*. Here's an example from John McIntyre's *You Don't Say* blog[16] showing brackets used for the same purpose:

> The program has not been announced, but a preliminary list of speakers has been posted at the EAC website, among them [cough] me.

Or you might see other characters:

(gasp!)

<claps>

:: evil laff ::

Bounding asterisks and their kin are common in online contexts like such as Facebook, Twitter, instant messaging apps, and online forums. But they long precede social media and even computers. For example, the lexicographer Ben Zimmer has traced them back to comic strips.[17] As he recounts, when early comic-strip authors needed to indicate non-verbal noises like "sniff" or "cough," they put them in parentheses. As one of the images shows in Zimmer's research, a *Li'l Abner* strip from 1935 put stars around "gulp." Charles Schulz, the author of *Peanuts*, used bounding asterisks for the many instances of "sigh" that the character Charlie Brown emitted over the years.

One reason that bounding asterisks developed in both comics and social media is that they're both implicitly about speech. Text in comic strips is mostly in speech bubbles; social media posts have the same flavor of dialog—you're talking to your audience. (Facebook used to prompt users with a textbox that said things like "What's on your

---

[16] Sadly no longer available on the *Baltimore Sun* site (McIntyre is now retired).
[17] http://languagelog.ldc.upenn.edu/nll/?p=4466

mind?") Playwriting has conventions for indicating stage directions, which generally involve putting the instruction in parenthesis and on its own line. So the idea of setting off dialog from other text is well understood, but the restricted space and formatting options in comics and social media have required a little more ingenuity. But it all works out, and we can easily understand the intent of text that's in bounding asterisks.

Related terms: grawlix

calque (loan translation)

There are a couple of ways to borrow terms from another language. One way is to just import the foreign word as is. This is referred to as a *loanword*. English has borrowed thousands of loanwords, with words from Norman French (*pork, beef*), Latin (*cheese, wine*), Arabic (*algebra, lute*), Hindi (*pundit, karma*), Chinese (*ketchup, wok*), German (*ersatz, kitsch, kindergarten, delicatessen*), Spanish (*bodega, cafeteria*), Turkish (*bulgur, yurt*), and too many more source languages to list here. To quote the lexicographer and language scholar Robert Burchfield, "One cannot but be impressed by the amazing hospitality of the English language."

Another way is to import the word but change it to sound sort of English-like. We did this with words like *crayfish* and *woodchuck* via the process of folk etymology.

Yet another way is to translate the term word by word or piece by piece into an English equivalent, which is referred to as a *calque*. For example, we have the word *earworm*, which means a song that's so catchy that it's hard to get out of your head. We borrowed the word from German, but instead of importing their word directly (*Ohrwurm*), we first translated it into English (*earworm*). We did a similar thing with the word *superman*, which is an English translation of the German word *Übermensch*. (Although in that case we translated *über*, which means "over," into the Latin-derived *super*.)

In the world of science we have the word *thought experiment* to refer to a way of testing theories by working out their logical consequences without hard experimental proof. This English word was calqued from the German word *Gedankenexperiment* in a translation of a paper by the German physicist Ernst Mach.

You can see why a calque is also sometimes known as a *loan translation*.

An example that might seem to be more obviously a calque is the term *paper tiger* to refer to an ineffectual person or country. This is a calque from the Chinese word *zhǐlǎohǔ*. You might also not be surprised to learn that *firewater*, referring to liquor, is a calque from Ojibwa, an Algonquian language. The term *blue blood*, referring to an aristocrat, is a calque from the Spanish term *sangre azul*. A calque that might surprise you is the word *gospel*. In English, this was originally *gōdspell*, or "good news," which is a direct translation of the Greek word *euangélion*.

Calquing isn't always done perfectly. We have some words in English that we half-calqued from German. One example is *liverwurst*, from the German word *Leberwurst*. We calqued the first half—*Leber* to *liver*—but didn't translate *wurst*. (We can speculate that enough English speakers already knew the word *Wurst*—German for "sausage"—that that word didn't warrant a full-on translation.) We also half-calqued *apple strudel* from German *Apfelstrudel*, translating *apple* but retaining *strudel*. Maybe we just didn't have a clear enough translation for *strudel*. For some reason we also half-calqued the name *bleu cheese*, retaining the French spelling for *blue*.

Interesting note: the psychologist Bruno Bettleheim made the argument that it's better to read Freud in the original German, because the words *ego*, *superego*, and *id* were *not* calqued from the German; instead, the English translations of Freud use Latin terms. Thus when Freud was translated into English, the German *das Ich* became *ego* instead of *the I*; *das Überich* became *superego* instead of *the over-I*; and *das Es* became *id* instead *the It*. As the scholar Curt Raney notes in the article "Freud as a Humanist":[18]

> [T]he American translation was an attempt to give Freud's ideas a scientific and medical quality that they did not possess in the original. Freud was a scholarly humanist in his writings. Forcing his words into a rigid, scientific mold has distorted the nature of his thinking.

---

[18] http://faculty.smcm.edu/ccraney/restricted/PDF/Freud_as_a_Humanist.pdf

Here's some more linguistics humor for you, courtesy of the linguist Danny Bate on Twitter: the word *calque* is a loanword (from French), and the word *loanword* is a calque (translated from the German word *Lohnwort*). You're welcome. :)

Related terms: folk etymology

capitonym

These two sentences look similar, but they mean quite different things:

> This march has been great.

> This March has been great.

The first sentence—the one with the lowercase *march*—seems to refer to a parade or demonstration, which apparently has gone well. The second sentence, the one with uppercase *March*, tells us that something about that month—maybe the weather was great, or perhaps a sports tournament turned out well. Although the words *march* and *March* are homophones, there's no way you'd confuse them when you see them written.

The words *march* and *March* are examples of *capitonyms*: words whose meaning depends on whether they are capitalized.

We have other examples like this:

- *august* (esteemed) and *August* (the month)
- *herb* (the plant) and *Herb* (the person)
- *job* (your work) and *Job* (long-suffering Biblical personage)
- *polish* (to shine up) and *Polish* (of or pertaining to Poland)
- *turkey* (the bird) and *Turkey* (the country)

Some capitonym pairs have the same pronunciation: *march*/*March*, *turkey*/*Turkey*. In theory, this could result in ambiguity when the words are spoken, even if there's no ambiguity when the words are written. For example, if spoken aloud, the sentence "This march has been great" is ambiguous. In practice, and as with a great deal of spoken language, context generally determines meaning. And it's rarely ambiguous whether you're referring to *turkey* the bird or *Turkey* the country.

But some capitonyms do change pronunciation based on the capital letter. The word *august* has different stress ("aw-GUST") from the capitalized *August* ("AW-gust"). Or the difference might be in the vowel. In England, you might spend the evening *reading* (REE-ding), or you might visit the town of *Reading* (RED-ing). The verb *polish* is pronounced with a short *o*, but *Polish* has a long *o*. If there were some sort of technique invented in Poland for shining metals, you would not be misunderstood if you talked about a "Polish polish."

Capitonyms that are pronounced differently are not necessarily exempt from confusion, though. Nancy Friedman, a naming specialist, cites two examples. One is a business called Polish on Piedmont, which did not offer lessons in how to speak Polish but was instead a nail salon. Similarly, you might have to pause for a moment to wonder whether a business called Polish Nail Spa was owned by Poles, offered nail care in the Polish style, or (likeliest, though less linguistically interesting) just polished nails.

Other examples of capitonyms that change pronunciation are *tangier* (more tangy) and *Tangier* (the city). Because I have lived in the Seattle area for many years, my favorite capitonym pair is *rainier* ("more rainy") and *Rainier* (as in Mount Rainier, a volcano near Seattle).

Related terms: homonym, polysemy

clipping

I doubt that you'd blink an eye if you heard someone say the following:

> I got a phone call at the lab. My bro canceled the disco
> party at the condo 'cause his possum has the flu.

(Well, you might raise your eyebrows at the scenario, but probably not at the words themselves.)

The same is true for the following sentence:

> It's a photo that was posted by a fan of the musical gent in his undies who plays cello in the rec room.

For our purposes, what's interesting is not reports about sick pets or exhibitionist musicians. What's interesting is that both sentences show many examples of a phenomenon called *clipping*. As the word suggests, clipping is about cutting off parts of a word.

It's clearer when you see the same sentences with the clipped words marked:

> I got a *phone* call at the *lab*. My *bro* canceled the *disco* party at the *condo 'cause* his *possum* has the *flu*.

> It's a *photo* from a *fan* of the musical *gent* who plays *cello* in the *rec* room in his *undies*.

Here's how each word is clipped:

- *phone* from *telephone*
- *lab* from *laboratory*
- *bro* from *brother*
- *disco* from *discotheque*
- *condo* from *condominium*
- *'cause* from *because*
- *possum* from *opossum*
- *flu* from *influenza*
- *photo* from *photograph*
- *fan* from *fanatic*
- *gent* from *gentleman*
- *cello* from *violoncello*
- *rec* from *recreation*
- *undies* from *underwear* (*undies* is also an example of a hypocorism.)

Clipping can chop off the beginning of a word (*phone*), the end (*fan*), or both (*flu*). As you can see from the list, we like to clip words in English.

We use many words today without realizing that they're clipped. When you were reading the list above, were you surprised that *disco* was from *discotheque*, *flu* was from *influenza*, and *cello* was from *violoncel-*

lo? Other terms that were clipped that might surprise you are *bus* (from *omnibus*), *van* (from *caravan*), and *buff* (from *buffalo*). And we're still at it, in new words like *bot* (from *robot*) and *blog* (from *web log*). Clipping is one part of the *totesing* construction, where people use the forms *totes* for *totally* and *adorbs* for *adorable*. (In totesing, you also frequently add *s* to the clipped forms.)

A commenter on a *Language Log* blog post noted that clipping was fashionable in the 1920s.[19] As evidence, the commenter cites lyrics from the introduction to the Gershwin song "'S Wonderful," which rhymes the word *fash* (for *fashion*) with *pash* (for *passion*). P. G. Wodehouse had his character Bertie Wooster saying things like "So there you have my posish [position]" and "in my fogged condish [condition]."

Grammarians have occasionally complained about clipping. Back in 1710 Jonathan Swift was grumping about clipped words like *mob* (from the Latin *mobile vulgus*, "inconstant common people"). In 1915 or thereabouts, the style guide for the *Kansas City Star* was adamant that reporters should write *luncheon*, not *lunch*.

There are different types of clipping, and they have unique names. Cutting off the beginning of a word is known as *apheresis*. One common place we see *apheresis* is when the word starts with an unstressed vowel, as in *because* > *'cause*, *excuse* > *'scuse*, *especially* > *specially*, and *America* > *'Murica*. Historically speaking, we got some words in English when an initial unstressed vowel was removed. An example is the word *bishop*, which came from a Latin word *episcopus* (which separately got us the word *episcopal*). Another is *strange*, which we got in the Middle Ages from the French word *estrange*, and *scapegoat*, which was a clipped version of *escape goat*.

In some cases, apheresis involves only an initial letter that *isn't* a vowel. There are lots of dialects of English that drop an *h* at the beginning of a word, a phenomenon known as *H-dropping* or *aitch*-dropping. (For example, in the musical *My Fair Lady*, Eliza Doolittle initially refers to the professor as "'enry 'iggins.") Historically, apheresis is also responsible for words that are still spelled with an initial *k* that's no longer pronounced, like *knife* and *knight*.

---

[19] http://languagelog.ldc.upenn.edu/nll/?p=18983#comment-1494822

Apheresis can produce word variations that continue to live side by side in English, as with *opossum* and *possum*. And in some cases, apheresis can produce a new word that is distinct from its source. That's what happened with *esquire* and *squire*; *squire* was originally a variation with apheresis of *esquire*, but *squire* evolved into its own word.

Fun fact: Somewhat unexpectedly (to me, anyway), the word *till* is not the result of apheresis on the word *until*. According to the OED, *till* (or variants of it) go back as far as recorded English and probably came into English from Old Norse, independently of the word *until*.

As noted, we also cut off the ends of words, which has its own name: *apocope*. As with apheresis, apocope can form synonyms for existing words. In addition to the examples you saw earlier, such as *lab*, *photo*, and *disco*, you'll find many more in everyday English, including *abs* (from *abdominals*), *ad* (from advertisement), *cred* (from *credibility*), *deli* (from *delicatessen*), *fave* (from *favorite*), *fax* (from *facsimile*), and *pub* (from *public house*).

In some cases, a word formed through apocope can replace the original word. The following graph created by the Google Ngram Viewer (see corpus) shows how the word *pub* (top line, blue) has become more and more popular in comparison to the word *public house* (bottom line, red):

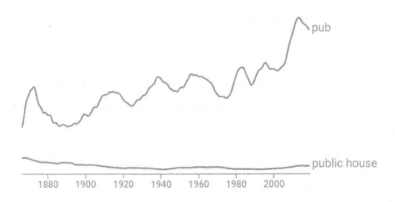

Another example is the word *piano*. The word *piano* was formed via apocope from *pianoforte* (which itself was a shortened form of *gravicembalo col piano e forte*, which means "harpsichord with soft and loud"). Today, the instrument you might have in your living room is just a *piano*. The original version of the instrument is still used when per-

29

formers want to replicate how, say, a Haydn concerto might have sounded in his day. To make it clear what they're offering, they might refer to the period instrument as the *pianoforte*. (Or to a *fortepiano*; both names were used.)

In the history of English, lots of words used to have syllables at the end that were removed by the process of apocope. Here are the first four lines of Chaucer's *Canterbury Tales*, showing words that originally had unstressed vowels at the end that have since disappeared:

Whan that Aprille, with hise shoures soote,
The droghte of March hath perced to the roote
And bathed every veyne in swich licour,
Of which vertu engendred is the flour;

These are *Aprille-April*, *hise-his*, *soote-sweet* (meaning "gentle"), *droghte-drought*, *roote-root*, and *veyne-vein*. In Old English (Anglo-Saxon, 450 to about 1100 CE), many of these *e* endings would have been more complex endings that marked the function of each of these words. By Chaucer's time (1300s), the endings had been reduced to unstressed syllables. And by our time, of course, they've disappeared. We still have traces of these endings in our archaic spelling system, but apocope has caused the sounds themselves to vanish.

Fun fact: *apocope* shares a root with *capon* (a castrated rooster). Speaking of "to cut off," I mean.

Related terms: epenthesis, haplology, hypocorism

collocation

In December 2018, the lawyer Michael Cohen was sentenced to prison for various crimes. The judge in the case, William Pauley, said that Cohen had pleaded guilty to "a veritable smorgasbord of fraudulent conduct." A lot of people who follow politics had questions about this fraudulent conduct. On the other hand, Twitter user Brendan Nyhan asked a question that a lot of language people were wondering about: "Why are smorgasbords always veritable?"

It's true, sort of. You hear *smorgasbord* referred to as *veritable* a lot. And in fact, that particular combination of words seems to be getting more popular, as this graph from the Google Ngram Viewer shows:[20]

veritable smorgasbord

Some terms just seem to go together: *crystal clear. Brilliant career. Sneak peek. Tight-knit community. Unsung hero. Desert island. Torrid affair. Arms akimbo. Once upon a time. Commit a crime. Feel free. Neither here nor there.*

The term for words like this that tend to occur as a unit is *collocations*. Or in the colorful description of Twitter user Kevin Paul Gregg, "Some words just fall in love with each other and decide to get married."

Another way of thinking about collocations is that they represent predictable groupings. Imagine you're asked to fill in these blanks:

_____ must go

_____ assembly required

There's a very good chance that you picked *everything* and *some*. These well-known expressions represent collocations.

Collocations aren't fixed phrases, because the elements in the collocation can appear in other contexts. (Although the expression *veritable smorgasbord* shows an affinity between *veritable* and *smorgasbord*, both of those words appear in plenty of other contexts.) And collocations are not idioms, because their meaning is directly derived from the combina-

---

[20] For more on the Google Ngram Viewer, see corpus.

tion of their parts. (In an idiom, the meaning of the individual words doesn't tell you the actual meaning of the whole.)

Collocations tell us something about the kind of constraint on word choice that makes English sound natural. For example, *quick* and *fast* are semantically similar, but if you say *She's a fast study* instead of *She's a quick study*, it sounds odd. In that expression, *quick* and *study* are the collocates.

A good example of collocation is the pairing of verbs with prepositions, which is idiomatic in a language. For example, in English we get *bored with* but *tired of* it. There's no clear reason why *with* is paired with *bored* and *of* is paired with *tired* when the meaning of the phrases is so similar. (But hold that thought.)

Collocations like this are particularly noticeable to—and frustrating for—people who are learning a language. And they differ by language, meaning that the instincts you have from your native language don't necessarily help you when you learn another language. For example, in English we say that someone is *married to* their partner; in Spanish, the expression is *casado con* ("married with"), which an English speaker would learn only by memorizing the expression.

Collocations help with computer-aided language—with machine translation or with predictive text on your phone. When you're texting, a program in your phone is searching for collocations based on what you've already entered and offering you the terms that it finds most statistically probable. For example:

Collocations can change over time. In standard English, we say "by accident." But a study[21] of collocations in vernacular English suggests that younger speakers tend to say "on accident," meaning that the collocation of *by* and *on* with *accident* is changing in the language. Similarly, the collocation *bored by* seems to be changing, and the collocation *bored of* seems to be taking over from *bored with*. This again shows that colloca-

---

[21] http://www.inst.at/trans/16Nr/01_4/barratt16.htm

tions are not fixed phrases, but just terms that, as the commenter said, are in love with another—but they might find themselves attracted to another word.

Related terms: fossil word

contronym (Janus word)

Suppose you ran across a sentence like this in a newspaper article:

> After an inquiry, the ethics board has sanctioned the mayor's behavior.

You'd have to read more in the article to learn whether the ethics board punished the politician's behavior or whether they approved of it. That's because the word *sanction* is a *contronym*—a word that not only has multiple meanings, but has two *opposite* meanings. A more colorful name for contronyms is *Janus word*, which refers to the Roman god of doorways and change, who had two faces that looked in opposite directions. (Also the source of the name *January* for the first month.)

Here are some more examples. The word *oversight* can mean "careless error" or "supervision":

> The accident was due to an oversight by the operator.

> The accident led to greater oversight of the operators.

The word *seed* can mean "to plant" or "to remove seeds from":

> After the field is plowed, the next step is to seed it with corn.

> After cutting the grapefruit, you should seed it.

The word *clip* can mean "to fasten" or "to cut a piece" from:

> After we've filled out the forms, we're supposed to clip them and put them in the envelope.

> We clipped the video to show just the interesting part.

It seems odd that a word can end up with an apparently opposite meaning, but it's happened quite a few times:

- *apology* (a statement of regret, a defense of)
- *bolt* (to secure, to run away)
- *cleave* (to split, to adhere to)
- *lease* (to rent from, to rent to)
- *peer* (a member of the nobility, your equal)
- *presently* (now, in a short while)
- *ravel* (to tangle, to unravel)
- *strike* (to hit, or to miss while trying to hit)
- *toss out* (to discard, to suggest)
- *wear* (to deteriorate, to endure)
- *with* (alongside, against, as in "to fight with")

A page on the DailyWritingTips site[22] lists more than 70 contronyms of different levels of oppositeness, so to speak.

For the most part, it's clear from context which meaning was intended, as some of the earlier examples show. For example, no one thinks that you're supposed to *add* seeds to a grapefruit after cutting it. But once in a while you do need to get clarification, as with the example about sanctions or the often-confusing *presently*.

In the children's book series about Amelia Bedelia, Amelia is a maid in a rich household who takes everything she's told literally. Contronyms play a role here. For example, when she's told to dust the furniture, she sprinkles powder on it, confusing the verbs *dust* "to remove the dust from" with *dust* "to sprinkle with a powder or dust." She later explains that she didn't realize that she was supposed to "*un*dust" the furniture. (She overcomes her employers' annoyance at these antics by baking delicious pies and cakes.)

How could we end up with so many words that have opposing meanings? One path is through the expansion of a word's meaning—that is, of semantic broadening. A word's meaning changes over time to become more general, and at some point the meaning (or one of them) comes to include an opposite meaning from the original sense. The Merriam-

---

[22] https://www.dailywritingtips.com/75-contronyms-words-with-contradictory-meanings/

Webster site uses the example of *peruse*,[23] which originally meant "to examine closely," but evolved to mean just "to read" and then "to browse." Result: opposite meanings.

In another case, what is seemingly one word today actually evolved out of two different words that ended up sounding the same. This is what happened with *cleave*, which is the result in modern English of the evolution of what were two different verbs back in Anglo-Saxon.

We're still developing contronyms. One example is the word *nonplussed*, which people use to mean either "unfazed" or "taken aback." (In formal writing, *nonplussed* is therefore probably a skunked term.)

Other contronyms arise in slang. During the 20th century with the word *bad*, which can mean "not good" but in slang usage can also be used admiringly ("The hero of that movie is one bad dude"). Other fairly contemporary examples are *wicked*, *killer*, and *sick*, which all have slang senses that are the opposite of what you'd find as the first sense in a dictionary. Or what about the word *drop* in "Netflix dropped the series." Does that mean that they made it available or that they canceled it? You'd need more context to be sure.

If you encounter a term that seems to suggest the opposite of what you think the speaker intends, you might need to stop and ask. If that seems embarrassing, consider having a peek at UrbanDictionary.com. But do be aware that words sometimes mean just the opposite of what you think.

Related terms: retronym, semantic broadening

conversational deletion

I bet you can imagine an exchange like the following:

> Person 1: Nice day today!
> Person 2: Supposed to be nice all week.
> Person 1: Well, better be going.
> Person 2: See you tomorrow.

---

[23] https://www.merriam-webster.com/words-at-play/peruse-usage

This is a perfectly normal conversation. Normal, except that all the utterances have elements missing. It's more obvious if you see them filled in:

> Person 1: *It's a* nice day today!
> Person 2: *It's* supposed to be nice all week.
> Person 1: Well, *I'd* better be going.
> Person 2: *I'll* see you tomorrow.

What's going on here? It's a phenomenon known as *conversational deletion*. If you picture a sentence written out, we can drop, or "erode," the left-most part of the sentence, which is why conversational deletion is also called *left-edge deletion*. Conversational deletion often involves leaving out pronouns; that particular kind of conversational deletion is referred to as *pro-drop* for "pronoun dropping."[24]

As the name implies, we engage in conversational deletion often in conversation. Here are a few more examples:

> Mind if I join you?

> Buddy of mine called yesterday.

> Who you gonna call?

It turns out that there are certain principles that guide what can and can't be eroded, and where the erosion can take place. As the examples show, conversational deletion allows us to remove the subject if the subject is a pronoun. But you can't drop the pronoun if it's stressed. If you're answering the question "Can you help me move tomorrow?" you have to include the pronoun in "I will be there." We can also erode words in negative sentences like "Don't get around much anymore" that we can't in their positive counterparts; we can't say "Do get around much" or "Get around much."

The rules of conversational deletion also allow us to sometimes drop auxiliary verbs—*Mind if I join you?* is missing *Do you*. In *See you to-*

---

[24] Technically, English is not a pro-drop language the way that Spanish is, or Latin. In pro-drop languages, the verb form is marked well enough that it's clear who or what the subject is. For example, in the Spanish sentence *¿Cómo estás?* the *s* ending on *estás* makes it clear that the sentence means "How are *you*?" English verbs are mostly not marked to indicate the subject (*How **are** you*, *How **are** we*, *How **are** they*), so we rely on pronouns to make that clear. Yet there are situations in which we can drop pronouns, like the ones discussed here.

morrow, the sentence is missing *I will*. We can also erode articles (*a*, *the*), as in *Buddy of mine ...*).

In questions, the deletion is more subtle than just removing the left edge of the sentence. In those cases, conversational deletion can occur after the question word, as in the *Who [are] you gonna call?* example.

Not surprisingly, there are also specific contexts in which conversational deletion can occur—it occurs in conversation, obviously, and in informal writing. In these situations, conversational deletion can be efficient. In a podcast (starting at 16:00) about conversational deletion[25], the linguist Daniel Midgley said, "When something's obvious, you don't need to say it." If you're literally in a conversation, there's always the option for your interlocutor to stop and ask "Wait, who do you mean?" although it's rarely unclear.

These days, informal writing includes emails and social media. But in previous decades when this phenomenon first came under the linguistic microscope, examples were often cited from diaries and letters. (Yet another name for conversational deletion is *diary drop*.)

In fact, conversational deletion is so marked for informality that it can be startling when you find it in a formal(ish) context. Not long ago I was surprised to find an example of conversational deletion in an unexpected place—an alert in Microsoft Outlook:

I don't know where *Do you* went, but it seems to be missing from this message.

Related terms: tag question

---

[25] https://talkthetalkpodcast.com/389-mailbag-of-pronouns/

corpus

A couple of interesting editorial questions came up recently among editors I know:

- What do people use as the past tense of *to mow*—is it *has mowed* or *has mown*?
- Can we use the term *customer-facing* to refer to a web page that anyone can see, not just people inside the company?

The traditional approach to answering these questions is to grab a reference book and see what they say. The Merriam-Webster dictionary says that *has mowed* and *has mown* are both acceptable past tense forms of *to mow*. As for *customer-facing*, at the time we were looking, Merriam-Webster didn't have an entry for that term. (Perhaps they do now.)

Looking in the dictionary might have answered our immediate question. But there are lingering issues. Sure, both *mowed* and *mown* are acceptable. But which one do people use *more*? And as an editor, I might be looking at a draft article where the author insists that everyone understands the term *customer-facing*. Is it possible that the dictionary is not the final story on this word?

Suppose that instead of looking at a dictionary, you could somehow search the language itself—search through English as speakers actually write it: books, magazines, maybe even social media. That is, in effect, what a *corpus* is: a collection—a database—of English. A corpus is built by having a computer scan thousands or millions of books, articles, scripts, social media posts, or other raw sources of written English. After some processing, the text is then available to be searched and analyzed. It's like taking the entire contents of a library—books, magazines, newspapers—and putting it online for easy search.

There isn't one single, searchable corpus that incorporates all of English. But there are many corpora that represent large and useful collections of the language. (Given their roots as academics, linguists use *corpora* as the plural.)

A well-known and easily accessible corpus is the collection that Google created by scanning as many books as it could from between the years 1500 and 2008. This enormous corpus—currently the largest in

English—is searchable by using the Google Ngram Viewer.[26] The graph below shows a Google Ngram Viewer search result for the terms *corpora* and *corpuses*. From this corpus search, we can see that in printed books, *corpora* (top line, blue) is more popular than *corpuses* (bottom line, red) as the plural of *corpus*.

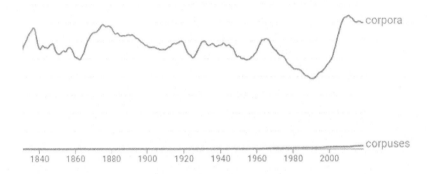

The Ngram Viewer allows you to search for individual terms, for contrasting sets of terms (as in the example), and for terms used as particular parts of speech, to name just a few of its many capabilities.

Another well-known corpus is the Corpus of Contemporary American English (COCA).[27] This includes about a billion words derived from newspapers, magazines, fiction, academic publications, and (some) spoken sources. Another corpus maintained by the same group is the Global Web-Based English corpus, which includes 1.9 billion words derived from English-language publications in 20 English-dominant locales.

The value of searchable corpora, of course, is that people who are interested in language questions don't have to wait till reference books like dictionaries catch up with how the language is currently being used. For example, in the old days, to get empirical data about emerging usages or dialectical variations, linguists used to interview subjects, which obviously is a process that's slow and limited. (A dialect survey done in 2003[28] that asked questions online got about 30,000 participants, which

---

[26] https://books.google.com/ngrams

[27] https://www.english-corpora.org/coca/

[28] http://dialect.redlog.net/

was a *huge* survey for its day.) Now anyone can search any of these corpora to get data about how people use the language.

I mentioned earlier that some of us editors had been asking about *mowed/mown* and about *customer-facing*. To get insight into those questions, I searched the iWeb corpus that contains 14 billion words. At the time I searched (corpora are always being updated, so things can change fast), I found this:

- The corpus has 134 instances of *have mowed* and 21 of *has mown*. I also found 52 instances of *has mowed* and 7 of *has mown*. I was able to conclude that *mowed* is the more popular past tense form of *to mow*.

- The corpus has 5,550 hits for *customer-facing* (3,323 for *customer facing* without the hyphen). The corpus lets you examine the sentences where words are used, and it also tells you the source of the text. By looking at that data, I got a sense of what types of texts the term *customer-facing* appears in. This in turn helped me judge whether the author was correct that readers for our document would understand the term.

In both cases, I feel like I know more than I would have if I'd just closed the dictionary and called it a day.

The linguist Lynne Murphy has a good example of using corpus searches to investigate a question about playing musical instruments. Which is more common: *play piano* or *play **the** piano*? And is one of these phrases more common in British English versus American English? She talks about her searches, including technicalities like looking for variants like *play*, *playing*, and *played*, in her blog post "playing (the) musical instruments."[29]

I usually use corpus searches to investigate usage questions that come up during editing. But corpora are used for all sorts of things. As more and more old publications are digitized and made available in corpora, dictionary makers can research more easily when words first appeared and how they were used. (Corpora make it easier to antedate a term— that is, find earlier occurrences than the earliest known example.) The

---

[29] https://separatedbyacommonlanguage.blogspot.com/2015/09/playing-musical-instruments.html

linguist Dennis Baron has been using corpora to research attempts over the centuries to devise a pronoun that means both "he" and "she"; that is, to find alternatives for singular *they*. Several linguists have been looking at corpora of historical English to try to figure out what the writers of the US Constitution meant by the phrase "bear arms."

Some linguists have started using Twitter as a kind of corpus. Although Twitter isn't directly searchable the way a corpus is, the linguists take periodic gulps from the Twitter firehose and then analyze what they've managed to capture. The immediacy of Twitter has allowed these linguists to see how people are using language nearly in real time. For example, the linguist Jack Grieve has used Twitter-based analysis to find new terms in American English almost as they're emerging and map them by region. (You can read one of Grieve's papers about his work with Twitter in the article "Mapping Lexical Innovation on American Social Media" in the *Journal of English Linguistics*.)

Corpora are also just fun to use. Everyone has questions about words, and it's easy to plug the words into a corpus search and see what you can learn.

Related terms: antedating

cranberry morpheme (cran-morph)

If you wander around the produce section of a grocery store, you'll find a variety of berries. At different times of the year you might find blueberries, blackberries, cranberries, and raspberries.

Leaving aside the deliciousness of berries, if you crack apart the names of the berries, you see that each name consists of two parts, like *blue* + *berry*. In language circles, these individual word parts are called *morphemes*; the term *morpheme* comes from roots that mean "form" + "unit." (Compare the word *morpheme* to the verb *morph*, meaning "to change form.")

The berry names all have two morphemes. The second one is *berry*. The first varies: *blue, black, cran, rasp*. The first two are obviously based on color: blueberries are blue, and blackberries are black. But what's cran-like about a cranberry? Or rasp-ish about a raspberry? For that matter, what's huckle-y about a huckleberry, another type of berry?

Basically, nothing—in modern English, these morphemes don't really have a meaning on their own.

Let's back up. Most morphemes carry a meaning that they contribute to the words that they're in. In the word *footballs*, there are three morphemes: *foot*, *ball*, and the *s* ending to mark a plural. Each of these morphemes appears in other words where it has the same sense as in *footballs*, such as **foot**wear, base**ball**, and *word***s**.

In contrast, we don't know what the *cran* part of *cranberry* is, but we know that a cranberry is different from a blueberry. Same for *rasp* and *huckle*. These morphemes don't appear in other words; for example, there are no other words with *rasp* or *huckle* in them in a way that corresponds to *raspberry* and *huckleberry*.

It was this special case of words like *cranberry* that provided a name for this phenomenon: a *cranberry morpheme*—or *cran-morph* for short. A cran-morph is a morpheme that doesn't have a meaning itself and whose only function seems to be to distinguish one word from another.

There are other examples of cran-morphs in English. Take the word *cobweb*. That's another word that's made up of two morphemes (*cob* + *web*). What does *cob* mean? Not really anything; it doesn't really add any meaning to the word *web*. You can't attach *cob* to another morpheme to create a new term from it. But a cobweb is specifically a spiderweb as opposed to some other kind of web. Other cran-morphs include *twi* in *twilight* and *cray* in *crayfish*.

Ironically, the *cran* part of *cranberry* is evolving away from being a cranberry morpheme. As noted, cranberry morphemes appear only in one word; they don't have a meaning of their own. But in the 1960s, a marketer named Edward Gelsthorpe was working at Ocean Spray, which is a company that harvests a lot of cranberries. Cranberries were traditionally sold only seasonally, and the company was looking for ways to generate year-round sales. Gelsthorpe blended cranberry juice, which is very tart, with apple juice in order to create a sweet drink. He named his invention Cran-Apple juice. It sold big, so he went on to invent Cran-Grape juice and products like Craisins (dried cranberries, as in *cran* + *raisin*).

You can probably see what's happening here: the *cran* in *cranberry*, which was once a cran-morph, has broken away, developed a standalone meaning, and made itself available to be combined with other words. For example, today you can also get a *crantini*, which is a martini with cranberry juice. Or to put it another way, *cran* has evolved from a cranberry morpheme into a libfix, which you can read about elsewhere in this book.

A fairly recent example of a word that highlights a cran-morph is in the word *repeat*. Although the *re* prefix means "again," the *peat* part doesn't really mean anything. Or does it? In the sports world, they talk these days about as *three-peat*, where a team wins three championships, especially if they're in a row. What was once a cran-morph (*peat*) has evolved slightly toward becoming a libfix that means something like "repetition" or maybe "time."

One final note. In case you were wondering, cranberry morphemes don't have a real meaning today, but they often did historically. The *cran* in *cranberry* is related to the word *crane*, for the bird. The *cob* in *cobweb* comes from *coppe*, an obsolete word for spider. And so on—many cran-morphs are just fossils of older words. (But not all. For more about the *cray* in *crayfish*, see folk etymology.) But as you saw, cran-morphs, even if they're fossils, might not be content to sit still forever.

Related terms: fossil word, libfix, unpaired word

crash blossom

A friend of mine has an amazing eye for news headlines like these, which he sends me regularly:

> Liquefied Natural Gas Protesters Build Longhouse Blocking Utility Headquarters

> Police Shoot Man with Dementia

You might need to read that first headline more than once to grasp that it's the natural gas that's liquefied, not the protesters. As for the second headline, as my friend said, "I guess it's better than shooting him with bullets."

You could call these types of headlines *ambiguous headlines*, which is clear but maybe a little boring. It turns out there's a much more interesting name: these headlines are all examples of *crash blossoms*.

Why *crash blossom*? It goes back to one particular headline that appeared in 2010 in the newspaper *Japan Today*:

Japan Violinist Linked to JAL Crash Blossoms

As with the earlier examples, maybe you need to read this more than once to figure out what it means. If so, you're not alone. On an online discussion forum for editors, one of the editors asked, "What's a crash blossom?"

As it turned out, a *crash blossom* in the headline isn't a thing. Instead, *blossom* is an action; it described what the violinist was doing—in other words, her career was flowering. The headline also attempted to capture a different fact, namely that some years earlier, her father had been on a JAL flight that had crashed (thus she was "linked to" the flight).

During the discussion on the editor's forum, another editor suggested that *crash blossom* would be a good name for these ambiguous headlines. The term caught on, and how. The linguists who post and comment on the *Language Log* blog now routinely use *crash blossom* when new examples come up (which they do often), and dictionaries now include the term.

There are many examples of crash blossoms; if you keep an eye out, you can find them pretty regularly. Here's an example that someone posted on Twitter, where the ambiguity is in the words *bans* and *face*:

Chris Steller
@chris_steller

What are face lawsuits?

Another example from Twitter is the following headline, where it's easy to misread *just misses*:

Douglas Cheape
@CheapeDouglas

Poor thing.

In the following headline, I stumbled on *building fire*, in which *building* is intended as a noun, not a verb:

Crews make progress on building fire in Seattle's White Center neighborhood

By FOX 13 News Staff | **Published** July 16, 2022 2:26PM | News | FOX 13 Seattle

There are also well-known examples that might be apocryphal, like these:

> Squad Helps Dog Bite Victim
>
> Red Tape Holds Up New Bridge
>
> March Planned For Next August

Crash blossoms are a form of garden-path sentence, which is a sentence that can lead you astray (down the garden path, as they say) because of some sort of ambiguity. The ambiguity can be in the meaning of words—for example, in "Red Tape Holds Up Bridge," *holds up* can mean either "suspend" or "delay." Or the ambiguity can be syntactic—that is, in the sentence structure. That's what happened in the original crash-blossom headline—*blossom* is intended as a verb, but the word is easily read as a noun.

Headlines are particularly prone to this issue. To save space, headlines often omit words that would otherwise clarify the meaning or provide clues about the parts of speech for each word. It's quite an art to write in headline-ese, and given the constraints of space and time that editors work under, it's no wonder that sometimes the result is a little wonky.

I wonder whether journalists sometimes deliberately craft ambiguous headlines for their own amusement. Someday I'll take a newspaper editor out to eat and get the inside story. Or as the headline might read, "Man Grills Editor at Lunch."

Related terms: attachment ambiguity, garden-path sentence, noun pile, squinting modifier

cutthroat compound

What do the words *turncoat, pinchpenny, pickpocket,* and *cutthroat* have in common? Well, for starters, they describe people you probably don't want to associate with. Nor do you probably want any of these descriptions to appear on your résumé.

But they also have an interesting structural similarity: they're words that are consist of a verb plus a noun:

- A *cutthroat* cuts throats
- A *pickpocket* picks pockets
- A *pinchpenny* pinches pennies (metaphorically)
- A *turncoat* turns their coat (again, metaphorically)

It turns out we have over a thousand of these verb + noun words in English. This fact caught the interest of the linguist Brianne Hughes. She named them *cutthroat compounds,* using an example of the phenomenon as the name of the genre. As she notes, the compounds had been discussed before using names like "verb-noun compounds," but Hughes, in addition to her work in finding cutthroats, has come up with a much more interesting name.

Hughes collects cutthroat compounds assiduously. The last time I looked, she had more than 1,200 of them, listed in a PDF file on her personal site.[30]

The examples I listed earlier all described bad people. But not all cutthroats are negative. Here are some others:

- *breakfast*
- *ceasefire*
- *hush-puppy*
- *jump-rope*
- *scarecrow*

Many cutthroat compounds are nouns, but some are adjectives (a *tell-all* story, a *do-nothing* Congress). Some are names, like *Dudley Do-Right* and *Silence Dogood,* the latter of which was a pen name for the young Benjamin Franklin.

---

[30] http://www.encyclopediabriannica.com/wp-content/uploads/2017/04/1273Cutthroats.pdf

Admittedly, many of the cutthroat compounds that Hughes has found are archaic terms, like *hanghead*, *makesport*, and *rake-hell*. Among the more obscure cutthroats are loan translations (calques) from other languages, especially French. We even have a few that are still in their original language. From French we have *amuse-bouche* ("gratify the mouth") and *mangetout* ("eat all," a British name for snow peas). From Spanish we have *Chupacabra* ("suck-goat").

Cutthroat compounds aren't very "productive," as they say in word circles; that is, we don't use this type of verb + noun compounding to create new words. Or at least, not very much—but we sometimes still see it in brand names like *Armor All* and *Disposall*, a brand of garbage disposal manufactured by GE.

It's fun to keep an eye out for cutthroat compounds. Several times I've found one and relayed it to Hughes. Each time I've done that, she already has that one on her list. But I keep hoping that I'll find one that's new to her.

Related terms: cranberry morpheme, libfix, portmanteau word

demonym, endonym, exonym

Let's start with an easy one: what do you call the inhabitants of Russia? *Russians*, of course. What about someone who lives in California? A *Californian*. Still pretty easy. What do you call the residents of Los Angeles? Someone might have to tell you that these are *Angelenos*. What about people who live in Liverpool in the UK? Those are the not-entirely-intuitive *Liverpudlians* or the entirely opaque *Scousers*.

These terms—*Russians*, *Angelenos*, *Liverpudlians*—are examples of *demonyms*, or names for the people who inhabit a place. That's one name; this type of label is also referred to as a *gentilic*, a *denizen label*, and a *municipal onomastic*.

Wikipedia uses the word *demonym*, and demonyms are frequently in the sidebars in entries for geographic locations. For example, the entry for Manila in the Philippines tells you the demonyms for inhabitants of

Manila in various languages. From that, you can learn that the demonym in English for Manila residents is *Manileño/Manileña* or *Manilan*.

Population (2020 census)[7][8]	
• **City**	1,846,513
• **Density**	48,000/km^2 (120,000/sq mi)
• Urban	24,100,000[6]
• Metro	13,484,482
• **Metro density**	22,000/km^2 (56,000/sq mi)
• Households	409,987
Demonym(s)	English: Manileño, Manilan; Spanish: *manilense*,[9] *manileño(-a)* Filipino: Manileño(-a), Manilenyo(-a), Taga-Maynila

Many demonyms (not all) are the same as the adjective form of a place name. We have a variety of ways to create these in English, generally by adding a suffix to the place name. For example, we can do the following (sometimes with changes to the stem):

- Add *(a)n*: *Italian, Nebraskan, Chicagoan, Manilan*
- Add *ian*: *Oregonian, Parisian, Glaswegian* (for Glasgow)
- Add *(e)r*: *New Yorker, Portlander, Londoner*
- Add *ite*: *Seattleite, Manhattanite, Muscovite* (for Moscow)
- Add *ese*: *Javanese, Viennese* (for Vienna)
- Add *i*: *Israeli, Nepali*

There are others as well (*Earthling, Cypriot*).

It's not always clear how to form a demonym, even to people who live in an area. A reporter who lives in Salt Lake City, Ben Winslow, took to Twitter to ask what residents of that city should be called: "Salt Lakers?" "Salt Lake Citians?" "Saltines?" There were lots of great replies, although it seems that the accepted demonym is the straightforward *Salt Laker*. (But how great is *Saltines*?)

Similarly, if perhaps less amusing, people who live in the state of Michigan have variously referred to themselves as *Michiganians* and *Michiganders*. In 2017, though, the state decreed the official demonym as *Michigander*. To help avoid confusion of this sort, the *U.S. Govern-*

ment Publishing Official Style Manual includes a list of the demonyms that they recommend for publications by the federal government:

5.23. In designating the natives of the States, the following forms will be used.

Alabamian	Kentuckian	North Dakotan
Alaskan	Louisianian	Ohioan
Arizonan	Mainer	Oklahoman
Arkansan	Marylander	Oregonian
Californian	Massachusettsan	Pennsylvanian
Coloradan	Michiganian	Rhode Islander
Connecticuter	Minnesotan	South Carolinian
Delawarean	Mississippian	South Dakotan
Floridian	Missourian	Tennessean
Georgian	Montanan	Texan
Hawaii resident	Nebraskan	Utahn
Hoosier	Nevadan	Vermonter
(Indiana)	New Hampshirite	Virginian
Idahoan	New Jerseyan	Washingtonian
Illinoisan	New Mexican	West Virginian
Iowan	New Yorker	Wisconsinite
Kansan	North Carolinian	Wyomingite

They also include a list of nationalities so you know their thinking about how to refer to the residents of places like Burkina Faso, the Faroe Islands, and San Marino.

Knowing the demonym for people in a region can be a kind of shibboleth that can mark you as an inside or outsider. That's especially true for non-obvious demonyms, like *Scouser* for Liverpool residents, as noted earlier, or like *Hoosier* for residents of the state of Indiana in the US. Although I've lived in Seattle for decades, I discovered only recently that the residents of the Fremont neighborhood in our city refer to themselves as *Fremonsters*.

Demonyms can also be controversial. For example, people in Hawai'i are sensitive to the use of the term *Hawaiian*. The issue is that not everyone who lives in Hawai'i is ethnically Hawaiian. Therefore, some people in Hawai'i consider it important to make a distinction between the adjective *Hawaiian* (of or pertaining to ethnically Hawaiian people) and the demonym *resident of Hawai'i*.

Similarly, there's the question of what to call people who live in the United States. The most frequently used demonym is of course *Ameri-*

can. That's what Wikipedia lists in the entry for United States, with footnotes citing its sources. But the western hemisphere contains North America and South America, so a lot of people are not necessarily happy to let *American* define only residents of the US. There are formal demonyms in other languages for *American*, such as *états-unien* in French and *estadounidenses* in Spanish. In Mexico, residents of "the north" are often referred to as *norteamericanos*. (That said, these languages also have the words *americain* and *americano* that are used as the demonyms.)

The problem is that the name of the country—*United States of America*—doesn't lend itself to easy adjectivization, hence to an obvious demonym—certainly not in English. In any event, it's wise for, um, Unitedstatesians traveling abroad to be sensitive in telling people their country of origin.

Demonyms can also change. A couple of centuries ago, the typical demonym for someone from England would have been *an Englishman*. But *man* is no longer considered ungendered (it's no longer a hypernym for "person"), so today you'd want to use a term like *an English person*.

And history can catch up with demonyms. A couple of generations ago, people from a specific part of central Europe could be referred to as *Yugoslavs*. But the country formerly known as Yugoslavia broke up in the 1990s, and the people who live in that area now use a variety of demonyms, including some that reflect historical ethnic ties, like *Croats*, *Serbs*, *Slovenians*, and *Macedonians*. A lesson from these changes is that before using a demonym to describe someone, you'd want to check with them first.

A couple of special cases of demonyms are *endonyms* and *exonyms*. An *endonym* is the name that a people use for themselves, for geographic features of their region, or for their language. This is also known as an *autonym*. An *exonym* is what other people call them or their region. This is also known as an *xenonym*.

For example, English speakers refer to the residents of Wales using the exonym *Welsh*; the people of that country refer to themselves using the endonym *Cymry*. The words *Wales* and *Welsh* derive from an old Germanic word that originally referred to the people in the Western Roman Empire who didn't speak Germanic, and that was used by the Anglo-Saxons to refer to their Celtic Briton neighbors. Related words are *Cornwall*, *Walloon*, and *walnut*. The words *Cymru* and *Cymry* derive from a

Celtic term that means "fellow-countryman," which is how the, er, Cymry view themselves. (You'll sometimes see *Wales* and *Welsh* listed as deriving from an old Germanic word for "foreigner," but the Welsh linguist Gareth Roberts disputes this theory.[31])

The linguist James A. Matisoff, who coined the term *autonym*, suggests that endonyms for the name of a people are often egocentric, associating the group with mankind in general, and that exonyms tend to be pejorative. For example, the name *Inuit* for the people who live in Greenland and in the polar regions of North America is an endonym that means "people." In contrast, the word *Eskimo* is a term that was probably a pejorative term in the language of the neighboring Algonquin people. These examples show how endonyms and exonyms are often a matter of the eye of the beholder.

Related terms: eponym, onomastics, toponym

descriptivism

Imagine that you've landed on an alien planet whose inhabitants, remarkably, speak a language that's similar to human languages. (This seems to be a necessary condition for many *Star Trek* episodes.) There's no English-to-alien translator, so you have to learn the alien language by full immersion.

You listen to the aliens speak and gradually discern patterns. You figure out when they're talking about something that happened yesterday and something that'll happen tomorrow. You deduce when they're talking about themselves or about others. You sort out their counting system. You learn how they refer to everyone in their extended families. You study how they talk differently at home, in their alien workplaces, and when they're giving alien speeches while running for alien president.

To help other earthlings who visit the aliens, you write all these facts down in a book, which you call *The Grammar of the Alien Language.*

---

[31] https://tinyurl.com/4nytwyjt

What you're doing is called *descriptivism*: an approach to language that seeks to describe how it works. The discipline of linguistics is fundamentally a descriptivist enterprise. In this regard, linguistics works by the same principle as any science: empirical observation. Its approaches and interests are much like those of psychology, sociology, and anthropology—sciences that aim to study human (or alien) behavior.

Descriptivism is sometimes contrasted with *prescriptivism*, which is an approach to language that focuses on recommending, or "prescribing," the proper way to use the language. When you study language arts in school, you're usually following a prescriptivist agenda, which focuses on correct spelling, when to use *affect* and when to use *effect*, and the best way to write a persuasive essay. These are useful skills, but they're not the focus of descriptivist-oriented linguists, who are less interested in making sure you keep *affect* and *effect* straight than in questions like how we ended up with this pair and whether there's evidence that native speakers are merging the terms.

Think about that grammar book that you wrote about the alien language. Your grammar is more like a physics or chemistry textbook: it describes the mechanics of a system, like how the verbs work, how to form plurals, and the terms that the aliens use for counting. That's what a *grammar* is to a linguist. Your (prescriptivist) grammar textbook for English class mostly doesn't bother with that sort of thing; after all, you already know how to speak English. Instead, the grammar book in your school is about how to refine your English for specific situations—generally, English for use in professional contexts. In one sense, your English-class grammar textbook is a kind of etiquette manual that tells you how to dress up your English for various formal occasions.

Although it's sometimes characterized that way, descriptivism is not "the opposite" of prescriptivism. At least, not any more than a sociologist who studies the dynamics of behavior at a cocktail party is "the opposite" of someone who advises people on how to network at parties. One observes and discovers and describes; the other recommends.

Descriptivists and prescriptivists do sometimes find themselves at odds about what constitutes "correct" language. A good example is in how each group approaches the question of dialects. There are hundreds of dialects of English, from so-called Queen's English to Scots English to Jamaican English to New England English to African American English

(AAE) to the varieties of English spoken in Canada, Southern California, Australia, India, and many more places. The dialects differ in what words they use, how words are pronounced, and even in their grammar. (Even this is simplified. Speakers in these speech communities or regions don't have a single dialect or way of using English. The general point is that there are many varieties of English and they all have differences from "standard" English.)

Prescriptivism generally focuses on one acceptable dialect, whatever the prestige dialect is of the country in question. In England, for example, prescriptivism might hold up so-called Queen's English as the one correct dialect and might then consider all other dialects to be incorrect. In contrast, descriptivists as a rule don't believe that a specific dialect is *inherently* more correct than another. Instead, they're interested in the mechanics of each dialect—how it works, how it differs from other dialects. (People are sometimes surprised to learn that dialects like AAE have grammatical elements that aren't in other dialects, including standard American written English.)

These days, dictionaries are generally written on descriptivist principles. Lexicographers research how people use the language today and dutifully record what they've learned. For example, they do a lot of research in corpora. As a result, words get into the dictionary that some people consider invalid. Take the word *irregardless*. The Merriam-Webster dictionary includes an entry for *irregardless*, which many people consider "not a word." But from a descriptivist point of view, people do use *irregardless*, so it must be a word, and the dictionary's job is to record what people say and write. The dictionary entry for *irregardless* does label the word as "nonstandard," which is a judgment call, but still one that's based on the research that lexicographers do.

Because descriptivists base their analyses on how people use the language in everyday speech and writing, they're sometimes accused of having an "anything goes" attitude toward what constitutes correct English. This is a misrepresentation of the descriptivist approach. It's true that the language of native speakers is considered the ultimate guide to how English works. But language is a communal act, and it's how a *community* uses language that defines it. Whether something is right or wrong is a matter of whether someone is following the rules of that community when interacting with that community. To use a fashion-based analogy, neither swimsuits nor ballgowns are correct or incorrect. But if you wear one to an event that calls for the other, you've made an error.

To be clear, linguists (i.e., descriptivists) certainly understand the *social* implications of using a privileged dialect versus using a stigmatized one. And in fact, the social implications of using different types of language are the purview of a branch called sociolinguistics.

The topic of descriptivism, and especially its relationship to prescriptivism, is a large and fraught one, since it tends to follow the contours of questions about "right" and "wrong" behavior. The important point is that linguists are, for the most part, not in the business of telling people how to speak their own language. Mostly they're interested in trying to figure out how language actually works.

Related terms: prescriptivism

double genitive (double possessive)

A friend of mine occasionally sends me examples of English that he thinks are illogical. One construction that bugs him is a phrase like *a friend of my mother's*. The phrase contains *of*, he explains, so it doesn't also need the possessive version of *mother* (*mother's*).

If English were built on logical principles (pro tip: it's not), his argument would be unassailable. You can argue that *She's a friend of my mother* is perfectly understandable, and that yes, adding the possessive to *mother* is gratuitous.

But that's not the way English works. People *do* say "a friend of my mother's." They also say "a friend of mine" and "a friend of hers." They might say "a friend of my mother," but they definitely don't say "a friend of me" or "a friend of her." Logic aside, we seem to be comfortable with the word *of* plus the possessive. If the possessive word is a pronoun, we're more than comfortable with this construction; in that case, using both *of* and the possessive is mandatory.

As you might guess, there's a name for this combination: the *double genitive* or *double possessive*.

Let's take a short step back. We have two ways in English to indicate possession. In grammatical terms, possessive is also known as *genitive*. One way to indicate possession is to add apostrophe + *s* to a noun, as in *my mother's pen*. Another way is to use *of*, as in *the pen of my mother*, which is referred to as *periphrastic possessive*, referring to the indirectness of the possessive. Double genitives use both: *It was a pen **of** my mother's*.

To complicate things, there are a few cases where using or not using a double genitive changes the meaning of a phrase. A typical example is this:

a picture of Harry's

a picture of Harry

In the first example, you're talking about a picture that belongs to Harry; he possesses it. In the second example, the picture is one in which Harry is the subject of the picture. Notice that this is different from the examples earlier about friends (*a friend of my mother* or *a friend of my mother's*), where including or not including the second possessive doesn't change the meaning.

Like I said, English sometimes doesn't follow algebraic-type logic. Even so, English speakers implicitly understand the set of rules for using (or not using) double genitive. As the word historian Michael Quinion notes on his World Wide Words site about the double genitive, "the rules are precise and strict and are understood and followed by every speaker of idiomatic English."[32]

I should note that just because double genitive is a recognized feature of English, that doesn't mean people always agree about whether it's the best way to express possession. For advice, consult your local editor.

Related terms: pleonasm

---

[32] http://www.worldwidewords.org/qa/qa-dou3.htm

double modal (multiple modal)

A colleague swings by your desk and asks if it would be possible to squeeze in a project on short notice. After you look at your calendar, you think you probably can do it, so you say, "I *might be able* to do that."

But if you live in certain parts of the English-speaking world, perhaps you say, "I *might could* do that."

The second example is not considered standard English because it uses what's called a *double modal*.

Modal verbs are a class of auxiliary ("helper") verbs, like *can, will, may, might, should,* and *could.* These verbs express ability (*can, could*), possibility (*might*), permission (*may*), or obligation (*shall, should*).

The modal verb appears in the normal position for a verb (for example, immediately following the subject), and the main verb follows. Here are some examples of the standard use of modal verbs, where the modal is in bold.

> I *can* help you.
>
> We *might* be able to go.
>
> She *should* check with them.

In a double modal construction, more than one modal verb appears, as in these examples:

> She *might could* go with you.
>
> He *must not can* hear us.

Probably the most common example of a double modal is *might* with a second modal, as in *might could go* or *might should eat.*

Dialecticians also refer to these as *multiple modals*, because occasionally speakers use more than two modals, as in *He might will can't come.*

Some scholars at the University of South Carolina have created the MultiMo database to track examples of multiple modals.[33] At the moment, they have over 2200 entries, which you can filter to find combina-

---

[33] https://artsandsciences.sc.edu/multimo/

tions you're curious about, to learn how and where they collected examples, and so on.

I'm going to note that some linguists—most notably Geoff Pullum, co-author of the monumental *Cambridge Grammar of the English Language*—observe that double modals act in ways that standard modals don't and that they are therefore might not be verbs at all, but something more like adverbs (for example, *might could* is a lot like *maybe could*.) However, the *might could* construction and similar are most often called double modals, so that's what I'm going with here.

Double modals are a feature of dialects from the American South and some other non-urban dialects. They also appear in northern England and Scotland. They're often stigmatized by people who don't have these constructs in their dialects, even though double modals can be "more efficient"—that is, use fewer words—than the equivalents in standard English.

Double modals are more interesting than just being a variant on how to form verb phrases. For starters, they have their own internal grammar; there's a right way and a wrong way to create double modals. For example, you can say, "She **might could** go, but you can't say, "*She **must might** go," even though the second example is also a construction with two modals. The *general* pattern is that you can combine (in this order):

1. One of *might*, *may*, or *must* plus ...
2. One of *can*, *could*, *would*, *should*, or *will*.

So *must can* is legit, but **might must* is probably not correct. There are also rules about how double modals can be negated (*might shouldn't*) or turned into questions (*Could you might go?* or *Might should we have called?*).

However, I say that these are general patterns because double modals are used in many speech communities, and they aren't necessarily used exactly the same everywhere. I played around with different combinations of modals in the MultiMo database, but there weren't many with zero entries. (I should also note that double modals are not part of my dialect, so I don't have an intuitive feel for what is and isn't correct in trying to use them.)

Double modals are also interesting because they can convey a different sense than what the equivalent standard verb phrase does. As one linguist writes, double modals are "used for hedging, politeness, being noncommittal, and expressing certainty without wanting to show certainty."[34] For example, telling someone that they *should* do something might be a bit bossy-sounding, but telling them that they *might should* do it says the same thing, but a little more politely. The linguist Suzette Haden Elgin, who comes from the Ozarks, stood up for double modals when she felt that they had been "sassed" by a post on the *Language Log* blog and provided an explanation of how *maybe* and *might could be* had different connotations for her.[35]

As I said, double modals are often stigmatized as incorrect or at least uncouth. But that can work both ways. In that *Language Log* blog post, Ben Zimmer has a citation from then-governor Mike Huckabee of Arkansas, who at one point in an interview says, "They might would have had a different conclusion." Huckabee can hew closely to standard American English if he wants to, but there are times when it might have served him to inject some double modals to speak in the voice of his constituents.

Related terms: personal dative

eggcorn

Many years ago, I noticed that some people wrote the phrase *for all intents and purposes* as *for all intensive purposes*. And somewhere else along the line I encountered *It's a doggy-dog world* in place of *It's a dog-eat-dog world.*

Being younger and more callow, I found these mis-writings to be mock-worthy. I thought it would be interesting to collect similar examples, and to that end I even briefly owned the domain AllIntensivePurposes.com.

---

[34] If you have access to the journal *Lingua*, you can find it as J. Daniel Hasty, "We might should oughta take a second look at this: A syntactic re-analysis of double modals in Southern United States English," *Lingua* 122 (2012): 1716–1738.

[35] https://ozarque.livejournal.com/471118.html

I never did anything with the domain, which is just as well. Instead, I learned more about language. Linguists had noticed this phenomenon, of course, but it turned out there wasn't really a good name for it. During one discussion, someone brought up the example of *eggcorn*, which some people write in place of *acorn*. The linguist Geoff Pullum suggested that people just use the term *eggcorn* for this type of and it caught on. The word *eggcorn* even now appears in some dictionaries, including Merriam-Webster.

Eggcorns arise when people hear a term or expression but don't understand it correctly. In interpreting what they hear, they reanalyze it using words that sound the same or very similar. Although eggcorns originate in speech, they become noticeable when people write out the new interpretations. Here are some more examples:

- *deep-seeded* instead of *deep-seated*
- *new leash on life* instead of *new lease on life*
- *old-timer's disease* instead of *Alzheimer's disease*
- *a shoe-in* instead of *a shoo-in*

At first glance, an eggcorn might look like another type of error, namely a malapropism. They're not quite the same, though. A malapropism is using the wrong word, like saying *derangement* instead of *arrangement*. Eggcorns instead are the result of misinterpreting the *sound* of a phrase—for example, *deep-seated* and *deep-seeded* sound the same, at least as pronounced by most Americans. If you don't know that the idiom is *deep-seated*, it's easy to hear it as *deep-seeded*. It's a matter of interpreting the constituent words of a phrase differently.

Another feature of eggcorns is that they sort of make sense, even if at times you have to squint a bit. For example, *old-timer's disease* is a sensible substitution for *Alzheimer's disease* because it's a malady that affects older people. Similarly, as an idiom, *new leash on life* isn't any less sensible than *new lease on life*. And *eggcorn* is a reasonable name for an acorn, because an acorn really does look like a little egg with a cap on it, like this:

As Pullum says, eggcorns are "imaginative attempts at relating something heard to lexical material already known."

As I said earlier, I never set up a website devoted to *all intensive purposes*, but some other folks did. The linguist Chris Waigl created The Eggcorn Database, an online catalog of eggcorns.[36] The database tracks examples and citations and lets you search either by the "right" or the "wrong" term (for example, "shoe" or "shoo").

In the following episode of *Dinosaur Comics*, a comic strip that exhibits a keen language sensibility, T-Rex is schooled about his use of eggcorns:[37]

---

[36] http://eggcorns.lascribe.net/
[37] Source: Dinosaur Comics #1841, used with kind permission by Ryan North.

Eggcorns are part of a larger taxonomy of language errors, which are fascinating for what we can learn about how people hear, interpret, and produce language. For more on some of these errors, see these entries:

- Folk etymologies are words borrowed from other languages that have been "English-ized" to make them more like familiar words.
- Malaphors are mangled idioms.
- Malapropisms are the use of the wrong word, either as a slip of the tongue or because the user doesn't know the right word.
- Mondegreens are misheard song lyrics.
- Rebracketing is hearing the division between words incorrectly (*I scream/ice cream*).

Related terms: folk etymology, malaphor, malapropism, mondegreen, rebracketing

epenthesis

I was at the hardware store once when I overheard a customer ask a clerk where to find a *masonary bit* for his drill, with an *a* between *mason* and *ry*. This didn't sound right to me, so I went home and looked it up, and sure enough, the word is *masonry*, no intervening *a*. (But I did have to go look it up.)

I didn't hold it against the man who was looking for the drill bit. Trying to say the *n* of *mason* followed by the *r* of *ry* involves moving the tongue in the mouth in a slightly awkward way, like making a quick chord change on guitar that moves several fingers. In these types of pronunciation situations, people will occasionally insert a helper sound that smooths the transition. Linguists have a name for this practice of inserting extra sounds into a word: *epenthesis*.

Epenthesis is common. Lots of people say *ath-a-lete* for *athlete*, for the same reason that the hardware-store guy said *mason-a-ry*, namely, to ease the transition from one consonant to the next. In some dialects of English, people say *fill-um* for *film*. Maybe you've heard someone say "real-a-tor" for *Realtor*. Some people pronounce the name *Henry* as *hen-e-ry*.

In these examples, epenthesis results in a vowel to bridge consonants. Epenthesis can also refer to inserted consonants. Lots of people pronounce the word *hamster* as *hampster*, using an inserted *p* to bridge the *m* and the *s*. Keep an ear out—you're likely to hear someone say *some-p-thing*, with a *p* between *m* and *th* in the word. You'll also hear an extra *t* in *prin-t-ce* (*prince*). Fun fact: extra consonants like this are called *excrescent consonants*.

In non-rhotic accents (accents where people tend not to pronounce the *r* sound), some speakers add an epenthetic *r* between vowels, referred to as a *linking R* or *intrusive R*. For example, people will say *pastar and sauce*. As another example, while they would normally pronounce *far* as *fah*, when they say *far away*, they will pronounce it *with* the *r* sound to avoid the awkward pronunciation of *fah* + *away*.

Some words today show evidence of historical epenthesis. For example, Old English had the word *thunor* for loud sky-sounds. Over the years, enough people inserted a *d* that by the Middle English period, the word had become *thunder*. (In German, *thunder* is the word *Donner* as in *Donner und Blitzen*; unlike English, German didn't add that epenthetic *d*.) Similarly, *tremble* was originally *tremulare* (compare *tremulous*), but we added a *b* in the middle. Yet another example is the word *messenger*, which was originally *messager* before we added the *n*. The word *empty* in Old English was *æmteg*, with no epenthetic *p*.

Even if people don't use epenthesis for words in their everyday speech, they might add sounds when a situation seems to call for it. A place you'll often hear epenthesis is when people sing. For example, the Rolling Stones have a song named "Tumbling Dice." When they sing the chorus, you can clearly hear them pronounce it as "tumb-e-ling dice," which not only bridges the *b* and *l*, but fits the rhythm of the song quite well.

Related terms: metathesis, rhotic

eponym

Can you name what the highlighted words in the following sentences have in common?

> While soaking her sore *Achilles tendon* in the *jacuzzi*, she enjoyed a *sandwich* and some *pralines* dipped in *boysenberry* sauce.

> The *gargantuan diesel* engine has a high *wattage* rating, but wear earplugs, because it produces over 90 *decibels*.

> The restaurant was *ritzy*, but I think I got *salmonella* from the *nachos*.

You might have guessed that all of the highlighted words are *eponyms*: words based on names. The word *eponym* is from Greek: *epo* ("upon, after") + *nym* ("name, word").

We have a *ton* of eponyms in English. Some are obvious, like *Achilles tendon*. But you might have been surprised that some of the words I highlighted are from names. *Salmonella*? Named for Daniel Salmon, who was part of a group that isolated the pathogen. *Jacuzzi*? An Italian inventor. *Ritzy*? From the Ritz hotel, which was built by the Swiss hotelier César Ritz. *Boysenberry*? A hybrid berry created by Rudolph Boysen in Anaheim, California in the 1920s. *Nachos*? A dish attributed to Ignacio ("Nacho") Anaya in Piedras Negras, Mexico in the 1940s.

Many eponyms are based on real people. They can be based on discoverers, like *salmonella*, or inventors, like *diesel* (for Rudolf Diesel) or *nachos* or *saxophone* (for Adolphe Sax, the Belgian who invented the instrument). In some cases, the credit is indirect. For example, during the French Revolution, heads rolled due to the *guillotine*, which was named for a doctor (Joseph-Ignace Guillotin) who merely suggested the device as an alternative to messier forms of execution.

An eponym might be named *for* someone, like *sandwich*; that word purportedly comes from the 4th Earl of Sandwich, who once impressed someone by spending 24 hours gambling, his only sustenance being some meat between slices of bread.[38] The word *praline* is also named for someone, though in this case it was a cook who invented the confection in the 1600s and named it for his employer, the Marechal du Plessis-Praslin. You might not know that the *teddy bear* was named for the American politician Theodore Roosevelt, who once spared the life of a bear cub. The *leotard*, a type of tight-fitting clothing, is named for Jules Léotard, a 19th-century French acrobat.

Some eponyms capture notoriety that their namesake might not appreciate. The Marquis de Sade, who died in 1814, lent his name (and inclinations) to *sadism*. Along similar lines, *masochism* is derived from a published case study of the writer Leopold von Sacher-Masoch. The verb *boycott* comes from the name of a land agent in Ireland named Charles Boycott who refused to lower rent and who was then, well, boycotted. To *bowdlerize* a text—that is, to censor it—is a word based on Thomas Bowdler, a 19th-century editor who took it on himself to remove all the parts from Shakespeare that he thought were not family-friendly. The verb *lynch* comes from *Lynch Law*, named for William Lynch, a Virginian vigilante during the 1780s. Reaching a bit further back, the term *draconian* to mean "very severe" remembers the Athenian Draco (around 650 BC), who pioneered a written code of laws for Athens that imposed harsh penalties, like a death sentence for minor theft.

The scientific world has eponyms all over the place. *Euclidean geometry*, *Newtonian mechanics*, the *Copernican system*, *Morse code*, *Feynman diagrams*—these are named for mathematicians and physicists. *Pasteurization* is named for Louis Pasteur, who invented the process. Something that pleases me is that many units of measure in science are eponyms: *ampere*, *angstrom*, *farad*, *gauss*, *joule*, *ohm*, *roentgen*, *volt*, and *watt* all honor scientists and engineers. A somewhat surprising eponym is that the *bel* part of the word *decibel* is named for Alexander Bell, inventor of the telephone.

We've also gotten a lot of words from mythology and literature. The *Achilles tendon* mentioned in the first example refers to the mythical Greek hero Achilles, whose mother dipped him in the River Styx to make him invulnerable. But she had to hold him by his heel, which left him

---

[38] This means that the word *sandwich* is ultimately a toponym—the Earl of Sandwich is associated with the parish of Sandwich in Kent in the UK. Sandwich in turn derives from Anglo-Saxon *Sondwic*, meaning "market town in a sandy place."

with a weak spot that was his eventual, you know, Achilles heel. All things *martial* refer to Mars, the Roman god of war. Something that's *quixotic* is referring to Don Quixote, Michael Cervantes's impractically chivalrous hero. A *scrooge*, of course, is someone who acts like the miserly protagonist of Dickens's *A Christmas Carol*.

Seriously, I could list eponyms all day long. To give you an idea of just how many we have, I'll just list some more along with where we've gotten them and leave out the backstory on each one, although I urge you to investigate them via your local dictionary.

- More historical figures: *bloomers, Cyrillic, derrick, dunce, Elizabethan, maverick, limousine, Molotov cocktail, shrapnel, silhouette, Victorian*. A fun eponym is *gerrymander*, a portmanteau of "(Elbridge) Gerry," a 19th-century American politician, with "salamander," because a map of a voting district created under his administration sort of looked like a salamander. Another one is *nicotine*, which is named for Jean Nicot, the French ambassador to Portugal in the 1550s who introduced tobacco to France.

- More mythology and literature: *gargantuan, herculean, jovial, Kafkaesque, mausoleum, museum, narcissistic, odyssey, serendipity, stentorian, tantalizing*. A literary eponym that I discuss elsewhere is the term *malapropism*. Some people might not know that it was Dr. Seuss (Theodor Geisel) who invented the word *grinch*.

- Botanists and horticulturalists: *dahlia, gardenia, lobelia, loganberry, magnolia, poinsettia, zinnia*. One way to remember how to spell the flower (and color) *fuchsia* is that it's named for the German botanist Leonhard Fuchs.

- Biblical characters: *Christian, Judas, onanism, semitic, Solomonic*. The word *maudlin* comes from Magdalena, which was the Latin name for Mary Magdalen.

The collection of eponyms in English is hardly static. People make up new eponyms all the time—*Clintonesque, Bushism, Trumpian*. A recent eponym is the verb *to Kondo-ize*, meaning to organize one's belongings, named for the consultant Marie Kondo.

Although eponyms are based on names, it's not always clear whether to capitalize them. The eponymous roots of some terms have become obscure enough that no one thinks to capitalize them. In fact, most of our eponyms are not capitalized.

A good rule of thumb is that if you need to know who the person is in order to understand the word, you capitalize it. Thus the adjectives *Freudian*, *Kafkaesque*, *Leninism*, *Dickensian*, and *Elizabethan* don't make much sense unless you know who the names refer to. But people can get by fine without knowing the names behind *diesel*, *quixotic*, and *herculean*, or even that these are terms based on names. When in doubt, of course, look the word up in a dictionary.

Related terms: aptronym, mononym, onomastics, patronym, toponym

etymological fallacy

You've probably encountered the word *decimate* in a sentence like "The virus **decimates** a patient's ability to fight off sickness." And there's some chance that you've heard someone say that *decimate* is being used wrong in this sentence.

The argument goes like this: in Latin, *decimate* meant "take one-tenth of." (There's a story that to punish mutiny in the Roman army, every tenth man was put to death.) Therefore, it's incorrect to use *decimate* in a sense like "to reduce drastically, especially in number" or "to cause great destruction or harm," as Merriam-Webster does.

And yet those two definitions represent how most people use *decimate* today. In the example sentence (which came from the *Washington Post*), *decimate* has the sense of "drastically reduce."

People who maintain that *decimate* can *only* mean "take a tenth of" are engaging in something called the *etymological fallacy*: insisting that a word's original meaning dictates its only true meaning.

Sure, knowing a word's roots is frequently a good clue as to what it means. If I'm confused about what *nonplussed* means, as a lot of people are, it can help to know that it's based on the Latin *nōn plūs*, meaning "no more, no further," and therefore means something like "perplexed" ("can't even"). If I really know my classical roots and encounter the word *tyromancy*, I might be able to determine its roots (*tyro* = "cheese" and *mancy* = "divination") and then guess that it means "to tell the future by reading cheese," whatever that might entail.

But in many cases, a word's meaning has meandered over time. *Nice* once meant "foolish." *Gymnasium* comes from a Greek term meaning "to train naked." *Persona* originally referred to the mask that an actor wore in classical drama. In American cuisine, the *entrée* is the main course, and not, as the etymology suggests, an "entry" dish. These are not the meanings we use today, even though they are the original meanings.

Still, many online lists of "words you're using wrong" will tell you that you're not using a word correctly because you're not using it in its original sense. In addition to the examples above, another word that often appears on such lists is *peruse*. People use *peruse* to mean "to look over casually." But the "you're using it wrong" lists will point out that the original meaning of *peruse* was "to use up, or deal with in sequence" and that *peruse* therefore actually means "to read carefully." Another word that's frequently on these types of lists is *ultimate*. This comes from Latin for "last" or "final," and the list will insist that you're using *ultimate* wrong if you use it to mean *highest* ("ultimate goal") or *best* ("ultimate vacation destinations"). These scoldings are examples of the etymological fallacy.

When lexicographers write dictionaries, obviously they investigate the roots of the words that they're defining. But they can't write definitions based only on roots; they have to define words according to how people actually use those words. Otherwise, if I read an article in the newspaper that talks about a virus "decimating" a victim's immune system, and the dictionary tells me that it means "reduce by one-tenth," I'm not really going to understand what the writer meant.

A word blogger once summed up the problem with the etymological fallacy:[39]

> Knowledge of etymology is completely unnecessary for using a language. What's necessary is not what words used to mean, but what words mean now. [...] Sometimes it is claimed that an earlier meaning

---

[39] Unfortunately, the blogger—"bradshaw of the future"—seems to have removed his informative and entertaining blog about words.

of a word is its literal or real meaning, but really all that can be said is that an earlier meaning is an earlier meaning.

In addition to not attending to how a word is used today, people who engage in the etymological fallacy tend to be selective. No one is proposing that *December* is properly the name for the tenth month, even though the *Dec-* part not only means "ten" in Latin, but December has that name because it originally *was* the tenth month. Not a lot of people insist that *myriad* means 10,000, although that's what it means in Greek. When medical professionals impose a *quarantine*, it isn't necessarily for 40 days, in spite of the word's origin as "period of forty days." And I am a little sad (or is it relieved?) that when I go to the *gym*, I don't see people adhering strictly to its original sense of training in the nude.

So here's a rule of thumb. Anytime someone proposes that a word's "real" meaning is based on its etymology and not on how people actually use the word today, you're probably looking at an example of the etymological fallacy.

Related terms: absolute adjective, pedant's veto, skunked term, zombie rule

etymythology (false etymology)

When I was a kid, sometimes we'd go to a steakhouse that had paper placemats with an illustrated history of the word *sirloin*. The story went that a king had been so impressed with the cut of beef he'd been served that he knighted it and it became "Sir Loin." The placemat had a cartoon of a guy with a crown tapping a steak with his sword.

I didn't know it at the time, but this was a perfect—perhaps *the* perfect—example of an *etymythology*: a made-up word history. You might think that this story is so fanciful that no one would really believe it. But you'd be wrong; Snopes.com posted an article debunking it. (The word folk etymology is sometimes used to describe this phenomenon of made-up etymologies. However, that term also has a more specific definition, which is covered separately in this book.)

But even if you don't believe that particular etymythology, you might have heard others. Perhaps you've read that the word *posh* comes from "port outward, starboard home," supposedly the preferred cabin arrangement of someone sailing between England and India. (It's not certain where the word *posh* came from, but it *definitely* does not derive from an acronym.) Another popular etymythology is that the word *tip*, as in the little extra that you slip to your restaurant server or to the luggage wrangler, is an acronym for "to insure promptness." No. As Cecil Adams of the *Straight Dope* column once said, "the cuteness of the story is in inverse proportion to the likelihood of its actually being true."[40]

The word *etymythology* was invented by the linguist Laurence Horn, who describes it as "the lexical version of the urban legend, a fable—or more generously a piece of culturally based arcane wisdom—not transmitted by scholarly research but passed on by word of mouth (or computer)." Passed on by word of mouth and sometimes by steakhouse placemats. Another and less interesting word for this is *false etymology*; yet another term I've heard is *fauxtymology*.

The appeal of etymythologies is that they tell a good story. The stories for *sirloin* and *posh* and *tip* conjure up scenes that are fun to imagine. An old etymythology for the word *pumpernickel* has it that it was bread that a Frenchman scornfully declared was only *bon pour Nicol* ("good for Nicol"), where Nicol was a horse—in some versions of the story, it was specifically Napoleon's horse. In this supposed history, *bon pour Nicol* then became the name of the bread. A great story, no? (The actual etymology is, for a change, just as good: the name of the bread derives from some regional German words that mean "farting devil.")

My favorite etymythology is about the word *kangaroo*. In this story, Captain Cook asked a native in Australia what the name was for that animal that was bouncing around. The native answered *kangaroo*, which supposedly meant "I don't know" because he didn't understand what Captain Cook was asking. Thus, the etymythology goes, we use a word today for the animal that really means "I don't know." Great story, but not true.

---

[40] https://www.straightdope.com/21341670/what-s-the-origin-of-kangaroo-court-is-kangaroo-aborigine-for-i-don-t-know

These stories are also appealing because they make a kind of sense. For example, you'll sometimes hear that the word *doozy* comes from Duesenberg, a company that made luxury cars until the late 1930s. That's such an obvious connection that it *has* to be true … doesn't it? As it happens, no; the word *doozy* appeared at least a decade before the cars did, as the lexicographer Kory Stamper explains in a blog post.[41]

People seem particularly fond of etymythologies that involve acronyms like the examples above. It's not hard to find "explanations" of the supposed origins of words like *swag* ("stuff we all get") and *cop* ("constable on patrol") and *fuck* ("for unlawful carnal knowledge"). In the same blog post I noted earlier, Kory Stamper has a useful rule of thumb about these types of explanations: "Acronymic etymologies are, by and large, total horseshit." Jonathan Lighter, the editor of the *Historical Dictionary of American Slang*, has used the term *retropseudoacronyms* to refer to etymologies like these that are falsely claimed to be acronyms.

Corporations sometimes promote etymythologies that involve their products. As an article in the *New York Times Magazine* explains, Keds claimed to be the first company to create *sneakers* (false; the word existed before the company did).[42] And Hershey liked to say ("it's a popular theory") that their chocolate kisses came from the sound of the machine that made them, a claim that a candy historian called "strategic corporate forgetting."

False etymologies have even left their mark on how we spell certain words. The word *victuals* in English is pronounced "vittles." That's because when the word entered English in medieval times, it came to us from the French word *vitaile*. Somewhere along the line, though, a scholar assumed that the etymology was the Latin word *victus* and somehow convinced everyone that the word should be spelled *victuals*, with a *c*— even though no one pronounced it that way. This type of false etymological thinking is also how we got the *c* in *Arctic* (real source was French *artike*), the *s* in *island* (originally French *ile*), the *b* in debt (French *dette*), and the *b* in *doubt* (French *dute*). This type of "fixing" of a word's spelling to make it more "correct" is also known as a *hypercorrective spelling* or *etymological spelling*.

---

[41] https://korystamper.wordpress.com/2014/12/19/answers-i-wish-i-could-send-etymology-edition/
[42] https://www.nytimes.com/2010/05/02/magazine/02FOB-onlanguage-t.html

The next time you hear a particularly entertaining word history, you might consider the source. Is it from someone who heard it from someone who read about it once? Does it involve a clever acronym? Is it in an advertisement? Is it on a steakhouse placemat? If it's any of these things, you're probably hearing an etymythology.

Related terms: backronym, folk etymology

familect (familiolect)

My wife and I cannot function without morning coffee, so it's important that we don't run out. But we have irreconcilable tastes in coffee. We frequently add coffee to the grocery list, but to make sure we don't get the *wrong* kind of coffee, we developed the habit of writing *moffee* (*Mike* + *coffee*) for my kind of coffee, and *soffee* (*Sarah* + *coffee*) for her kind.

This proved so useful that it's been extended to other words. I now write *moothpaste* on the list when I run out of my special toothpaste and *meese* for the kind of cheese that I particularly like.

These words—*moffee*, *soffee*, *moothpaste*, and *meese*—have become part of our *familect* or *familiolect*. They're words that make perfect sense to us, but that are presumably baffling to anyone who visits our house and glances at the whiteboard where we write our list.

The linguist David Crystal has described a familect—another term is *kitchen table lingo*—as constituting "a fascinating group of the private and personal word-creations that are found in every household and in every social group, but which never get into the dictionary." Along similar lines, Gretchen McCulloch has proposed the word *friendlects* for the private language of a group of friends.

Here's another example. I heard a story once about a family that had a pair of Jack Russell terriers who went nuts whenever they heard the word *squirrel*. (This was long before the movie *Up* and the dog who said "Squirrel!!!") It became so bad that the family had to invent a new word for squirrels (*squak*, I was told) to be able to talk about the animal without riling up the dogs. (In an interesting case of linguistic transmission, after I heard this story, our family incorporated *squak* into our own familect.)

As Crystal says, every family has its own familect. They might be deliberately crafted words (or semi-deliberately, like *moffee*). Or they might come from mistakes that have been institutionalized within the family, often mistakes made by children. They might reference inside jokes, and they might constitute personal names used only within the family.

The *New Yorker* cartoonist Roz Chast talked about how she and her husband started saying "Should we just fend?" to mean poking around in the kitchen to see what they could assemble into a meal. Kathryn Hymes, writing in *The Atlantic*, describes how she once mangled the Turkish phrase for "Happy birthday," and now she and her partner annually wish each other "two pigs."

In January 2018, the editor Iva Cheung posted a tweet asking for "words, expressions, or pronunciations that are unique to your familiolect." She got many responses, and the Twitter thread was picked up by *BuzzFeed*. There were some great familectical terms, many of which originated with children; here are a few:

- *broom-shove* for a dustpan
- *distructions* for *instructions*
- *knee pits* for the back of the knee
- *pizza bones* for the leftover crusts
- *shaky cheese* for grated parmesan cheese

And it seems like every family has their own name for the TV remote.

Familects are generally a lot of fun. But as with any dialect, there can be issues. For one thing, the terms in a familect belong to the family or to the social group where they were invented, and using the familect is a marker of belonging to that family. It can be weird if a casual friend hears a familectical term and starts using it with members of the family. (If I ever met anyone from the family that invented the word *squak* for "squirrel," I'd never presume to use the term in their presence; it's their term.)

And familectical terms can of course be a bit embarrassing if used outside the family, especially terms based on childish mistakes. My own daughter has a nickname that came about because her then-toddler brother couldn't pronounce her name properly. When she went away to school, we eventually discovered that she never tells anyone about that nickname. Fair enough.

Related terms: shibboleth

flat adverb

If there's one thing that you probably learned about adverbs when you studied English in school, it's that they end in *ly*. *He's a **slow** runner* (*slow* is an adjective), but *he runs **slowly*** (*slowly* is an adverb). Right? Yes and no. Many adverbs certainly do (and indeed must) end in *ly*:

> She performed that move ***brilliantly***.

> It's an ***intelligently*** written account of a little-known historical incident.

> They left ***immediately***.

> The cat ***tenderly*** groomed the baby squirrel.

But as with so much in English, the story isn't quite that simple. Is the word *slow* an adjective or an adverb? It can be both:

> He moves ***slowly***.

> He moves ***slow***.

> He's a ***slow***-moving fellow.

In the first example, *slowly* is obviously an adverb. In the second example, it's hard to argue that *slow* isn't functioning as an adverb. And in the third example, *slow* again is clearly working as an adverb; it modifies *moving*.

When an adverb can have an *ly* ending but doesn't, it's known as a *flat adverb*. Or to put it another way, a flat adverb has the same form as an adjective. The adverb *slow* is a good example. So are *quick* (*she moves quick*), *bright* (*the stars shine bright*), *safe* (*drive safe!*), and *tender* (*love me tender*).

You might object that adverbs like *slow*, *bright*, *quick*, and so on are incorrect, and that they should have an *ly* on them when they're used as adverbs. (I'm pretty sure I was taught this.) But there are a number of problems with the objections to flat adverbs.

For one thing, using these adverbs in their flat form is widespread. The examples I showed earlier are widely attested, including ("Love Me Tender") in the title of a huge Elvis Presley hit. A common road sign simply says "Slow," and they don't mean that as an adjective.

Then there is the issue that for some words, the *ly* variant of an adverb actually means something different from the flat variant:

- *close/closely*
- *hard/hardly* ("Working hard, or hardly working?" as the joke goes)
- *near/nearly*
- *smart/smartly*

In certain compounds, it's even a mistake to use the *ly*-less version, as in *quick-thinking player*.

To make things even more complicated, there are a bunch of adverbs that don't even have *ly* forms. You can't *drive fastly*, you can't *run farly*, you can't *visit again soonly*, you can't *hang toughly*, and you can't *aim lowly*.

Finally, there is the weight of the history of English. Flat adverbs were more common in the past, as these examples from the 17th century illustrate:

> And I will make thee **exceeding** fruitful (*King James Bible*, Genesis 17:6)

> Old John of Gaunt is **grievous** sick, my lord (Shakespeare, *Richard II*, Act I, Scene 4)

> Well, thou hast comforted me **marvellous** much (Shakespeare, *Romeo and Juliet*, Act III, scene 5)

> I was **horrid** angry, and went out of doors to the office (Samuel Pepys, *Diary*)

In each of these cases, we'd use an *ly* form today.

Among the best-known instances of a flat adverb must be the famous advertising campaign from Apple Computer that featured the expression

Think Different. Some people claim that this offended grammar purists, who believed it should have been *Think Differently*. Jobs and others defended *different* in this context, and the results of the ad campaign certainly were successful.

So the story with adverbs is a little bit more complicated than that they end in *ly*. Flat adverbs are not only common, but they can be quite useful, as you can see when you *go deep*.

Related terms: absolute adjective

folk etymology

You might not have given much thought to the word *crayfish*. If you did, you might have thought that it was a little odd. The animal that goes by the name *crayfish* is a crustacean, a sort of small, freshwater lobster. It's not a fish, really. Still, a crayfish does live in the water, so maybe *fish* makes sense, sort of. But what does *cray-* mean?

Basically nothing. The original name, which we got from Old French back in the Middle Ages, was *crevice* (*ecrevisse* in modern French). But that wasn't a word in English (at least, not for a freshwater crustacean), so over time English speakers wrangled the French name *crevice* into something that seemed more English-like. Result: *crayfish*. Or in some dialects *crawfish*, same difference. (Because the prefixes *cray* and *craw* don't mean anything in themselves and serve only to distinguish the name from other types of fish, they're examples of cranberry morphemes.)

Assimilating an unusual or foreign term into English—or at least, into more familiar English—results in something known as a *folk etymology*. People like their words to make sense, and given a chance, they'll coerce an unfamiliar one into a more familiar form. As a certain George Wakeman observed in 1869, "The common people are all amateur etymologists, and they like to put into every word some familiar glimmer of sense." Or as Peter Sokolowski put it in a *Word Matters* podcast, there's a "gravitational pull toward a more common word" to make unfamiliar words more familiar.[43]

In particular, the *fish* of *crayfish* part shows how folk etymologies work, since the animal is a little bit fishy. Or at least that made more sense than the Old French term—*crevice*—from which *crayfish* derives.

The *crayfish* example shows one example of folk etymology at work on words that we've gotten from other languages. Another example is *Jerusalem artichoke*, which refers to a vegetable that's the root (tuber) of a species of sunflower. Guess what, Jerusalem artichokes don't come from Jerusalem. Instead, the *Jerusalem* part is folk etymology for the word *girasole*, which is an Italian word for "sunflower" (*girasole* combines "to turn" + "sun"). In fact, *Jerusalem artichoke* is a kind of double folk etymology, because *artichoke* is *also* an assimilation: it comes from the Arabic *al-karsufa*. The word went through Spanish and then Italian before landing in English, being transformed at each step in each language until settling into English in a way that was friendly to our ears.

A technical term for folk etymologies is *phono-semantic matching*. Per one definition, in phono-semantic matching, a word's "non-native quality is hidden by replacing it with phonetically and semantically similar words or roots from the adopting language."

A word you might occasionally hear for the phenomenon of folk etymologies is *Hobson-Jobson*. This was the title of a glossary published in 1903 that listed many words that had come into English from South Asian and East Asian languages. Per the authors of the glossary, the title refers to "an Anglo-Saxon version of the wailings of the Mahommedans as they beat their breasts in the procession of the Moharram—"Yā Hasan! Yā Hosain!"" The word extended to refer to any similar borrowing that was Anglicized. As you might be able to tell by the authors' own definition of *Hobson-Jobson*, their efforts reflected colonial and patronizing attitudes toward other peoples and other languages. It's useful to know about this word, but I much prefer *folk etymology*.

A folk etymology that I particularly like is the word *hoosegow*, meaning "jail." ("He was sent to the hoosegow for a long time.") This word is an Anglicization of the Spanish word *juzgado*, meaning "judged" and

---

[43] https://www.merriam-webster.com/word-matters-podcast/episode-58-folk-etymology

used to mean a court or "a place for adjudicated individuals." In other words, it meant jail. Americans adapted *juzgado* into the slightly more English-sounding *hoosegow*.

There are many words whose entry into English involved folk etymologies. Other examples are *junk* for the Chinese-style ship (from Javanese) and *paddy* as in *rice paddy* (from Malay), *mary jane* for marijuana (from Spanish), and *mongoose* (from Marathi). The woodchuck and muskrat got their English names as folk etymologies of the indigenous words for those animals.

A somewhat more recent example is the word *antivenom*. The word was originally *antivenin*, based on Latin *anti-* plus *venene* ("poison"), but morphed quickly into *antivenom*, a more familiar compound to English speakers. (A Google Ngram search shows *antivenom* overtaking the *antivenin* in the 1980s. For more about this type of search, see corpus.)

You can see folk etymology at work in real time, so to speak, in the word *chaise-longue*. We borrowed this term from French, where it means "long chair." But through the process of folk etymology, the word is in the process of becoming *chaise-**lounge***. As with folk etymologies in general, the reinterpretation makes sense. The word *longue* doesn't mean anything in English, but *lounge* does, and moreover *lounge* seems like it's suggested by the horizontal nature of the chair in question.

Place names can reflect folk etymology as well. *Sing Sing*, the infamous prison, was named for the village where it was built in, which in turn came from the Sintsink natives in the area. (When the prison became notorious, the residents of the village decided to rename it *Ossining*.) I live in the state of Washington, where many contemporary names are English adaptations—that is, folk etymologies—of Native American names. A well-known example in our state is the name *Seattle*. This was named for a chief of the local Duwamish and Suquamish tribes. English-speaking settlers in the area couldn't pronounce his name properly, which is variously rendered as Sealth, Seathl, See-ahth, or Si'ahl. The name *Seattle* is just a best approximation. Some other Washington cities that reflect folk etymologies are *Walla Walla* and *Humptulips*. There are many more throughout the Americas. In Mexico, a great example is the city of Cuernavaca. The name literally means "cow horn" in Spanish, which was the best approximation the Spanish could do of the original name, *Cuauhnahuac*.

The term *folk etymology* is also used sometimes to mean a fanciful (but incorrect) etymology—that is, an etymology invented by common folk. For more about that sense of the term, see etymythology.

Related terms: calque, eggcorn, phonotactics

fossil word

I bet you know what *sleight of hand* means—it refers to being able to do clever and tricky things with your hands; prestidigitation. But what exactly does *sleight* mean? Do soccer players exhibit sleight of foot? Is Einstein's theory of relativity just sleight of brain?

Or a co-worker stops by your desk to tell you that the boss is in a *high dudgeon*. You know you should keep your head low, at least until the boss is, er, out of their dudgeon.

The words *sleight* and *dudgeon* are examples of *fossil words*: words that are pretty much extinct in English but that are preserved in the amber of idioms and stock phrases. (Many of them are in collocations—a set of words that are frequently used together.) You will search long for examples of *sleight* that aren't part of the phrase of *sleight of hand*. Similarly, when you encounter *dudgeon*, it's almost always going to be in a phrase like *in high dudgeon*.

There are more fossil words than you might think, like these:

- *look **askance***
- *in fine **fettle***
- ***gird** one's loins*
- ***kith** and kin*
- ***spick** and **span***
- *short **shrift***
- *in the **throes** of*
- *out of **wedlock***

These days, few people can give you a precise definition for words that are fossils—ask among people you know what *dudgeon* or *kith* or *shrift* mean.

Most fossil words were once normal parts of English. For example, *sleight* used to be a noun form of the adjective *sly*. The word *kith* was part of Old English, and it survived in the sense of "people you know" until the 19th century.

Similarly, *shrift* refers to the Catholic rite of confession and absolution. It's related to the verb *to shrive*, which we still see in the name *Shrove Tuesday*—the day before Ash Wednesday. (*Shrove Tuesday* is therefore another name for Mardi Gras.) A *short shrift* is one where the confession is quick. In *Richard III* (Act III, Scene 4), Sir Richard Ratcliff advises Lord Hastings to "Make a short shrift." That use of *short shrift* was literal, but over time the phrase evolved to mean something like "give little effort or attention to."

The enduring popularity of Shakespeare and the King James Bible has helped some fossil words survive:

> much ***ado*** about nothing (Shakespeare play of that name).

> one ***fell*** swoop (*Macbeth*, Act IV, Scene 3). Fun fact: *fell* means "fierce" or "malevolent" and is related to the *fel* in *felon*.

> for Adam there was not found an ***help meet*** for him (Genesis 2:20).

> ***Gird*** up thy loins now like a man (Job 40:7).

> hoist with his own ***petard*** (*Hamlet*, Act III, Scene 4). Fun fact redux: *petard* refers to an explosive device and derives from a word that also gave us "to fart."

> For ye ***suffer*** fools gladly (2 Corinthians 11:19).

As with the earlier examples, you'll almost always hear words like *fell* and *gird* and *petard* and *suffer* embedded in these stock phrases. And if you press people on what, say, *fell* or *petard* means, there's a good chance they won't know. We can use these terms in idioms even so, because we understand the idiom as a whole, without having to understand what each word in the expression means.

Related terms: collocation, cranberry morpheme

garden-path sentence

Some sentences force you to stop and rethink what you're reading. Here's an example:

The government plans to raise taxes were defeated.

You start reading about how the government is planning to raise taxes, and then you get to *were defeated*. Wait, what? You have an aha! moment and start over, because now you realize that the word *plans* is not a verb, as you'd first thought; it's a noun. The plans were defeated. Here's another one:

The cotton clothing is usually made of grows in Mississippi.

You probably start by thinking this sentence is about clothing. But it's actually about cotton, which you don't realize until you get to *grows*. Then you have to go back and re-read the sentence so that it makes sense.

These are examples of *garden-path sentences*, which are sentences that lead you "down the garden path" toward an incorrect interpretation. Try the following example:

The horse raced past the barn fell.

You start out thinking that the horse had been in a race, but when you get to *past*, things go weird. If you restart the sentence and read it was *The horse **that was** raced past the barn fell*, it makes more sense. (It's not a great sentence even then.)

Or what about the following sentence:

Writing clearly is hard.

Here, you might start off thinking that the sentence is about how to write clearly. But you then get to *is hard* and you might decide that the sentence isn't about writing clearly; it's that clearly, writing is hard.

Psycholinguists are interested in garden-path sentences because they help illustrate how people parse and understand sentences. We read (or hear) sentences word by word, building an interpretation in our heads of the sentence's structure and meaning. For the most part, this works great—in fact, when we're listening to someone, we can often mentally race ahead and anticipate where the sentence is going. In conversation, we might even finish their sentence for them. (Not that they necessarily like that.)

But a garden-path sentence upends the mental construction we have of the sentence. Our parsing apparatus hits a dead end, and we have to go back and start over.

Many garden-path sentences are the result of attachment ambiguity, where the ambiguity is syntactical (what modifies what) rather than semantic (what a word means). In the sentence about cotton clothing, we initially assume that *cotton* is modifying *clothing*, and that's a reasonable guess, because we've heard *cotton clothing* before. We eventually realize that *cotton* is not attached to *clothing*; instead, the phrase *clothing is made of* is attached to *cotton*. (This would be clearer if the word *that* appeared here: *The cotton **that** clothing is made of … .*)

Headlines for news articles are rich sources of garden-path sentences, in part because they often leave out words (like the *that* in the cotton example) that clarify the sentence structure. You can read more about the special case of headlines under crash blossom.

By the way, the sentence *Writing clearly is hard* is also an example of a squinting modifier, where the ambiguity is whether *clearly* modifies the word preceding it or following it—that is, what *clearly* is attached to.

Related terms: attachment ambiguity, crash blossom, squinting modifier

genericization, generonym

Here's a strange (and contrived) little story:

> When I saw smoke behind the building, I googled "dumpster fire." I thought it was a kerosene fire, but it turned out to be dry ice!

This isn't a particularly interesting story on its own. But it's interesting from a word perspective, because several words—*to google, dumpster, kerosene, dry ice*—are based on brand names.

You probably recognize *to google* as based on the company name Google. But *dumpster*? *Kerosene*? *Dry ice*? Yes, these are words that have long since experienced the process of *genericization*: turning from brand names into generic words that have lost the power of trademark. That is, they've become *generonyms*.

As with eponyms, there are more of these generonyms in English than you might think, like these examples:

- *aspirin*
- *laundromat*
- *linoleum*
- *thermos* (bottle)
- *trampoline*
- *yo-yo*
- *zipper*

Companies that own trademarks have a complicated relationship with the public's wide use of their brand name as a generic term. On the one hand, what company doesn't want their brand to be the go-to word for the market that they're in? From that perspective, every time people use *google* to mean "to search on the web" or *xerox* to mean "to photocopy," the brand name is reinforced: *Google* is synonymous with search, *Xerox* is *the* brand of photocopier.

But of course the danger is that if the word becomes genericized, the company can lose its trademark protection. The trademark office uses what they call the *primary significance test* to determine whether a trade name has become generic. What they look for is whether people know whether terms like *google* and *xerox* still refer to companies.[44]

For example, people no longer travel on Escalator™ brand moving staircases. Thanks to a lawsuit in 1950 that declared that *escalator* had become generic, any company that builds a revolving staircase can refer to it as an escalator. We can probably assume that Bayer, the pharmaceutical company, is not eager to point out that the word *heroin* was once their trademark. The process of losing a brand name in this way is called *trademark erosion*, or more colorfully, *genericide*.

---

[44] If you need advice about your own branding questions, please don't rely on what you read here; consult a qualified professional.

Even if you know that a word is a trademark, it can sometimes be difficult to remember what truly generic term to use in its place. What *do* you call that thing that's often known as a *Q-Tip?* ("swab") Or *Scotch tape?* ("transparent tape") Or *Velcro?* ("hook-and-loop fastener")

To prevent genericization of their brands, companies need to police them. Companies like Google often have a trademarks page where they list the way they would like people to use their trademarks, like this from the Google trademarks page:

Google™ search or search engine

To help protect its trademarks, Xerox has periodically run ads that remind people that its name is not a verb. Here's an example:

If a trademark is misused it could come undone.

If you didn't know zipper was a trademark, don't worry, it's not. But it used to be. It was lost because people misused the name. And the same could happen to ours, Xerox. Please help us ensure it doesn't. Use Xerox only as an adjective to identify our products and services, such as Xerox copiers, not a verb, "to Xerox," or a noun, "Xeroxes." Something to keep in mind that will help us keep it together.

xerox.com   Ready For Real Business **xerox**

The folks at Velcro Companies, the entity that owns the Velcro brand, made a surprisingly funny video—one that looks like it might feature real lawyers—telling people not to use *Velcro* generically.

but if you keep doing it our trademarks go away.

They also tell you not to use certain other names, like [censored] for bandage, and [censored] for inline skates.[45]

Even so, many words live in a murky zone between trademark and generic term. In some areas of the United States, people use the word *coke* to mean any soft drink, although there seems to be no danger of the Coca-Cola Company losing this brand anytime soon. (Per the previous description, it's hard to forget that Coke comes from Coca-Cola, the company.)

In Britain, *to hoover* is used generically to mean *to vacuum*. Terms like *Band-Aid, Chap Stick, Crock-Pot, Fiberglass, Formica, Frisbee, Jacuzzi, Jell-O, Memory Stick, Muzak, Ping Pong, Photoshop, Plexiglas, Popsicle, Realtor, Rolodex, Saran Wrap, Scotch tape*, and *Zamboni*, while often used generically, are still trademarks. A brand name that got a big workout as a generic term in the last few years is *Zoom* to refer to virtual meetings conducted on any platform.

Editors and others who want to be vigilant about such things need to look up terms to be sure that they're using trademarks correctly, or to decide whether to substitute a true generic term (*tissue*) for a trademarked name (*Kleenex*). Dictionaries will often note that a name is a trademark—if you look up *Polaroid* or *Velcro* or *Kleenex* in a Merriam-Webster dictionary, it will explicitly say "trademark" next to the word.

---

[45] https://www.velcro.com/dont-say-velcro/

Now and again a term is officially genericized, so to speak. For example, the 2013 edition of the AP style guide advises journalists that the word *dumpster*, which did originate as a trademark, can be used generically and no longer needs to be capitalized. If you want to write about a lowercase-*d* dumpster fire, you can do so in good conscience.

Related terms: minced oath, onomastics, semantic bleaching

glottal stop

Try this: slowly say *Uh-oh!* as if you'd just belatedly remembered an appointment. If you say *Uh-oh* very carefully, you'll notice a tiny hitch at the beginning before *uh* and another one in the middle between *uh* and *oh*. This little hitch is called a *glottal stop*.

English has a number of consonants that are *stops*, as linguists refer to them, including the sounds *p*, *b*, *t*, *d*, and *k*. These sounds are called *stops* because when you say these sounds, you're literally stopping the air in your mouth. For example, if you say *supper* carefully, when you get to the *p* sound, your mouth is completely closed. (In contrast to stops, there are also *fricatives* like *s* and *sh* and *th*, which produce sound using friction in your mouth's airstream rather than stopping it altogether.)

A glottal stop is like other stops, except that you stop the air way in the back of your mouth. (*Glottal* is the adjective form of *glottis*, which is part of the larynx.)

When writing English, we sometimes represent glottal stops as an apostrophe or backward apostrophe. For example, in the name *Hawai'i*, the apostrophe represents a glottal stop between the last vowels. However, in many languages—including English—there's no official letter for the glottal stop, the way there is for stops like *p*, *t*, and *k*. Therefore, when linguists were devising the International Phonetic Alphabet (IPA), an alphabet to represent every possible sound in human language, they gave the glottal stop its own letter. They settled on using the character ʔ, which is similar to a question mark. (By the way, the glottal stop *is* a letter in the Hawaiian alphabet, where it's called the *'okina*, and is written as ', a character that looks like somewhat like an apostrophe.)

In some contexts a glottal stop is optional. For example, as noted, the correct pronunciation of *Hawaiʻi* includes a glottal stop ("huh-wah-ʔee"). However, you can pronounce it as Hawaii ("huh-wah-ee") with no glottal stop, and people understand what you mean, even if you are technically mispronouncing the name.

But sometimes a glottal stop is not optional. For example, you can't actually say the expression *Uh-oh* without a glottal stop. If you don't precede the *o* sound with a glottal stop, it has more of a sighing quality and doesn't mean the same thing.

Although we don't formally recognize the glottal stop as a letter in English, it shows up not only in expressions like *Uh-oh*, but in many dialects of English, usually in place of a *t* sound. For example, in some dialects in England, a *t* sound in the middle of a word is pronounced as a glottal stop. Thus the formal pronunciation for *water* is *wah-der* or *wah-ter*, but in the UK you can frequently hear it as wah-ʔer. (Or *wah-ʔah*, since many dialects in England are non-rhotic.)

In a word like *wah-ʔer*, the glottal stop is considered a nonstandard pronunciation, but as linguist and language teacher Alex Rotatori says, "glottal stop is now firmly embedded in English pronunciation at all social levels."[46] Indeed, the glottal stop lurks in many words that have a *t* at the end of a syllable. For example, it's common for many English speakers (including Americans) to pronounce the words *football*, *button*, *smart*, and *cart* with a glottal stop for the *t*. The linguist John Wells uses the example of *start button*, which very few people pronounce with a clear *t*, and most pronounce as *starʔ buʔon*. And if you listen carefully, you can hear a glottal stop at the beginning of words that we think of as starting with a vowel, like *apple* and *elegant*.

We *do* need distinct letters for sounds like *p* and *b* in English because speakers need clues about whether to choose one or the other. There's a difference between *putter* and *butter* and between *pat* and *bat*. But we don't need a letter for glottal stops because we don't distinguish words based on whether they include that sound (duly acknowledging the correct pronunciation of *Hawaiʻi*.) English speakers don't have to choose to

---

[46] http://alex-ateachersthoughts.blogspot.co.uk/2013/01/glottal-stops-in-standard-english.html

produce a glottal stop—it just comes out naturally in certain contexts, like when we say *Uh-oh!*

Related terms: epenthesis

grawlix (obscenicon)

When you encounter something like "Why, you dirty #@$%*!" in a comic, you don't know exactly what the character is saying, but you get the idea. The character is cursing, but there's nothing on the page that can get the author in trouble with people who might be offended by the real thing. All those punctuation marks aren't a real curse word—they're a *grawlix*.

This delicacy is no accident. Grawlixes started showing up in newspaper comics about 100 years ago. Comic-strip authors had plenty of need to show characters who were angry, or who had hit their thumbs with hammers, or were otherwise in positions where you might expect some richly appropriate cursing. But the comic pages are family-friendly, and in that era and in that context a curse word was never going to be allowed to appear in print. So the artists invented grawlixes.

The term *grawlix* was coined as a satirical term in 1964 by Mort Walker, best known as the author of the comics "Beetle Bailey" and "Hi and Lois." Walker went on to develop a whole vocabulary for various marks used by cartoonists, such as *biffits* for the clouds left by running, *indotherm* for the rising wavy lines that represent heat, and *squeams* for the stars and circles that represent being drunk or dazed. He collected his invented terms in the book *The Lexicon of Comicana* in 1980.

Grawlix is a term primarily known among cartoonists. The lexicographer Ben Zimmer has proposed the alternative term *obscenicon* (a portmanteau of "obscene" + "icon"). The word *obscenicon* has some advantages. For example, it's pretty clear what it means just from looking at it, plus it echoes the familiar word *emoticon*. Other terms sometimes used for this phenomenon are *symbol swearing* and *profanitype*.

Grawlixes sometimes show up in non-comics contexts. In 2009, Justin Halpern started a Twitter account with the name "Shit My Dad Says," which purported to cite the cranky but amusing things that Halpern's father pronounced. Someone at the CBS network inexplicably thought this would make a good TV show, but the title was a problem. In the end, the show was titled *S#*! My Dad Says*. The TV network AMC created a show named *Kevin Can F**K Himself.* The naming consultant Nancy Friedman has also written about jeans with the brand names *Crazy B#@!h, Skinny B#@!h,* and *F#@k Me B#@!h.*

A small problem with grawlixes is that if you're reading out loud, it's not obvious how to pronounce them. As I noted earlier, when you see a grawlix, you know that a character is cursing, but you don't necessarily know what they're saying. The linguist Arnold Zwicky thought about this problem and observed that we actually do have a convention for these things: we say "bleeping" or "blankety-blank" or some other minced oath.[47]

The line between a grawlix and the more generic avoidance character isn't always clear. My advice: if you want to keep things distinct, consider grawlixes to be limited to comics.

Related terms: avoidance character, bounding asterisks, minced oath

greengrocer's (or greengrocers') apostrophe

At the end of 2019, a UK-based organization known as the Apostrophe Protection Society (APS) shuttered its doors. The organization had worked diligently for two decades at "preserving the correct use of this currently much abused punctuation mark," to quote their website. On their page about the correct use of apostrophes, the society states in unambiguous terms that "Apostrophes are NEVER ever used to denote plurals!"

This is rule 3 of 3 on their page, and as you can see, it focuses on how *not* to use apostrophes. As a general principle, if you're shouting at people not to do something, it usually means that they're already doing it. And that's the case here. In fact, using an apostrophe before a plural s—

---

[47] http://itre.cis.upenn.edu/~myl/languagelog/archives/002461.html

apple's and *orange's*—is so common that it has its own name: the *green-grocer's apostrophe*.

The word sleuth Paul McFedries traces the term *greengrocers'* (or *greengrocer's*) *apostrophe* to 1992,[48] but using an apostrophe to mark the plural has been earning derision for much longer.

And holy moly, does this usage ever irritate people. For example, at one point, someone went to the trouble of creating the following mug emblazoned with "Every time you use an apostrophe to make a plural, a puppy dies." (The mugs seem to be no longer available.)

But this proscription didn't always exist. It might seem to us today that the uses for the apostrophe are of long standing. But the thinking about apostrophes and plurals was in flux for a long time. For one thing, people have been writing English for more than 1200 years, but the apostrophe only showed up in the mid-1550s. In the 17th and 18th centuries, many printed works included apostrophes in plurals. For example, John Dryden, who was a stickler about his texts, used them. By the 20th century, of course, opinion on this usage had changed.

And the APS notwithstanding, it's not like apostrophes are *never* used for plurals. Even the *Chicago Manual of Style* (CMOS), the go-to guide for a lot of editors working on commercial content, declares that single letters are pluralized using an apostrophe: *mind your p's and q's.* (Take

---

[48] http://wordspy.com/index.php?word=greengrocers-apostrophe

the apostrophes out and observe why the CMOS experts have ruled this way: reading *mind your ps and qs* just looks weird.)

Anyway, apostrophe rules are a bit of a mess. As Elizabeth Sklar said in her textbook *College English*, "The apostrophe is the stepchild of English orthography."[49]

You use apostrophe + *s* to mark the possessive, but strangely, not in pronouns (*yours*, *his*, *hers*). In fact, if you *do* add an apostrophe to the possessive pronoun *its* (that is, you write "it's"), you get another load of trouble from apostrophe-watchers.

Another use for apostrophes is contractions—that is, to mark letters that are omitted. But what's omitted exactly in the possessive? A theory you'll occasionally encounter is that the apostrophe + *s* stands in for *his*: *John's car* is a shortened form of *John his car*. This is implausible for a number of reasons, starting with the fact that the possessive for the feminine is *her*, and we don't say *Sarah'r car*. But more to the point, the historical record makes it clear that the possessive in Old English was formed by adding *s* or *es* to the end of words (though they got by fine with no apostrophe to mark this, as noted). If anything has been left out of a possessive *s*, the only candidate would be the *e* in *es*.

It's not really that surprising that a lot of people haven't mastered this arcana, and of course a great many just don't care. And among those people we can count greengrocers, it seems.

Related terms: umlaut

hapax legomenon

Pick a substantial book off your bookshelf—maybe a nice, fat novel—and take a glance through it. As you look, think about this: what are the odds that the text contains a word that appears only one time in the entire book? Would you take a bet that there is such a word?

---

[49] If you have access to JSTOR, the journal storage site, you can read the chapter "The Possessive Apostrophe: the Development and Decline of a Crooked Mark."

I hope you did take the bet, because the odds are good, even in a big book. A famous example is the novel *Moby-Dick*, which has over 200,000 words. If you pull out all the words and rank them according to how often they appear, 44% of the words appear only once. Or so claims a user named Radagast3 who plotted the distribution of words in *Moby-Dick*.[50] I don't know about you, but to me this seems like a surprisingly high percentage.

(What might be even more surprising is that when you count the frequency of words in texts, the distribution of the words is similar across different texts. For example, in most texts, about 50% of the words appear only once. The frequency follows a so-called power law, which for the distribution of words is known as *Zipf's law*.)

A word that appears only once in a text, or in an author's collected works, or in a language at large is known as a *hapax legomenon*, or just a *hapax* for short. The term *hapax legomenon* is a Greek expression that means "something said only once." The reason we use a Greek term is that the word originated in Bible studies when people were poring over old texts in Hebrew and Greek in order to translate them. The New Testament, which was written in Greek, has over 650 hapax legomena (to use the plural), and 25 of those didn't appear anywhere else in the Greek of the time (that is, in koine Greek). The Old Testament, written in Hebrew, has about 1500. *The Iliad* has over 1,000 hapaxes.

If you're reading *Moby-Dick* and you run across a term that you don't recognize, you can at least turn to a dictionary—that is, you can take your question about a hapax legomenon that appears in a single text and try to find it in a larger body of work, like the entirety of English. For example, in *Moby-Dick*, one of the hapaxes is *baboon*, which is unique within that text, but which you can find elsewhere in English.

But if you're translating old texts in Greek or Latin or Hebrew or Mayan or Ancient Egyptian, your hapax legomenon might be the only instance of the word that we know about, period. A surprising example is the word *daily* in *give us this day our daily bread*, which is a translation of the Greek word *epiousios*. But the two Bible verses that include the word (Matthew 6:11, Luke 11:3) are the only place where the word *epiousios* appears anywhere. There is disagreement about what *epiousios*

---

[50] https://en.wikipedia.org/wiki/File:Moby_Dick_Words.gif

means, and by no means do scholars agree that it means "daily." (You can read more about the interpretations of *epiousios* in the Wikipedia article about that word.)

When you encounter hapax legomena in old texts, obviously it can be a problem because you might not have any other way to determine what the singular word means. In practice, though, it might not be as opaque as it seems. Sometimes the word is similar enough to known words, or is compounded from known roots, so that its meaning is clear. For example, the Old English translation of 2 Maccabees 6:18 contains the only known instance of the word *offrung-spic*, in a verse in which the Jewish elder Eleazar refuses to eat something forced on him by a cruel ruler. Based on the roots, *offrung-spic* translates as "offering bacon"; modern renderings use terms like *pig's flesh*, *swine's flesh*, or just *pork*.

But sometimes we have to speculate. An example I like is that the Latin text for *The Satyricon* contains the hapax *apoculamus*. Some scholars think this is a made-up compound *apo* ("away from") and *culum* ("butt"): "to haul ass." But not everyone agrees with this analysis, in spite of how awesome that explanation is.

Now and then we can guess that a hapax is just a mistake. A poem in Middle English from the 1400s includes the hapax *snowcrie*. The word is dutifully listed in the OED, but the entry just says "meaning uncertain." There's a good chance that this was just an error—a scribal typo, so to speak—and maybe it was supposed to be *sorcerie*, meaning "sorcery." At any rate, that seems like a reasonable explanation for this otherwise unknown word.

But for some hapaxes, we might never know their exact meaning. This is depressingly true for highly fragmented texts, like the relatively few instances of texts that we have for various dead languages. Even Middle English, which was spoken approximately between the years 1100 and 1500, has many hapaxes. The people who compiled the Middle English dictionary reckon that about a third of their entries are hapaxes.

But having to guess at the meaning of a hapax can be true even for modern texts. Authors have always felt free to invent new words—nonce words—that are initially hapaxes. Depending on who's counting, Shakespeare invented (or at least used) anywhere between 400 and 1,700 words not seen elsewhere. Dickens likewise was a prolific word-coiner, having come up with *sawbones* (for a doctor), *ugsome* (for "horrible"), *whizz-bang*, and *flummox*.

Many of these nonce-word hapaxes by these authors have been adapted into English. But even with these well-known authors, we sometimes have to guess at the meaning of a hapax in their works. Dickens used the word *sassigassity* in one of his stories, probably to mean something like "audacity"). We're not sure, and there is no place we can check.

Occasionally the author goes out of their way to create a hapax. You might recognize some of the hapaxes in a poem by Lewis Carroll that starts this way:

'Twas brillig, and the slithy toves
    Did gyre and gimble in the wabe:
All mimsy were the borogoves,
    And the mome raths outgrabe.

The words *brillig* and *slithy* and *outgrabe* do now appear more than once in English, hence they're technically no longer hapaxes. But the other references to these words just come back to the poem, and the words' meaning remains as impenetrable as that of any hapax in an ancient text.

Related terms: mountweazel, nonce word, unpaired word

haplology, liquid dissimilation, syncope

You've probably heard people say "probly" when they mean *probably*. Or maybe you've heard "libry" for *library*. If you listen to people who have a particular British accent, perhaps you've heard "febry" for *February*.

These are all instances of a kind of shortening known as *haplology*. Haplology is a specific kind of leaving-out of sounds: the sounds that are left out are entire syllables, and the syllables are next to each other, and they're very similar. The word comes from the Greek for "single" + "word."

Look at the haplology for *probably*:

*pro-**ba**-bly*
pro-bly

As you can see, the *ba* syllable that's left out is pretty similar to the *bly* syllable at the end. Similarly, in the haplologized "libry" pronunciation, it's the middle syllable (*lib-**ra**-ry*) that's left out due to its similarity to the *ry* syllable that follows.

You might think of these as "incorrect" pronunciations, but it's possible that you have a few examples of haplology in your own speech. A common example is *authoritative*, which many people pronounce "au-THOR-i-tive," leaving out *ta* before the last syllable. Word people like to wryly note that the word *haplology* is often pronounced "hap-lo-gy."

The sometimes-mysterious pronunciations of place names can show evidence of haplology. For example, if you've only ever seen the name *Worcestershire*, which is the name of a county in England, you'd have no idea that it's pronounced "woos-ter-shire," or that *Leicestershire*, another county name, is pronounced "les-ter-shire." You have to hear it to know that an entire syllable is dropped in each case. My wife is from Worcester, Massachusetts, which the locals refer to as "woo-ster." (Actually, since the town is in Massachusetts, they refer to it as "woo-stah," because they have a non-rhotic accent.)

Some words show a historical influence of haplology. Speakers over the centuries wore down some syllables, and the words as we know them today no longer even show the syllables that were squeezed out. Examples include *humbly* (originally *humblely*), *simply* (originally *simplely*), and *nobly* (originally *noblely*). The Germanic tribes that invaded the British Isles 1500 years ago included the *Angli* (various spellings), who gave us the *Anglo-* part of *Anglo-Saxon*. The name for their new homeland was *Angla-land*, but as you can see, through haplology this evolved into *England*.

Haplology is one of several ways in which people make pronunciation easier. A similar type of sound modification is *liquid dissimilation*, which removes instances of the letters *l* or *r* when they appear near each other (*library* as "liberry"). The linguist Nancy Hall made a list of words that show liquid dissimilation, which includes many examples that I'd heard, possibly even from myself:

95

- *ape[r]ture*
- *be[r]serk*
- *f[r]ustrating*
- *gove[r]nor*
- *hi[er]archy*
- *lib[r]ary*
- *lit[er]ature*
- *prost[r]ate* (not to be confused with *prostate [cancer]*)
- *vete[ri]narian*

Dissimilation for *l* is less common than it is for *r*. But I found a nice example in a listing for a recording of Pachelbel's Canon, where the first *l* had disappeared:

The Glory of the Baroque
Pachelbel Canon & Gigue

Pachebel: Canon
Emerald Ensemble, Rog
From the Album The Glory of t

As is so often true, there are also historical examples. The word *pilgrim* comes from the Latin *peregrinus*; the shift from *r* to *l* to produce *pilgrim* is another example of dissimilation. Similarly, *purple* comes from the Old English word *purpure*.

Another way that sounds are squeezed out of words is *syncope*, which is a general contraction of sounds. We see this in *camera > camra, didn't > dint, vegetable > vedgtable*, and *Wednesday > Wenzday*.

Sometimes we drop sounds, sometimes we add them (epenthesis), sometimes we switch them metathesis. Pronunciation can be hard!

Here's something fun: the writing equivalent of *haplology* is called *haplography*, with *graph* for "writing." A common example is writing *Missippi* for *Mississippi*, or *rember* for *remember*. If you've ever done this, you can take comfort from history. This type of error appears to be universal—haplographic errors appear in the Dead Sea Scrolls.

If you do hear someone say "fustrating" or "libary," you might still consider it wrong, but at least now you know where their pronunciation comes from.

Related terms: clipping, epenthesis

homonym, homophone, heteronym

Our spelling system in English is, let's face it, a bit of a mess. By one count, we have 205 different spellings for our 44 sounds.[51] Some studies suggest that the weirdness of our writing system significantly slows kids down as they learn to read when compared to children learning to read in other languages. One might marvel at times that we learn to read fluently at all.

We have two fundamental problems: one involves spelling and another involves sound, which can lead to these potentially confusing situations:

- Some words are spelled the same and sound the same, but mean different things (grizzly **bear**, **bear** a burden).
- Some words sound the same but are spelled differently (deer, dear).
- Some words are spelled the same but sound different (to **lead**, a **lead** weight).

In casual use, people refer to all these types of words as homonyms ("same" + "name"). But we can get more precise than that! We can use terms that make it clear where the overlap is with these types of words, whether it's spelling (-graph for "writing") or pronunciation (-phone for "sound").

Same spelling, same sound, different meaning (homonyms)

Let's start with homonyms. As I was saying, a broad definition of homonym encompasses words that sound the same even if they're spelled differently, like deer/dear. However, to keep things ultra-distinct, I'm going to limit homonym to words that sound the same and are spelled the same, like bear/bear.

Here are a few more homonyms:

- bug: an insect; an error in a computer program; to bother (someone)
- mean: the middle; cruel; to intend

---

[51] http://literacyproblems.blogspot.com/2017/12/reading-problems.html

- *bark*: the covering on a tree; what dogs do
- *rock*: a big stone; a style of music; to move back and forth
- *rose*: a flower; past tense of *to rise*

There are hundreds and hundreds of homonyms in English. As readers, we can generally tell from context what the intention is. You can see, for example, that homonym pairs often consist of a verb and a noun. This means that it's usually clear from how the word appears in a sentence which meaning is intended.

Different spelling, same sound, different meaning (homophones)

There's also a large number of words that sound the same but are spelled differently, like *deer* and *dear*. What's interesting about these is their common pronunciations, so we can say they're *homophones*. (Because they're spelled differently, we can also say they're *heterographs*.)

Let's look at some examples of homophones:

- *ate* and *eight*
- *bear* and *bare*
- *carat* and *caret* and *carrot*
- *medal* and *meddle* and *metal* and *mettle* (in American English, anyway)
- *moan* and *mown*
- *nun* and *none*
- *principal* and *principle*
- *site* and *sight*
- *their* and *they're* and *there*
- *to* and *too* and *two*

One reason to think about homophones separately from homonyms in general is that homophones are a source of a lot of spelling errors. You can find many pages on the web that aim to help you untangle confusable homophones like *capitol* and *capital*, *compliment* and *complement*, *cord* and *chord*, *palette* and *palate*, *pedal* and *peddle*, and *principle* and *principal*. There are probably very few of us who have *never* confused *to*, *too*, and *two* when we're writing quickly. And who hasn't encountered examples of confusion between *their, they're,* and *there*?

Unlike the homonyms listed earlier, homophone pairs are often the same part of speech—a pair of nouns or a pair of verbs. *Pedal* and *peddle* are both verbs; *principle* and *principal* are both nouns. This makes it easier for someone to slot in the wrong word when they're writing—there are two similar words that are both nouns, say, and a person just picks the wrong one.

And it's just hard to keep some of the pairs of homophones straight. People learn mnemonics to try: "The principal is your pal," is supposed to help you remember that *principal* can refer to a person. The editor Stan Carey suggests a mnemonic for *compliment/complement*: remember that *compliment* contains an I ("I compliment you") and that *complement* is about *comple*ting something.

Sometimes the word pairs consist of a common word and one that's more obscure, which makes it even harder to keep them straight. This is the case for the homophones *bait* ("to entice," as in "bait a trap") and *bate* ("to restrain"—think *abate*). A search in the Corpus of Contemporary American English (COCA) shows that *baited breath* shows up about 26% of the time when someone presumably meant *bated breath*. That's a pretty high percentage of using the wrong homophone.

Same spelling, different sound, different meaning (heteronyms)

Another class of potential confusion is with words that are spelled the same (*homographs*) but sound different (*heterophones*) and mean different things—the *lead/lead* example from earlier. These are known as *heteronyms*. Here are some more examples:

- *address* (verb) and *address* (noun)
- *content* (adjective) and *content* (noun)
- *desert* (verb) and *desert* (noun)
- *excuse* (verb) and *excuse* (noun)
- *minute* (adjective) and *minute* (noun)
- *object* (verb) and *object* (noun)
- *permit* (verb) and *permit* (noun)

- *proceeds* (verb) and *proceeds* (noun)
- *sewer* (one who sews), *sewer* (waste stream)
- *wound* (adjective), *wound* (noun)

Many of our heteronyms come from the same source but have diverged for different functions. As one example, the noun *permit* was derived from the verb *to permit*. During this process, the stress pattern in the noun shifted. In the verb, the stress is on the second syllable ("per-MIT"), but in the noun, the stress is on the first syllable ("PER-mit"). Result: heteronym. By the way, this pattern of a verb changing to a noun and undergoing a change in the stress is common enough that it has its own name: *initial-stress-derived noun*.

Sometimes the heteronyms were borrowed from other languages, but at different times. That's what happened with *minute* ("small") and *minute* ("60 seconds"). Both words came from Latin (*minutum*), but their different senses entered English at different times for different purposes and somehow ended up with different pronunciations.

Sometimes heteronyms come from different origins but end up with the same spelling in English. A medical *wound* (pronounced "woond") goes back to an Old English word *wund* that meant the same thing. The adjective *wound* (pronounced "wownd") was derived via a normal process in Old English from the past tense form of the verb *to wind*. The word *sewer* to mean "one who sews" is pronounced differently from *sewer* to mean a waste conduit, and those words have completely different origins.

The verb *to desert* and the noun *desert* to mean "arid region" both come from a Latin term that means "abandoned." But we also have *desert* as in *just deserts*, which comes from an old French word meaning "to deserve." The chess piece *pawn* is related to the word *peon* from Latin, whereas the verb *to pawn* comes from an old Germanic word that seems to have meant something like "pledge."

A few words are heteronyms for some people but aren't for others—it can depend on how the person pronounces the words. For example, some people pronounce the verb *to import* as "to IM-port," but other people pronounce it as "to im-PORT." For people who say the verb as "to IM-port," the noun *import* isn't a heteronym. (Instead it's a homonym.) That can also be true for *address*, *insult*, *excise*, and some others.

A special case of heteronyms is a capitonym, in which the words are distinguished by capitalization (*polish/Polish*). That's covered elsewhere in this book.

Bringing it all together

If you're like me, you might have a hard time keeping straight variations of the different terms for "sounds like" and "written like." To help me keep it all straight, I made myself the following chart.

Name	Spelling	Sound	Examples
homonym homophone *and* homo-graph)	Same	Same	*bear* (animal)/*bear* (to carry) *rose* (flower)/*rose* (from "to rise")
homophone (heterograph)	Different	Same	*nun/none* *to/too/two* *site/cite/sight* *ate/eight*
heteronym (homograph *but not* homophone)	Same	Different	*permit* (n)/*permit* (v) *lead* (n)/*lead* (v) *desert* (n)/*desert* (v)

The Wikipedia page for homophone has a great Venn diagram that shows the relationships and overlaps of homonyms, homophones, homographs, heteronyms, and heterographs. If you've still got questions, I recommend that you have a look.

Related terms: capitonym, International Phonetic Alphabet (IPA), polysemy

hypercorrection

A classic case of trying too hard is the (possibly apocryphal) telephone receptionist's "Whom shall I say is calling?" That instance of *whom* sounds fancy, but it's incorrect; it should be *who*, because grammatically it functions like *I should say [she] is calling*.

Using *whom* like this is a good example of *hypercorrection*: using a word form or pronunciation incorrectly (or dubiously) in an effort to sound formal. To quote the linguist Michael Erard, hypercorrection results when someone has attempted to mimic high social class "but couldn't fulfill its linguistic expectations"; Alistair Cooke called this the "Grammar of Anxiety."

Another example of hypercorrection pertains to the "correct" plurals for words of foreign origin. For example:

At the aquarium we saw several ***octopi***.

Using an *i* as the plural ending instead of saying "octopuses" is a way of sounding formal. But in a strict sense, the plural *octopi* is etymologically incorrect; the word *octopus* is from Greek, but the *i* ending for a plural is from Latin. (We borrowed the term via Latin, which is how it ended up with an *i* ending.) The form *octopi* has become a conventional alternate plural form to *octopuses*, but using *octopi* can look a lot like an attempt to sound formal and you can call it a hypercorrection—especially if someone *insists* that it's the correct plural for *octopus*.

A place you'll find hypercorrection is in the overuse of *I* in place of *me*, or *she/he/they* for *her/him/them*. Patricia T. O'Connor subtly poked fun at this habit with the title of her book *Woe Is I*. Even the grammar book we used way back when I was in high school English allowed that *It's me* was correct English. (Hold on to this thought for a minute; there's more to this story.)

Another example of hypercorrection is awkwardly avoiding stranded prepositions—that is, having a preposition at the end of a sentence—in the mistaken belief that it's wrong. An example is changing "Where did you come from?" to "From where did you come?" Stranded prepositions were declared an error by 18th-century grammarians who wanted to follow Latin, in spite of ample evidence that prepositions at the end of a sentence have been used in English since forever. (Read more on the "rule" about prepositions in the entry for zombie rule.)

By the way, the famous joke-example is "This is nonsense up with which I will not put," which *absolutely, positively* was not said by Winston Churchill.[52]

One of my older relatives was taught that it's incorrect to use *people* as the plural for *person*. (It's not.) I never once heard her say something like "I saw those people"; she would say something like "I saw those persons." But I thought that I was unlikely to talk her out of this habit, given how entrenched this hypercorrection was in her speech. And it wasn't just her; someone on Twitter had a more recent experience with the same hypercorrection:

The Layman's Linguist
@LaymansLinguist

One time in 5th grade English class we had a quiz on plural nouns but when we got them back the next day, we'd all been marked wrong for putting <PEOPLE> instead of <PERSONS> so if you ever wanna see 23 small children unite to absolutely RIOT against prescriptivism—that'll do it.

2:58 AM · Aug 24, 2022

Some examples of hypercorrection involve pronunciation. For example, pronouncing the *t* in *often* is often (ahem) cited as an example of hypercorrection. The *t* was originally there in English, but its pronunciation had disappeared in medieval times. In the 19th century the sounded-out *t* started creeping back, but only in *often*, not in words like *soften* or *fasten*. In 1926, H. W. Fowler thought that pronouncing the *t* in *often* was an affectation among academics and a practice by "uneasy half-literates who like to prove that they can spell." (Fowler was nothing if not opinionated.) Even so, eventually so many people had added the *t* back in that it's now a standard alternate pronunciation.

Along similar lines, for American speakers, an exaggerated articulation of *t* in words like *button* or *kitten* is a hypercorrection. Hyperarticulated *t* in these examples shows that hypercorrection can be relative. If a

---

[52] http://itre.cis.upenn.edu/~myl/languagelog/archives/001715.html

speaker's accent normally calls for a *t* in the middle of a word to be carefully articulated, then doing that is not hypercorrection. It's only hypercorrection if the speaker is pronouncing words in a way that aspires to an accent that is not native to them, presumably to sound more prestigious.

A construction that's often proposed as an example of hypercorrection is to use *I* in place of *me* in compound objects—sentences like *They gave it **to Sarah and I*** or *It's just **between you and I***. (Per traditional grammar, these should be *They gave it to Sarah and me* and *It's just between you and me*.) This sure looks like hypercorrection, doesn't it? Like someone shooting for something like "It is I" instead of "It's me" and overdoing it.

If so, it's been a hypercorrection for a very long time. The expression *between you and I* appeared in Shakespeare:

> [...] since in paying it, it is impossible I should live, all debts are
> cleared between you and I
> (*The Merchant of Venice*, Act III, Scene 2)

And *you and I* as an object was also used by Pepys, Defoe, and Mark Twain.

It seems likely that constructions like *between you and I* or *to you and I* aren't hypercorrections so much as more evidence that pronouns in English just don't work the way they're "supposed" to. Consider also ***Me and my friend** went to the movies*, where *me and my friend* is widely condemned as wrong, but is also a construction that's in very wide use. There's definitely something going on with pronouns joined with *and* that goes beyond hypercorrection.

Related terms: eggcorn, malaphor, malapropism

hypernym, hyponym

We live in a world of deep hierarchies; each level of the hierarchy is the child of the level above it, and the parent of the level below it. However, I don't want to contemplate the philosophical implications of this possibly profound observation. We are here for the names.

So: a *hypernym* (also, *hyperonym*, both Greek for "over-name") describes a class of things that has child categories: *color*; *dog*; *tree*; *bird*; *game*. Another term for hypernym is *superordinate*, which suggests how these terms pertain to a kind of semantic hierarchy. (*Super* is Latin for "above.") In more everyday language, this is also known as an *umbrella term*.

The corresponding term *hyponym* ("under-name") describes the subcategories under the hypernym:

- Blue (hyponym) is a type of color (hypernym).
- Chess (hyponym) is a type of game (hypernym).

Each level of the hierarchy is in turn part of a larger hierarchy. A name that's a hypernym in one context can be a hyponym in another:

- A beagle (hyponym) is a type of dog (hypernym), but a dog (hyponym) is also a type of canine (hypernym), and a canine (hyponym) is a type of carnivore (hypernym).
- A Douglas fir (hyponym) is a type of tree (hypernym), but a tree (hyponym) is also a type of plant (hypernym).

The terms can apply to nouns, as you've seen. But this type of semantic categorization and hierarchy can apply to verbs as well. For example, *to saunter* and *to stroll* are hyponyms of *to walk*. And *to walk* is in turn a hyponym of *to locomote*.

For the most part, these relationships are easy to grasp and don't raise many linguistic eyebrows. But hypernymy and hyponymy have a couple of interesting wrinkles. As noted in the examples, some words can be both hypernyms and hyponyms, depending on the context in which they're being used. This type of word is called an *autohyponym*. I suspect you can considerably enhance your word-nerd cred by tossing that one around at a party someday.

There's also an interesting issue with terms that can be hypernymic but are also sex-marked, like *cow*. In English as spoken by people who don't raise livestock, a *cow* (hyponym) and a *bull* (hyponym) both fall under the generic hypernym *cows*. ("Look at those cows in the field.") We also use *dog* generically to refer to domesticated canines; in casual usage we don't distinguish male dogs (*dogs*) from female ones (*bitches*).

A discussion we've been having for about the last century is whether words like *mankind* and (especially) *man* should function as hypernyms for both *man* and *woman* in expressions like *That's one small step for mankind* and *Man does not live by bread alone.* Usage has been moving away from this hypernymic use of *man* and *mankind*, and these days we're apt to see *people, person,* and *human* or *humankind* as preferred hypernyms. Similarly, the masculine pronoun (*he, him, his*) has been used to represent all people (*A fool and **his** money are soon parted*), but singular *they* (*Everyone should bring **their** own lunch*) is becoming more acceptable in standard English.

Along those lines, the words we use for professions are becoming more hypernymic. Not that long ago, people who performed on the stage or in movies were either *actors* or *actresses*. These days many women refer to themselves as *actors*—that is, the word *actor* is moving from toward being a hypernym for both "male actors" and "female actors." Similar shifts have created non-sex-marked terms like *flight attendant* as hypernyms for *steward* and *stewardess* and expanded one formerly sex-marked term to encompass both (*author* for *author* and *authorette, hero* for *hero* and *heroine*).

Although the concept of hypernyms and hyponyms seems simple when you first look at it, you have to look closely. And you have to keep track of how they're used in our ever-shifting language.

Related terms: polysemy, singular *they*

hypocorism

When I was still a young person, the makers of Life cereal ran a TV commercial about their product. In the commercial, some kids were astonished that their younger sibling, Mikey, liked a cereal that was nonetheless "supposed to be good for you." The tagline was "Mikey likes it!" For many years afterward, people seemed to think that I would enjoy being called Mikey. (They were mistaken.)

A pet name or nickname like *Mikey* is known as a *hypocorism*. We have many hypocorisms in English that you surely know:

- *Eliza, Beth, Liz, Bess, Betty,* and *Libby* for *Elizabeth*
- *Madge, Maggie, Margie, Marge, Megan,* and *Peggy* for *Margaret*
- *Moll, Molly,* and *Polly* for *Mary*
- *Rick, Ricky,* and *Dick* for *Richard*
- *Bill, Billy, Liam, Will,* and *Willy* for *William*
- *Dubya* for *George W. Bush*

As you can see, hypocorisms often involve using a diminutive like *Betty* or *Margie* or *Billy*. But they can also just involve shortened (clipped) versions of a name, like *Will* for *William*. Some hypocoristic shortenings aren't always obvious, like *Peg* for *Margaret* or *Molly* for *Mary*. (There's a whole grammar of how we form nicknames like these which I won't get into here. The linguist and editor Jonathon Owen has a good Twitter thread about it, though.[53])

The term *hypocorism* comes from Greek, where it refers to using child talk. And this is a clue for where we get some of these names: they're based on the way children might shorten or play with names. Some hypocorisms arose as rhymes: *Dick* rhymes with *Rick* (short for *Richard*); *Bob* rhymes with *Rob*, short for *Robert*; *Peg* rhymes with *Meg*, short for *Margaret*.

Hypocorisms can also reflect pronunciation difficulties that young children have. David Bowles, an author and translator, notes that there are hypocorisms in Spanish that don't seem obvious, such as *Pancho* for the man's name *Francisco* or *Conchita* for the woman's name *Concepción*. But as he explains in a Twitter thread, there are underlying phonetic rules that help derive the hypocorisms from the original names, even if the rules aren't obvious.[54]

The word *hypocorism* also covers names that aren't derived from a person's name. Terms of endearment like *Honey* or *Sweetheart* or *Baby* are also considered hypocorisms—that is, they're what we sometimes call pet names.

Hypocorisms aren't limited to names for people. We use words like *doggy* and *kitty* and *piggy* to refer to animals, regardless of their age or

---

[53] https://tinyurl.com/43tdf2xh
[54] https://tinyurl.com/28vs6mpw

size. Notice that these are diminutives of common nouns, not of names. In Britain, people refer to the television as the *telly* and to a drink as a *bevvy*.

The real enthusiasts for hypocorisms in the English-speaking world seem to be Australians. Many of the words that are considered stereo-typically Australian English (or *Strine*, as it's sometimes hypocoristically called) are hypocorisms, like *barbie* (barbeque), *brekkie* (breakfast), *mozzie* (mosquito), and *footy* (football). It seems that the hypocoristic word *selfie* was coined in Australia. A recent coinage is *pando* for "pandemic."

As the linguist Chi Luu points out, it's not that other English speakers don't use hypocorisms; it's that Australians "seem to regularly do it so much more, and in much wider social and speech contexts."[55] The writer Dan Nosowitz uses this sentence as an example of an "only slightly weird" sentence in Australian English:

> I had an avo sammie in the arvo with my sparky mate Daz at the servo.[56]

Nosowitz proposes the theory that Australians are fond of hypocorisms because Australian society is particularly unstratified. Because English doesn't have good ways to indicate equality, Australians developed a kind of uber-informality by using first names and nicknames, even for people like politicians. The flip side is that this style of language becomes a dialectical way to indicate membership.

By the way, before you use any hypocoristic names, check with the person in question. A William you know might not want to be known as Willy, and a Victoria might not want to be known as Vicky. Just like I didn't want to be called Mikey.

Related terms: clipping, demonym, familect, mononym, onomastics

---

[55] https://daily.jstor.org/australians-obsessed-nicknaming/
[56] https://www.atlasobscura.com/articles/australian-nicknames

infix, tmesis

I'm sure you know what a *prefix* is: it's when you add something to the front of a word, like *un* to *friendly* to form *unfriendly*, or *anti* to *climax* to form *anticlimax*. And you also know that a *suffix* is when you add something to the end of the word, like when you add *ness* to *friendly* to form *friendliness*, or *ship* to *owner* to form *ownership*, or *ish* to *noon* to form *noon-ish*.

But what about words like these?

- *edu**ma**cated*
- *shi**z**nit*

In these words, the added part is in the middle of the word. Not unreasonably, these are called *infixes*. (All three together—prefix, infix, and suffix—are referred to collectively as *affixes*.)

A closely related word is *tmesis*. This term also refers to inserting something into the middle of a word, but for tmesis, the inserted part is a whole word, not just a bit like *ma* or *izn*. The Merriam-Webster definition for *tmesis* uses the example of *what place soever*, where the word *place* has been inserted into *whatsoever*.

For the most part, unlike prefixes and suffixes, infixes and tmesis aren't a grammatical feature of English—that is, we don't conjugate words using infixes, or typically form new words using tmesis, or anything like that. In other languages, infixes *do* have a grammatical role.

There are a few examples of a sort of stock infix, like *edumacated*, which is a word that's generally used ironically. The rapper Snoop Dogg invented an entire idiolect that uses *iz* infixation, like *shiznit* and *crizazy*. And a verbal trait of the Simpsons character Ned Flanders is that he uses *diddly* as an infix in words like *Hi-diddly-ho!*

A place where we really see infixes in English is in what's referred to as *expletive infixation*. As the name suggests, it's where we drop a curse word into the middle of another word:

- *abso-**bloody**-lutely*
- *un-**frickin**-believable*
- *fan-**fucking**-tastic*

In these cases, the infixed expletive works as an intensifier: *abso-bloody-lutely* is more emphatic than just *absolutely*.

There are rules about infixation, including expletive infixation. Speakers are not free to insert any infix anywhere in the word. For starters, only certain words can be dropped into expletive infixes, mostly words like *bloody* and *goddamn* and *fucking* (or their variants) that already have freedom of movement in a sentence.

On top of that, there seems to be a rule that any infix precedes the stressed syllable, so that these are typical patterns:

> *edu-CA-ted* > *edu-**ma**-CA-ted*

> *fan-TAS-tic* > *fan-**frickin**-TAS-tic*

Whereas the following doesn't work for English speakers:

> *fan-TAS-tic* > **fan-TAS-**frickin**-tic*

Infixation and tmesis is not a new phenomenon in English. Shakespeare used the infixed *how heinous e'er* in *Richard II* (Act V, Scene 3). The OED has cites for *abso-blooming-lutely* going back to 1909. So infixation has a long history in English, and as we've seen with Snoop Dogg and Ned Flanders, it continues doing fine in English today.

Related terms: libfix, portmanteau word

International Phonetic Alphabet (IPA)

Every English speaker (reader) knows that the correspondence between sounds and letters in our alphabet is ... imperfect. For example, letters that stand for vowels can be pronounced in a variety of ways:

- *sit, library, pique*
- *cat, fate, pa*
- *mere, met, her*
- *clothes, honey*
- *cube, push, but*

On top of that, speakers of different dialects often pronounce these vowels differently.

And the same sound can be represented by different letters:

- *cat, kitty*
- *shoot, nation*
- *phone, feet*

And there are other weirdness, like silent letters, or single letters that represent multiple sounds, like *box* (*x=ks*) and *use* (*u=ee-u*).

The English alphabet clearly isn't a great tool for precisely capturing the subtleties of how people pronounce language. In Act I of his play *Pygmalion* (which was the basis for the musical *My Fair Lady*), George Bernard Shaw makes an initial effort to represent the speech of the London flower girl Eliza Doolittle as she sounds when Henry Higgins first encounters her:

Ow, eez ye-ooa san, is e? Wal, fewd dan y' de-ooty bawmz a mather should, eed now bettern to spawl a pore gel's flahrzn than ran awy at-baht pyin. Will ye-oo py me f'them?

... though after this transcription, he adds "Here, with apologies, this desperate attempt to represent her dialect without a phonetic alphabet must be abandoned as unintelligible outside London."

And that's just English. Using our alphabet, how might you represent people speaking French or Russian or Mandarin or the click languages of Africa? A normal alphabet just isn't up to the task.

Thus in the late 19th century, linguists began devising an alphabet that assigns one symbol to each unique sound in every human language. This included many sounds that aren't in English; the goal was to have a single alphabet for all of human language. The result—the *International Phonetic Alphabet*, or *IPA*—consists of 107 letters with 52 diacritical marks, or marks that are used above, below, or within a letter.

To give you an idea of what the IPA is like, the following table shows a small selection of IPA symbols and corresponding sounds from English. (There are many more, even just for the sounds of English.)

ʌ	cup		b	boy
ɑ:	father		d	dog
æ	cat		j	yes
e	bed		k	cat
ɪ	hit		n	noon
i:	see		ŋ	sing
ɒ	hot		s	see
ɔ:	four		ʃ	she
ʊ	put		t	tea
u:	food		tʃ	church
aɪ	five		θ	think
aʊ	out		ð	father
eɪ	eight		z	zoo
ʊəʳ	cure		ʒ	measure

You can see that the IPA relies on some unfamiliar symbols. The sound of *a* in *father* and *a* in *cat* are distinct sounds, so they get distinct letters: ɑ: (father) and æ (cat). The two sounds represented by *th* in our writing system have different letters in the IPA: θ for the *th* in *think*, and ð for the *th* in *father*.

The beauty of the IPA is the absoluteness of the alphabet: one sound per character. If you say "to-MAY-to" and I say "to-MAH-to," the IPA has different spellings for our respective tomatoes, and we don't have to try to imagine how people pronounce things in different accents, and we don't have to write "may" and "mah" to represent the different pronunciations.

By the way, in the opening scene of *Pygmalion*, Henry Higgins is transcribing Eliza Doolittle's speech using what he calls "Higgins's Universal Alphabet," which clearly is a version of, or precursor to, the IPA.

Some dictionaries use the IPA to indicate the pronunciation of words. That's what the *Collins English Dictionary* does, for example. If you look up *tomato*, they give you this as the pronunciation:

təmeɪtoʊ

Dictionary.com lets you choose how you want to see the pronunciation. In one version, they show what they call the "phonetic respelling":

[*tuh*-**mey**-toh, -**mah**-]

But you can click a button to display the IPA version instead:

/ tə'meɪ toʊ, -'mɑ- /

In both of these dictionaries, and in many more, you can click the speaker icon to hear the word pronounced according to the spelling they provide, which is a handy way to practice your IPA skills.

Knowing the IPA is a fundamental skill for linguists. If you take an introductory linguistics class, they'll probably ask you to learn enough IPA to be able to transcribe some English utterances. I can tell you from experience that it definitely takes some practice.

Another group that has a keen interest in learning the IPA is opera singers. A singer might be called upon to sing operas whose librettos are in Italian, German, Russian, Czech, English, and other languages. Most singers don't learn all of these languages. Instead, they learn to pronounce them phonetically, for which a knowledge of the IPA is a good start. For example, they might use the IPA Source website to get IPA transcriptions of opera arias and Lieder.[57]

Even if you don't encounter the IPA in a dictionary, it's worth knowing if you think you'll ever read anything about phonology. The IPA Chart With Sounds page on the InternationalPhoneticAlphabet.org site lets you click symbols to hear how they're pronounced.[58] And a post called "How to remember the IPA vowel chart" on the *All Things Linguistics* blog provides handy hints for how to learn the IPA symbols for vowels.[59] As the author says, "The IPA vowel chart is a thing of beauty, a joy forever, and sometimes a bit of a pain to learn."

Related terms: homonym, spelling alphabet, umlaut

---

[57] https://www.ipasource.com/about/
[58] http://www.internationalphoneticalphabet.org/ipa-sounds/ipa-chart-with-sounds/
[59] http://allthingslinguistic.com/post/67308552090/how-to-remember-the-ipa-vowel-chart

libfix

Before September 1971, the word *Watergate* was familiar primarily to people in Washington, DC, as the name of a hotel and office complex. The name comes from the locale—there's an old canal nearby, with a dam ("gate") that regulates water flow.

On September 3, 1971, a burglary occurred in the office complex. As many people know, the break-in was the beginning of what became known as the *Watergate scandal*, or just *Watergate* for short.

There were political ramifications, of course, but also an interesting linguistic one. The *gate* part of *Watergate* broke off, so to speak, and became a thing you could add to the end of a word to suggest a scandal. There's a Wikipedia article named "List of -*gate* scandals and controversies" that lists dozens of *gate* scandals. Some that you might remember include *Deflategate* (NFL), *Dieselgate* (VW), *Emailgate* (Hillary Clinton), *Gamergate* (sexism in the video-game industry), *Troopergate* (three different scandals), and *Sharpiegate* (an altered weather map). Hardly a week goes by without some new *gate* hitting the news.

The linguist Arnold Zwicky coined the term *libfix* for this type of particle (morpheme). The *lib* part comes from "liberated," because the particle has been freed from its original word. The *fix* part comes from *affix* (prefix, infix, suffix) to mean something that you can attach to a word.

Libfixes are common, not to mention fun. Here are some more that you probably know:

- *burger* from *hamburger* (as in *veggieburger*)
- *franken* from Frankenstein (as in *frankenfood*)
- *splain* from *explain* (as in *mansplain*)
- *zilla* from *Godzilla* (as in *bridezilla*)

Something that's kind of amazing is how far a libfix can travel away from its origin. Take *burger*. This originally came from Hamburg, the city in Germany. In German, *Burg* is a fortress; there are many towns and cities in German-speaking regions with *burg* in their names, like Augsburg, Brandenburg, and Freiburg. (A related term that has come down to us in English is *borough*.)

For our purposes, the next step is that *Hamburger* came into English as *Hamburger Wurst*, which is to say, sausage (*Wurst*) in the style of Hamburg. The *er* ending on *Hamburger* is an adjective form in German for things like cities, so *Hamburger* means "of or from or belonging to or in the style of Hamburg."

In English, the meaning of the term *hamburger* shifted from "in the style of Hamburg" to describing instead the manner in which the sausage was presented: as a patty. This in turn shifted to referring to a patty served on a bun. From there, the final step was to generalize the "burger" part to mean any patty-shaped serving on a bun: a *cheeseburger*, a *fishburger*, or a *veggie burger*. As if that weren't enough, the *burger* libfix has taken on a metaphoric sense in words like *mouseburger* and *nothingburger*, where it has a sense that might be glossed as "whole lot of _____", with the prefix filling in the blank. That's a long journey: from a word meaning "fortress" to a patty and then on to "something resembling."

You can't predict what word particle will liberate itself to become a libfix, and then you can't predict where the libfix will go. Here are some more of recent vintage that you might recognize:

- *-holic* from *alcoholic* (as in *gameaholic*)
- *-nap* from *kidnap* (as in *dognap*)
- *-pocalypse* from *apocalypse* (as in *snowpocalypse*)
- *-versary* from *anniversary* (as in *dateaversary* and *blogaversary*)

Once you've become aware of libfixes, it becomes an interesting pursuit to look for them. You might be surprised at how often you'll find one.

Related terms: cranberry morpheme, folk etymology, portmanteau word

malaphor (idiom blend)

Perhaps you're contemplating a home project you've never done before and aren't sure how to proceed. You call a friend to ask about it. Oh, it's not hard, they reassure you: "It's not rocket surgery!"

What they *meant* to say was "It's not rocket *science*," but the metaphor got tangled up with "It's not brain surgery." The result is an *idiom blend*, or to use a term I personally like, a *malaphor*.

Here are some more examples:

> Keep your finger on the ball (keep your finger on the pulse + keep your eye on the ball)
>
> That's the way the cookie bounces (that's the way the cookie crumbles + that's the way the ball bounces)
>
> The early bird killed the cat (the early bird gets the worm + curiosity killed the cat)
>
> It's nerve-curdling (nerve-racking + blood-curdling)

The term *malaphor* (a portmanteau of *malapropism* and *metaphor*) first appeared in 1976. It was used by Lawrence Harrison in an article in the *Washington Post*, although the phenomenon had been noticed earlier.

Malaphors are different from *mixed metaphors*, which are a sequence of metaphors that are nonsensical ("You buttered your bread. Now sleep in it!"). They're also not quite malapropisms, where the speaker substitutes a similar-sounding but incorrect word, and which I cover elsewhere.

A malaphor is generally a mistake based on mixing two expressions that share some elements. As with some other word-based errors, linguists are interested in what malaphors might tell us about how people process language. For example, in the article "To Err is Human: To Study Error-Making is Cognitive Science," Douglas Hofstader and David Moser describe the process like this:

> One can liken the production of a malaphor to someone who reaches into a cookie jar, grabs two cookies at once, and then, trying to pull both out at once through the narrow neck, breaks each of them in two. What emerges is a hybrid of two cookies. [...] Often the two halves dovetail so seamlessly that we are unaware of having grabbed two different linguistic "cookies" or of having spliced them together.[60]

If you pay close attention, you'll discover that malaphors are pretty common. Someone who calls himself Davemalaphor keeps a blog on the Malaphors.com site, and he finds enough malaphors that he can post new

---

[60] https://quod.lib.umich.edu/m/mqrarchive/act2080.0028.002/53:8

ones a couple of times a week. He's collected a bunch of them into a book with, appropriately, a malaphor-based title: *He Smokes Like a Fish and Other Malaphors*.

Related terms: hypercorrection, malapropism, snowclone

malapropism

Sometimes we say something that comes out close to what we intended, but it doesn't quite hit the mark. The result is often funny, as in these examples:

> Texas has a lot of *electrical* votes. (Intended word: *electoral*)

> This is *unparalyzed* in the state's history. (Intended word: *unparalleled*)

> That might give you a little *inclination* of the problem. (Intended word: *indication*)

These are all examples of *malapropisms*: using one word for a different, similar-sounding one, usually with an amusing result.

The term *malapropism* came from French (*mal à propos* = "badly suited, inappropriate"). We got it in English via Sheridan's play *The Rivals*, written in 1775, which featured a character named Mrs. Malaprop who is given to this type of utterance. (Example: "Sure, if I reprehend [read: *apprehend*] any thing in this world, it is the use of my oracular [read: *vernacular*] tongue, and a nice derangement [read: *arrangement*] of epitaphs! [read: *epithets*]") A couple of centuries earlier, the Shakespeare play *Much Ado About Nothing* had included the character Dogberry, who had likewise provided comedy via malapropisms ("Our watch, sir, have indeed comprehended [read: *apprehended*] two aspicious [read: *suspicious*] persons"). The idea of malapropisms—and the people who make them—has been recognized for a long time.

In literature, malapropisms are used to signify a character who is trying to sound elegant but can't quite pull it off. Many malapropisms have also been uttered by real people, not necessarily from an effort to im-press, but simply as errors—for example, politicians and sports commentators sometimes utter malapropisms when they're speaking extemporarily.

In fact, everyone emits malapropisms from time to time through some sort of slippage of the mental gears. Among people who study such things, these are referred to as *Fay-Cutler malapropisms*, named for a couple of graduate students (David Fay and Anne Cutler) who identified these "production errors" in the 1970s and characterized them as "inadvertent use of the wrong word." These are slips of the tongue that a person might make inadvertently but would recognize as an error ("Did I just say *inclination*? Duh, I meant *indication*.")

In contrast, there are *classical malapropisms*, as the linguist Arnold Zwicky calls them. These are errors where the speakers intended the word they spoke; they just don't realize it's an error—"ignorance of the correct usage," as Fay and Cutler classified them. In *The Rivals*, another character describes how Mrs. Malaprop "deck her dull chat with hard words which she don't understand."

When malapropisms are used for comedic effect, as Shakespeare and Sheridan did, they're classical malapropisms, since it's not just what the characters say but their cluelessness about their utterances that makes them funny.

Malapropisms are more subtle than they might seem at first. They tend to follow their own set of rules: malapropisms tend to match the part of speech, number of syllables, and stress pattern of the word they aspire to. The word used by mistake is almost always a real word, even in classical malapropisms. Perhaps not surprisingly, malapropisms often have *some* semantic relationship to the word they're replacing. For example, in the quote from Mrs. Malaprop earlier, *derangement* was an antonym of *arrangement*, or at least it was back when Sheridan was writing *The Rivals*. It turns out, perhaps not surprisingly, that there's even a grammar of mistakes when we speak.

Related terms: eggcorn, folk etymology, hypercorrection, malaphor

metathesis

At a certain stage of their language development, young children tend to get the sounds in words mixed up—for example, they might say "pasket-ti" instead of *spaghetti*, "aminal" for *animal*, or "ephelant" for *elephant*. This type of transposition is common—so common, in fact, that there's a name for it: *metathesis*.

But metathesis is hardly limited to the speech of young children. You might have heard someone say "purty" for *pretty*—that's metathesis. An example I've heard a lot is when people say "asterix" for *asterisk*. You'll often hear people say "calvary" for *cavalry*.

You might even hear (or say!) some words with metathesis without re-alizing it. The linguist Anne Curzan has a story about how she was teach-ing a college class and was surprised to learn that many of her students said "larnyx" for *larynx*. (This anecdote stuck with me, I think, because I'm pretty sure that I, too, said "larnyx" till I heard the story.)

Given how common metathesis is, it's not surprising that words that we use today show evidence of metathesis at work in the past. The word *dirt* was *drit* back around 1300, but by around 1500 was showing up as *dyrt*. The word *bird* was originally *bryd* in Old English, but by medieval times, the variation *byrdes* was showing up. Similarly, the word *third* goes back to an Anglo-Saxon word *thridda*, based on *thri* (that is, "three"). But even as long ago as 750 CE, the variant form *thirdda* ap-peared in the *Lindisfarne Gospels*.

Another example of historical metathesis is the word *ask*; in some dia-lects of English, this is pronounced as *aks*. This is metathesis, clearly, but what's interesting is that the variation between these forms goes back about as far back as we have examples. In Old English, the forms *ascian* ("ask") and *acsian* ("aks") are both recorded. And the variation contin-ued for many more centuries. As the OED explains in its entry for the verb *ask*, the *aks* form ...

> is very well attested in Old English but is chiefly found in late West Saxon. However, in Middle English the [*aks*] forms are more widely distributed throughout the midlands and south. Such metathetic forms have long been regarded as nonstandard (the anonymous *Writing Scholar's Compan.* (1695) describes *ax* as vulgar), although they re-

flect the usual pronunciation of the word in many regional varieties of English.

That is, the *aks* form was widely distributed in England into the time that the New World was being settled, and it's still with us in some dialects.

Some people have proposed that metathesis is the reason that some people say "nucular" for *nuclear*. That seems like a reasonable explanation, but because they don't do this with other words like *molecular*, some linguists feel like metathesis is not what's at work in "nucular." (It might just be based on analogy to words like *muscular* and *binocular*.)

Here's a tidbit about metathesis that you can use the next time you're at a dinner party. In Shakespeare's *The Tempest*, there's a character named Caliban. It's been proposed that this name is an anagram for—that is, a metathesized version of—the Spanish word *canibal*, meaning "cannibal." Bon appetit!

Related terms: epenthesis, haplology

minced oath

Let's say you're in a meeting at work, and you spill an entire cup of tea on yourself. "Well … *shoot*," you say. "I dropped my … *darned* … cup." In another context, you might have used somewhat stronger language. But you're at work and with what's sometimes referred to as polite company, so you resort to *minced oaths*.

A minced oath is a euphemistic variant of a swearword. You know plenty of them, I'm sure, like these:

- *cripes* for *Christ*
- *effed up* for *fucked up*
- *goldurn* for *goddamn(ed)*
- *shoot* or *sugar* for *shit*
- *son of a biscuit* for *son of a bitch*

The urge for swearing is common; it's been estimated that people produce about 80 to 90 taboo words every frickin' day. But of course in many situations it would be considered inappropriate to emit the word you're *really* thinking of. Given that we feel the need to swear but are often in contexts where taboo words are, well, taboo, it's not surprising that we have a healthy collection of minced oaths to choose from.

Minced oaths are generally suggestive of the taboo word they represent. For example, they often use alliteration and assonance to suggest the taboo word: *dang* for *damn*, *heck* for *hell*, *cripes* for *Christ*. In *Atlas Obscura*, Dan Nosowitz explains how *goddamn it* became *dagnabbit* through the processes of metathesis and dissimilation.[61]

An earlier minced oath was the word *dashed*, which substituted for *damned*. In *Bleak House*, Dickens has one of characters say "Dash it, Tony. […] you really ought to be careful." A minced oath I learned from a colleague who'd been in the military is *Charlie Foxtrot* for *clusterfuck*, which combines alliteration with the standard spelling alphabet that's used in military communications.

An interesting, though limited, source of minced oaths is rhyming slang. Various sources say that the relatively innocuous British term *berk* ("a stupid or foolish person") derives from *Berkley hunt*, which was rhyming slang for *cunt*.

In earlier eras, the prohibition on "taking the Lord's name in vain" resulted in minced oaths like *Zounds* for *God's wounds* and *Gadzooks*, which is "perhaps," says Merriam-Webster, "from God's hooks, the nails of the Crucifixion." This form of minced oath seems to be a version of taboo avoidance, where some words or names are so powerful that people don't want to say them out loud.

These days, our taboos tend more toward sex, body functions, and race. In 1948, Norman Mailer's publisher used the word *fug* for *fuck* in the novel *The Naked and the Dead*. While the word *fuck* is now used pretty freely in print media, it's not accepted in prime-time TV. As a result, TV writers still need to use minced oaths. For example, in the TV show *Battlestar Galactica*, characters said the term *frak* (or *frack*) for *fuck*. Or if you're not a *Battlestar Galactica* fan, maybe you're a fan of Ryan North's *Dinosaur Comics*, where T-Rex starts a comic with a minced oath:[62]

---

[61] https://www.atlasobscura.com/articles/what-does-dagnabbit-mean
[62] Source: Dinosaur Comics #3065, used with kind permission by Ryan North.

A generic minced oath is the word *blank*, especially in the expression *blankety-blank* ("The blankety-blank computer is acting up again"). This is a bit meta, because it refers to the convention in printed materials of using avoidance characters to suggest but not actually spell out potentially offensive words, as in "Out, d——d spot!" We also use *bleep*, another meta minced oath, which comes not from print but from broadcasting—it suggests the sound that censors sometimes use to mask taboo words on radio or TV. For example, there's a movie whose title is *What The #$*! Do We know?!* The movie's website consistently refers to this as *What the Bleep Do We Know!?* Whatever it is we don't know, we don't want to say its name out loud.

Related terms: aposiopesis, avoidance character, grawlix, pejoration, semantic bleaching

misle

When I was a kid, I was visiting a friend who had a lot of comic books. I was looking through his collection and plucked one out and read the title. "Tales to Asto Nish?" I asked, to his great amusement. Somehow I'd read *astonish* as "asto-nish," even though it made no sense and I was perfectly familiar with the word *astonish*.

This experience of wrongly parsed word is familiar enough that it has a name: a *misle*. This term (pronounced "missle" or "my-zzle" with a long *i* sound) is a back-formation from the word *misled*, the past tense form of *to mislead* ("They were misled by the headline").

Some people have looked at the word *misled* and gotten it into their heads that they were looking at the past tense form not of *mislead*, but of an otherwise unknown verb *to misle*. ("Today he misles, yesterday he misled, tomorrow he will misle.") The term *misle* has therefore come to be the label for any similarly misparsed word.

To be fair, *to misle* actually once existed in English, as a variant of *to mizzle*, meaning *to drizzle*. But it's obscure to the point of invisibility; good luck finding it in any dictionary shy of the OED.

Even if you've never misread *misled*, you might recognize some other common misles:

- *coworker* parsed as *cow + orker*
- *potash* parsed as *po + tash*
- *sidereal* as *side + real*
- *sundried* parsed as *sundr(y) + ed*

During the 2022 Winter Olympics, Nancy Friedman read *freeskier* (one who free-skis) as a misle and asked "who's the freeskiest?"

Nancy Friedman 🎿
@Fritinancy

I saw "freeskier" and wondered who's the freeskiest.

9:21 AM · Feb 10, 2022

She was probably kidding, but it's nonetheless a good example of a misle.

Some misles cause confusion for a lot of people, such as *disheveled* and *biopic*. Others are idiosyncratic, where one reader trips over the word while others don't. People have reported the words *codenamed*, *goatherd*, *riverbed*, and *underfed* as misles. They might never have given *you* any trouble, but at least someone parsed them wrong at some point.

Misles aren't necessarily the same as words that we mispronounce because we've only ever seen them in print—words like *albeit, antecedent, epitome*, *calliope*, and *hegemony*. Those are what the people behind the *Because Language* podcast once called *only-read-it-isms*—words whose pronunciation you don't know because you've never heard anyone say them out loud. In contrast, a misle is a word that you do know, but somehow while reading it, you just mentally carve it up wrong and get confused.

There's an old joke that involves misles:

Q: How can you tell the difference between a plumber and a chemist?
A: Ask them to pronounce *unionized*.

The humor is that a plumber will pronounce it as "union-ized" and the chemist will pronounce it as "un-ionized." Note that you can't *tell* this joke, you have to read it, because misles.

A comparatively recent source of misles has been domain names for the web. There are a number of notorious domain names where the company did not anticipate some amusing reinterpretation. One example is whorepresents.com, which is the Who Represents site, but can easily be read a different way. Another is (was) expertsexchange.com, the domain for Experts Exchange. The folks who ran that site did eventually get wise, and the URL is now experts-exchange.com. In one case, someone set up a site that supposedly sold pens from an island (uh-huh, sure), the goal of which seemed primarily to be able to use the domain name penisland.com and play on our ability to read a misle. (It works, obviously.)

Related terms: mondegreen

mondegreen

I'm willing to bet that there is no one who has not misheard a song lyric. You're with friends, belting out some familiar tune. Maybe you're singing a Jimi Hendrix song and come out with "'scuse me while I kiss this guy." Or you're singing along to an ABBA tune and sing "See that girl, watch her scream." Or at Christmas time you go caroling and sing "O come, holly faithful." (Due to copyright restrictions on song lyrics, I can't give you the originals of these misheard lines.)

A friend stops you and says "Uh … that's not how it goes."

Awkward.

You can take comfort from the fact that there's a word for a misheard lyric: a *mondegreen*. The word has a great history that derives from, well, a misheard line in a poem.

The American writer Sylvia Wright coined the term *mondegreen* in 1954 in an article in *Harper's Magazine*. She writes how her mother used to read her a poem that, as Wright understood it, went like this:

Ye Highlands and ye Lowlands,
Oh, where hae ye been?
They hae slain the Earl Amurray,
And Lady Mondegreen.

In fact, the last line of the ballad is "And layd him on the green." In the *Harper's* article, Wright describes that she did learn this, but still preferred her version, and along the way, coined the term *mondegreen*:

I know about this, but I won't give in to it. Leaving him to die all alone without even anyone to hold his hand—I won't have it.

The point about what I shall hereafter call mondegreens, since no one else has thought up a word for them, is that they are better than the original.

Although I introduced the term *mondegreen* to refer to misheard song lyrics, you can see that Wright uses it to refer to misheard lines in a poem. Dictionary definitions suggest that a mondegreen is *any* sort of misheard line, whether in a song, poem, or just ordinary speech. In this last and most generous sense, mondegreens can be considered the basis for eggcorns. But the linguist Mark Liberman proposes to keep the word *mondegreen* for mishearings of "part of a song or poem or similar performance," and I like that distinction.[63]

A kind of tabula rasa for mondegreens is the song "Louie, Louie" in the version recorded in 1963 by The Kingsmen. In the recording, the lyrics are basically incomprehensible. But many adults were very concerned

---

[63] http://itre.cis.upenn.edu/~myl/languagelog/archives/000018.html

that the lyrics were obscene, to the point where the FBI investigated. I can personally attest to at least one copy of the record being smashed on the living room floor by a disapproving parent who was convinced that whatever the lyrics were, kids in *that* household were not to be listening to such filth.

I wonder sometimes whether mondegreens might become less prevalent in the future. When I was young, we listened to pop music on crappy AM radios, and it was surprising we could make out any lyrics at all. But even when radio got better, all we had were our ears and possibly the help of cool friends who seemed to know things like song lyrics. If we were lucky, an artist might include lyrics in the liner notes for an album.

These days, of course, you can find almost any song lyrics online. But the correctness of online lyrics—especially for karaoke, my daughter tells me—is by no means a certain thing. And I suppose the fact that people keep contributing mondegreens to sites like KissThisGuy.com tells us that we'll be mishearing lyrics for as long as people sing (or say) them.

Related terms: eggcorn, malapropism, misle, rebracketing

mononym

Think about all the artists who've released records over the last century or so. Even so, if I told you, "Someone discovered a new Elvis recording," you'd probably know immediately who I was talking about.

The singer Elvis Presley achieved what few people have done in history: he became famous enough that he's referred to using a *mononym* ("one" + "name"), namely just *Elvis*. He's in good, if rare, company:

- *Cicero*, the Roman politician
- *Cleopatra*, the Egyptian queen
- *Confucius*, the Chinese philosopher
- *Madonna*, the singer
- *Napoléon*, the French general and emperor

Someone who can be identified by a single name is said to be *mononymous*. The mononym can be a person's actual name. For example, Cicero is the politician's surname; he was actually Marcus Tullius Cicero, and Madonna's name is her actual first name; she was born Madonna Ciccone.

Mononyms can also be nicknames, such as the musician Sting. His real name is Gordon Sumner, but he got the nickname "Sting" because at one point he favored a yellow-and-black sweater. The futból (soccer) player Pelé's nickname (real name: Edson do Nascimento) originated in his school days.

Some mononyms were invented by the mononymous person. "Voltaire" was actually the writer's pen name; he was born François-Marie Arouet. Similarly, the name "Saki" was the assumed pen name of the writer Hector Hugh Munro.

In some cases, the mononym isn't a name at all, strictly speaking. For example, many people refer to the sage Siddhartha Gautama as Buddha, although this is actually a descriptive title meaning "awakened one" in Sanskrit.

And some names look like mononyms but aren't intended that way. It might look like the Icelandic singer Björk has a mononymic name. But her name is actually Björk Guðmundsdóttir. In Icelandic, it's just a custom to go by your first name.[64]

Some mononyms are fleeting—widely understood at some point but perhaps not with the legs of a name like Cicero or Napoléon. Who knows if hundreds of years from now people will instantly recognize names like Cher or Madonna or Ye. Still, for now we know these folks by their single name.

Related terms: eponym, hypocorism, onomastics, patronym

---

[64] At least, according to "The peculiarities of Icelandic naming" by Katharina Hauptman (https://www.meer.com/en/2248-the-peculiarities-of-icelandic-naming).

mountweazel

Suppose that you spend years doing research and writing to compile a dictionary. At last you publish your dictionary and await the riches you'll earn from your work. But barely a year later, someone else publishes a dictionary that eats into the sales of your dictionary. You get hold of a copy of their book, and you're outraged—why, it sure *looks* like they copied a bunch of your entries! You did all the work, and they get profits from it?!

(By the way, this is not just a hypothetical example. The history of dictionaries is filled with actual plagiarism from older dictionaries, and charges of plagiarism from contemporary ones. As the lexicographer Kory Stamper notes about 19th-century dictionaries, "lexicographers of the era routinely borrowed from each other."[65])

So for your next edition, you decide to lay a trap: you'll include a fake entry—a word that doesn't exist, along with a fanciful definition. If that entry appears in the next edition of the rival dictionary, you'll have caught them red-handed. Red-worded, whatever.

You won't be the first person to think of this. The problem you're experiencing is one that's familiar not just to dictionary writers, but also to people who compile encyclopedias and who publish maps. And of course there's a word for it: you're creating something called a *mountweazel*. More prosaically, a mountweazel is referred to as a *copyright trap*. In the realm of mapmaking, a locale that appears on a map (whether as a copyright trap or just an error) is referred to as a *phantom settlement*.

The word *mountweazel* comes from the name Lilian Virginia Mountweazel. In 1975, the *New Columbia Encyclopedia* (NCE) included an entry for this interesting-sounding but short-lived person—among her many accomplishments, she created a photo essay of American mailboxes that was widely exhibited in Europe. Unfortunately, she died at age 31 in an explosion while working for—so ironic—*Combustibles* magazine.

But you might have a hard time finding more details on the photo essay, or about Ms. Mountweazel herself, anywhere except the NCE. That's because Ms. Mountweazel was entirely invented. The idea is that

---

[65] https://www.the-tls.co.uk/articles/the-dictionary-wars-peter-martin-reviewkory-stamper/

if another encyclopedia ended up including an entry for Ms. Mountwea-zel, the editors of the Columbia encyclopedia could cry foul.

A story in the *New Yorker* recounts how a mountweazel was included in the *New Oxford American Dictionary* (NOAD) in 2005.[66] Given a clue—it was in the E's—someone read through the thousand-plus entries and compared them to other dictionaries. In the end, the mountweazel turned out to be the word *esquivalience*, which NOAD defined as "the willful avoidance of one's official responsibilities." It seems like *esquiv-alience* did get picked up by at least another dictionary, whoops, al-though that, er, error has since been fixed.

Not everyone entirely buys the idea that an entry like *esquivalience* got into the dictionary as a mountweazel. Ammon Shea, one of the lexicog-raphers who hosts the Merriam-Webster podcast *Words Matter*, thinks that maybe *esquivalience* originated as a practical joke among the dic-tionary editors.[67] It somehow got through the editing process, and when the word was discovered in the final version, the editors claimed that oh, that—we put that in as a mountweazel. "An April Fools' joke gone awry," he proposes. But you never know. The dictionary editing process is rigorous, and it's not like a lexicographer can just slip an invented term into the book when no one is looking.

In any event, it's hard to keep a good word down. The name *mountweazel* might have been entirely invented, but here it is, doing ser-vice to describe the phenomenon it was invented for. And who knows, if enough people write about *esquivalience*, perhaps it, too, will slip into general use.

Related terms: hapax legomenon, nonce word, unpaired word

---

[66] https://www.newyorker.com/magazine/2005/08/29/not-a-word
[67] https://www.merriam-webster.com/word-matters-podcast/episode-100-how-did-we-get-here

Muphry's Law

Imagine that you've written something online, and some rando comes along and criticizes your grammar. Annoying, right? But suppose that in the course of calling out some error of yours, *they themselves* make a grammatical error. Satisfying, no?

People who deal with language professionally—especially editors—are well aware of this possibility. So much so, that there is not just one but several names for the phenomenon.

Probably the best-known term is *Muphry's Law*. If you look at that and think that the name looks familiar but not quite right, then you completely get it. The law is a deliberate misspelling of the well-known Murphy's Law ("Anything that can go wrong, will go wrong").

Stated generally, Muphry's Law is the proposition that any writing about language usage will itself contain usage mistakes. The term *Muphry's Law* was invented by John Bangsund, an Australian editor, who posited the following axioms, as originally published in the *Canberra Society of Editors Newsletter*:

> If you write anything criticising editing or proofreading, there will be a fault in what you have written;
>
> If an author thanks you in a book for your editing or proofreading, there will be mistakes in the book;
>
> The stronger the sentiment in (a) and (b), the greater the fault; and
>
> Any book devoted to editing or style will be internally inconsistent.[68]

As the page also notes, an additional axiom is that any such mistake will be obvious to everyone but you.

Jed Hartman, a writer and editor, independently formulated the idea as *Hartman's Law of Prescriptive Retaliation* in this way:

> Any correction of the speech or writing of others will contain at least one grammatical, spelling, or typographical error.[69]

---

[68] http://www.editorscanberra.org/muphrys-law/
[69] https://www.kith.org/words/1999/04/11/hhhyphen-comments/

Another formulation—McKean's Law—is named for the lexicographer and editor Erin McKean. Other variations (Skitt's Law, Bell's first law of Usenet) arose in internet forums, a rich source of both correction and error.

Experienced editors are familiar with Muphry's Law and try various ways to avoid it. One maxim you'll hear from editors, for example, is the reminder to look things up, even if you're pretty sure or maybe even almost positive. A suggestion for virtually every writer, whether they're writing about usage or anything else, is to set the text aside for a day or a week and then review it before publishing it. A little distance can help a writer find many of those errors that will be obvious to everyone else. And finally, of course, there's nothing like having someone else review what you've written.

There is one sure-fire way to avoid becoming a victim of Muphry's Law, of course, which is to refrain from criticizing the speech, writing, or usage of others. I may yet learn this lesson.

Related terms: prescriptivism

negative polarity item (NPI)

Think about whether you would ever hear (or say) the following:

I go there anymore.

She's here yet.

He would budge an inch.

Probably not, right? You might say *I **don't** go there anymore* or *She **isn't** here yet or He **wouldn't** budge an inch*, but those earlier sentences don't sound quite right.

Terms or expressions like *anymore* and *yet* and *budge* are said to be *negative polarity items*: they're generally used only to express a negative sense. Here are some more examples:

They don't care anymore

I'm not seeing anyone

> She doesn't give a hoot
>
> They won't lift a finger
>
> He didn't like it at all

As you can see from the examples, negative polarity items can be individual words (*anymore, anyone*) or phrases (*give a hoot, lift a finger, like at all*).

A negative polarity item generally doesn't have a positive counterpart. Think about some more examples of things people wouldn't say, like "I give a lot of hoots about that" or "He needed some help, so I lifted a finger" or "I liked that guy at all."

However, negative polarity can often be a matter of context; some negative polarity items don't always have negative polarity, just in certain expressions. In the example *I'm not seeing anyone, anyone* has negative polarity; you wouldn't say "I'm seeing anyone." (You'd say "I'm seeing someone.") But you can use *anyone* in other contexts without a negative sense, like "Did anyone call?"

Some terms that are negative polarity items in standard English are sometimes used in a non-negative way in informal language. For example, the term *anymore* normally has negative polarity, as in "They don't care anymore." But people sometimes use it in a non-negative way: "Anymore, English speakers say *totes* when they mean *totally*." For people who use *anymore* only as a negative polarity item, this can sound odd, and it underscores the negative-polarity-ness of the term.

People also play with the negative polarity. They'll take an expression like *don't give a fuck*, which has negative polarity; people don't say "I give a fuck" to mean they're enthusiastic about something. They'll then extend the literal sense of this idiom to create sentence like *I am out of fucks to give* or *No fucks were given*. Both of which, I should note, retain the negative polarity of the original.

Negative polarity items sometimes show up without the actual negative, as in "I could give a damn," which is interpreted as meaning "I *don't* give a damn." There are various explanations for how something like *could care less* somehow can mean *couldn't care less*. The linguist John Lawler has proposed that *could care less* works like *give a damn*—that these expressions that have no negative nonetheless represent "negation by association," as he calls it.[70]

Although they're harder to find than negative polarity items, there are also positive polarity items. Some of these are *some*, *somewhat*, and *blink of an eye*:

> I bought *some* flowers.

> He's *somewhat* good looking.

> She arrived *in the blink of an eye*.

As with negative polarity items, positive polarity items have no real negative counterpart. If you do try to negate these statements, you end up with dodgy stuff:

> *I *didn't buy some* flowers. (Usually *any*)

> *He *isn't somewhat* good looking.

> *She *didn't arrive in the blink of an eye*.

As with so many "rules" in English, even if something like negative (or positive) polarity seems complicated to describe, native speakers intuitively understand it and navigate it effortlessly. So much so that they can play with it to wring even more meaning out of it.

Related terms: unpaired word

nonce word

Do you have trouble understanding the bolded words in the following sentences?

> As far as I can tell, he lives exclusively on sodas. You could call him a *Diet-Coke-tarian*.

> We *COVIDed* away the months of quarantine by doing dozens of jigsaw puzzles.

---

[70] http://itre.cis.upenn.edu/~myl/languagelog/archives/001202.html

I'm guessing you understood these terms, even though I just made them up. These are examples of *nonce words*, or words that are invented for a specific, one-time use ("for the nonce"), without the intention that they should become a new word.[71] Or more succinctly, a one-off word. (Fun fact: *for the nonce* was a rebracketing (misdivision) of "for then ones." For more about this phenomenon, see rebracketing.)

People make up words *all the time*. Language is inherently an improvisational act, and word creation is one of the ways in which we exercise our improv skills. We do this when we want to capture a concept that in the moment doesn't seem to have a word, as with *Diet-Coke-tarian*. Most of our nonce words are like this, done on the spur of the moment for a particular situation.

Nonce words can extend to expressions as well. Someone might use a compound like *an **everything-but-the-kitchen-sink** approach* that they've invented on the spot, combining an idiom with a noun in a novel way. (Using *everything-but-the-kitchen-sink* as an adjective is an example of anthimeria.)

We can generally understand nonce words at first glance; usually, if we don't, the intent of the nonce word has failed. Most nonce words are therefore variations on or combinations of existing words, like *Diet-Coke-tarian* (based on *vegetarian*). Sometimes resemblance is enough; if I say that *his manner seemed, dunno, **smoily***, it might not be immediately clear what words I've combined, but I'm guessing that most people would understand that my impression of him was negative.

But some nonce words are made up wholesale with no apparent relationship to other words. You might consider the poem "Jabberwocky" by Lewis Carroll to be filled with nonce words like *brillig* and *slithy* and *vorpal*, not to mention the *Jabberwock* itself. Most words in the poem have pretty good sound phonesthemics—sound symbolism—so you can get a sense of what they mean, but ultimately we don't know their exact meaning. A more contemporary example of an opaque nonce term is the word *pompatous* in the expression "pompatous of love" from a song by Steve Miller. This is definitely a nonce word, though I suppose it's possible that it was an inadvertent one.

---

[71] An unfortunate aspect of the term *nonce word* is that *nonce* means "pedophile" in UK slang.

People sometimes make a distinction between nonce words and *nonsense words*. The words in "Jabberwocky" might have been intended just as nonsense words rather than as nonce words. The books of Dr. Seuss likewise have many nonsense words. (But also many nonce words, like *Sneetches* and *Lorax*.) The distinction is that nonce words have an intended meaning, even if they are made up on the spot. Nonsense words, on the other hand, don't have an intended definition. The difference is sometimes a subtle one; is a *vorpal blade* a nonsense word or does it refer to … well, something? You decide.

A fascinating story about nonce words involves the *wug test* that's well known in linguistic circles. A *wug* is an imaginary animal (a nonce animal) invented in 1958 by the linguist Jean Berko Gleason. She created a test that involved nonce words like *wug* and *gutch* and *spow* and then used them to see whether children could apply implicit language rules like how to form plurals of nouns or the past tense of a verb. For example, she created this test:

This is a WUG

Now there is another one.

There are two of them.

There are two _____.

Would children add *s* to *wug* to form *wugs*? All of the nonce words sounded like English words, but crucially, they were not real words, meaning that children could not have been exposed to them. Her research provided insights about the extent to which children generalize certain rules of English. (Results were uneven; children did better on some words than others.)

If you take the long view, all words were once nonce words. And that illustrates a point about word creation, namely that if a nonce word is useful, it can find life beyond the context that it was invented for. Many writers have created nonce words that we now use routinely, like *bloodstained* (Shakespeare), *serendipity* (Walpole), *flummox* (Dickens), *grok* (Heinlein), *catch-22* (Joseph Heller), and *cyberspace* (William Gibson). The writers for the TV show *The Simpsons* have given us the words

135

cromulent ("fine, acceptable") and *embiggen*. And Lewis Carroll might have invented *galumph* as a nonce word, but it's in dictionaries now.

I'd be willing to take a bet that a year from now we'll all be using a word that started recently as a nonce word. My odds are pretty good.

Related terms: anthimeria, hapax legomenon, mountweazel, portmanteau word, unpaired word

noun pile (noun stack)

Have a look at these expressions:

air bag malfunction safety recall follow-up notice

failed password security question answer attempts limit

reduced minimum operating system partition space available requirement

I'm guessing it took you a bit of effort, and maybe some backtracking, to figure out what each of these meant. Having seven terms in a row makes for a bit of a pile-up, which is why these are called *noun piles*. (Alternative names: *noun stacks*, or the more formal *complex nominal*.)

Noun piles are problematic because, as you saw, they can be hard to parse. In his book *The Sense of Style*, Steven Pinker has a chapter titled "The Web, the Tree, and the String" in which he explains the problem: "As long as the modifier is short, it poses no difficulty for the reader." It's easy to grasp expressions like *the recall notice* or even *the air bag recall notice*. Pinker continues: "But if it starts to get longer it can force a reader to entertain a complicated qualification before she has any idea what it is qualifying." In other words, you can have made it as far as *failed password security question answer* and still not know what the noun pile ultimately is about.

As noun piles get longer, it can also become more difficult to determine the relationships among the words. In the following example, you can draw relationships between the words in several ways:

data bound control table row action links

Is it *data-bound-control table*? Or is it *data-bound control-table*? Is it *row-action links* or *row action-links*? And so on.

Noun piles are generally found when "people try to cram a whole lot of information into a small space," as the linguist Arnold Zwicky has said. Technical writing, academic writing, and bureaucratic writing are all good sources for noun piles. In my experience as an editor, I find that people don't set out to create noun piles like these. Instead, the author is trying to achieve a high degree of precision, which leads to qualifying, and eventually over-qualifying, a noun. A technical writer once described it this way: "Somehow when you generate text, you have this idea that maybe some more explanation will help." And maybe it's true that adding explanation will help, but stacking it up in front of the noun like this often obscures rather than helping. (Two fixes for noun piles are to remove elements that aren't necessary, or to rewrite the sentence—for example, turning *reduced minimum operating system partition space available requirement* into something like *reduction in the requirement for the minimum space that's available on an operating system partition*.)

Another place you'll find noun piles is in newspaper headlines. In his explanation of noun piles, Pinker cites this example:

> Admitted Olympic Skater Nancy Kerrigan Attacker Brian
> Sean Griffith Dies

With headlines, the problem is often a space constraint. The headline writer is trying to get important details into the headline in the fewest number of words. And as noted under crash blossoms, headlines often omit function words that can help the reader sort out the relationship among the words.

Once you know about noun piles, you start spotting them as you read. Finding a particularly long one can help you see the problem that the author was wrestling with, and you can practice your editing skills by thinking about how you'd untangle the pile. If you're interested in how you might fix a noun pile, I've written about it in the entry "Fun (or not) with noun stacks" on my blog.[72]

Related terms: crash blossom

---

[72] https://mikepope.com/blog/DisplayBlog.aspx?permalink=2292

numeronym

What do these words have in common?

- *K-9* (for "canine")
- *gr8t* (for "great")
- *24/7* (for "24 hours a day, 7 days a week")
- *W3C* (for "World Wide Web Consortium")
- *i18n* (for "internationalization")

These are all examples of *numeronyms*, or words based on numbers. There's no formal definition for *numeronym*, so I choose to define the term in a very broad way to refer to any use of numbers for words (or vice versa).

You can see that some numeronyms use a number in a phonetic way— that is, as a homophone. *K-9* (sometimes just *K9*) is one example, one that goes back to World War II and that continues in the military and in police forces. The advent of texting on early-generation phones brought another wave of phonetic numeronyms like *gr8t* and *18tr* (for "later"). These were simply shortcuts to make texting easier when it was awkward to type out text messages on phones that had only number pads. Conventions for these types of numeronyms include using *2* for "to" (*2nite*) and 4 for "for" (*4EVA*).

Speaking of phones, a type of numeronym that you used to see frequently in the pre-online world is a phone number expressed as a word. The number pad (and earlier, the dial) for telephones has numbers, of course, and each number is associated with a set of letters: 2 with ABC, 3 with DEF, and so on through 9 with WXYZ.

This let people create words out of telephone numbers. Businesses used this as a form of advertising — for example, 1-800-PLUMBER (1-800-758-6237) is the phone number of a service that will get you a plumber, and 1-800-GOTJUNK (1-800-468-5865) connects you to someone who will haul away your extra stuff.

There is also the fun example of the 19th-century racehorse named *Potatoooooooo*. This name is a kind of reverse numeronym: the horse's name is pronounced "potatoes," which is more evident if you see the alternative spellings for the name, like *Pot-8-Os* and *Pot8Os*.

Some numeronyms include numbers that are actually used *as* words. This might include numbers in expressions like the following:

I did a *180* (a 180-degree turn; a U-turn).

What's the *411* on this? (information, from the conventional use of 411 as a number to dial for information).

I tried the link, but it *404'd* (resulted in a 404-Not Found error).

The personal ad said that they're *420*-friendly (code for marijuana).

Terms like *W3C* and *i18n* work a bit differently. They use numbers algorithmically, so to speak. The name *W3C* refers to the World Wide Web Consortium (note the three W's), which is the organization that gave us *www* at the beginning of web addresses. The numeronym W3C isn't just a cute way to refer to WWW; the organization uses W3C as its official abbreviation.

And then there's a word like *i18n* for "internationalization", along with words like *l10n* for "localization" and *a11y* for "accessibility." These numeronyms use a number to indicate how many letters are being left out of the word. There's an interesting history for this type of word. In an earlier era of the computer age, the computer company DEC had a system that didn't accommodate long account names. When they had to set up an account for an employee named Scherpenhuizen, the name was too long, so they just named the account using the abbreviation *S12n*.

The convention was useful, and people started using it to abbreviate other words that were unwieldy, especially if you had to write them frequently. (*Internationalization*, *localization*, and *accessibility* are all terms that are used frequently in the software business; imagine having to write these out on a whiteboard during meetings.) On the website for the venture capital firm Andreesen Horowitz (based in Silicon Valley), the company refers to itself as *a16z*; in fact, they use a16z.com as their web address.

The convention has appeared outside the software industry a few times, and for the same reasons it was adopted there. When the Icelandic volcano Eyjafjallajoku erupted in 2010, some news accounts referred it as *E15*.

Numeronyms also proved useful in another forum. Right about the time that texting got easier and it became less essential to use numeronyms for convenience in text messages, we got Twitter. In its original form, Twitter limited posts to 140 characters. This inspired some creativity to keep words short, including using numeronyms. When the translator Luke Spear posted on Twitter, he wanted to use a hashtag on his posts about translation. But *#translate*, that's nine characters for the word, plus the hash mark makes ten. Spear instead came up with the hashtag *#x18*—*x* for "trans" plus *18* for "late."

What all these numeronyms have in common is that they're a convenient (fast, small, easy-to-remember) way to write words. Since writing quickly is a perennial goal, who knows, we might see some other clever numeronyms in the future.

Related terms: backronym, syllable acronym

onomastics

Suppose that your job was to study people's names. You study trends in baby-naming, like how tens of thousands of American parents in the last 25 years somehow independently decided to name their babies Emma or Olivia or Noah or Liam. Or how names like Edith or Eunice or Homer or Herbert, which were once popular, are rarely heard on the playgrounds of today. Or how the name Robin, which is a boy's name in the UK, became a popular girl's name in the US in the 1960s.

If this were your job, your job would involve *onomastics*, or the study of names. (Is it just me, or is it great that there's a name for names and naming things?)

Onomastics certainly involves the study of people's given names or the names they're otherwise known by (like mononyms). It also studies people's family names (like patronyms)—how they're constructed, how they're handed down, and so on.

Beyond just these examples, onomastics is a wide field that includes basically anything to do with names. If it's been assigned a name, an onomastician has probably studied it (and might have even been involved).

For example, onomastics also involves the study of toponyms, which are names based on a location, like how the word *tuxedo* derives from Tuxedo Park, New York.

Onomastics includes *odonyms* (sometimes *hodonyms*), which is the word for the names of "travelways": streets, roads, highways, and other byways. An onomastician (odomastician?) can probably tell you what the heck the difference is between a street, road, avenue, boulevard, circle, court, way, lane, and the rest. Or they might be able to tell you the history of famous street names like Broadway and Wall Street in New York and Fleet Street in London. Or how Skid Road in Seattle, which was once a path along which logs were "skidded" to the waterfront, became *skid row*, the generic name for any town's run-down area.

On the commercial side, onomastics also encompasses the field of company and product names. Naming your company or product is by no means a straightforward task. Ideally, you want a name that's distinctive and memorable and that also has an emotional appeal. But the name also has to be something customers can confidently pronounce, and of course one that's legally available. Meeting the challenges of creating a good company or product name requires a kind of expertise that the principals in a company often don't have. So they hire a special kind of onomastician: a naming professional. As with personal names, so with company names; think about how there was a fashion for a while to drop vowels: Flickr, Tumblr, Scribd, Grindr. Or the plethora of names that end in *ly*: Humanly, Writerly, Weebly, Fundly, Oatly, Bubly.

I once attended a fascinating presentation about how property developers name their buildings and divisions. Pay attention to the names of those flashy new condo developments you see in your area, and you'll find that the names sound hip and modern (and often similar). But the buildings built 20 or 30 or 50 years ago, if they're even still around, have names that sound dated. Not to mention the old joke about how developers who turn farmland into housing subdivisions name the estate after the natural feature they obliterated, like Rolling Meadows and Pheasant Run.

This type of naming consultation isn't necessarily just for commercial names. The entrepreneur Lindsay Jernigan set up a business in China that helps Chinese people select an "English name"—a practice that many Chinese people follow, but that sometimes can result in a name that doesn't sound like a name to English-speaking ears. Jernigan guides people toward names that encompass traits that the speaker wants—things like special astrological symbolism or specific sounds to include or avoid—but that also are names that will not raise eyebrows abroad. The challenge is not unlike that of coming up with a good company or product name, but it's for a kind of personal brand.

There's even an onomastic component in the weather. The World Meteorological Organization has a formula for how hurricanes are named. Each season, names are assigned alphabetical names—the first storm of the season gets an *A* name, the second one a *B* name, and so on. The names alternate between traditionally men's names and traditionally women's names on a six-year rotation. However, if a hurricane is particularly forceful, the name might be retired—we'll never hear about another Hurricane Katrina, for example.

Going back to baby names, the Social Security Administration has some pages that let you see the popularity of first names in the US. That's where you can learn, for example, that *Noah* and *Emma* were the most popular names in the 2010s, whereas *James* and *Mary* were the most popular in the 1950s—and in fact have been the most popular in the last 100 years.

Related terms: aptronym, demonym, eponym, genericization, hypocorism, monomym, patronym, toponym

orphan acronym (orphan initialism)

In the United States, the organization AARP is an interest group for elderly people. The organization publishes a magazine, lobbies Congress on issues that affect older people, and makes available discounts on zillions of products and services. They seem very interested in the welfare of our older citizens, you might observe. But you might ask, "What does AARP stand for?"

Well, ahem. Once upon a time, *AARP* stood for *American Association of Retired People*. These days, though, *AARP* stands for ... nothing. That's right: officially speaking, it no longer stands for American Association of Retired People. AARP is what's called an *orphan acronym*.

This happens occasionally when a name outgrows its original purpose. In the case of AARP, in 1999, they decided that their focus was no longer exclusively people who are retired. (And rightly so; you can become an AARP member at age 50, and I sure don't know many people who feel that 50 is a retirement age.) So they sort of waved an onomastic wand, and presto, the initialism AARP no longer stands for anything.

Another orphaned acronym is *SAT*, a college-admissions test that many US high school students take. When the exam was originally conceived in the 1920s, it was called the *Scholastic Aptitude Test*, hence SAT. The name was changed in 1990 to the *Scholastic Assessment Test* (still SAT), and then several variants, and now it's just the *SAT test*. The College Board, the company that owns and administers the test, is explicit on this point. "Please note that SAT is not an initialism; it does not stand for anything," a spokesman said in the *New York Times*. "The SAT is the SAT, and that's all it is."[73]

The term *orphan acronym* (or *orphan initialism* if you want to make that distinction) seems to have been invented about 2005 by Dan Puckett when he worked at the *St. Petersburg Times*, who had an entry for them in that newspaper's style guide. An alternative term is *empty initialism*.

A surprising number of commercial enterprises have undergone acronym orphaning. You might believe that *AAA* stands for *American Automobile Association*, but you'd have a hard time finding this on their web-

---

[73] https://www.nytimes.com/1997/04/02/us/insisting-it-s-nothing-creator-says-sat-not-sat.html

site. Similarly, you might have grown up in an era when *IHOP* was the *International House of Pancakes*, but the only place the latter name appears on the IHOP site is on their Our History page.

ESPN? No longer official *Entertainment and Sports Programming Network. MTV* is no longer *Music Television. FFA* (now *National FFA Organization*) is no longer *Future Farmers of America*. (On the National FFA Organization's "About FFA" page, they do acknowledge the origin of FFA: "The letters 'FFA' stand for Future Farmers of America. These letters are a part of our history and our heritage that will never change.")

One orphan acronym/orphan initialism that might surprise you is *KFC*. As pretty much everyone knows, this stands for *Kentucky Fried Chicken*. Or does it? In the 1990s, people who marketed for the company had some concerns about whether the *Fried* part of *Kentucky Fried Chicken* could potentially put off the health-conscious restaurant patron. Moreover, the restaurant chain sells a much wider menu of foods than the original name suggests. So the company branding these days is all about *KFC*, although you will find an acknowledgment of the original name on their site. From a marketing perspective, the original name might be one that's hard to abandon.

Companies often want to keep a part of their name—the abbreviation—that's an important part of their brand recognition while trying to downplay (or best of all, forget) aspects that aren't compatible with the current company image. The IHOP chain originally played up the "international" and "pancakes" part of its name, both in its menu and its chalet-style architecture. Over time, the name *IHOP* became well recognized, but as the restaurant's menu changed and it moved into less distinctive spaces, a smart move was to keep *IHOP* but deemphasize pancakes, at least as part of the name.

Customers who remember the old, pre-orphaned acronyms might find the "It doesn't mean anything" explanation a little silly. (I quizzed my wife about all of these orphan acronyms, and she remembered the original names of all of them. And boy, wasn't she surprised to learn from me that they no longer stand for anything.)

But companies *can* leave their history behind. You might know the 3M Company as the company that sells things like Scotch-brand tape and Post-it Notes. Have you ever thought about what those 3 *M's* are? Since 2002, the company is just 3M, but it was originally the Minnesota Mining and Manufacturing Company. And if you didn't grow up with CVS pharmacies, you might be surprised to learn that the original name was *Consumer Value Store*.

I've gotten to the point now where I start questioning every company name that consists of initials and wondering whether it's an orphaned acronym. What about IKEA? Not really an orphan; it was just a made-up name based on combining the first letters of the founder's name, the farm he grew up on, and the nearby village. A&W? DHL? Just the founder's initials. IBM? Still International Business Machines. UPS? Still United Parcel Service. No luck so far, I just know that there are many more orphan acronyms out there waiting to be found.

Related terms: genericization, onomastics, syllable acronym

patronym, matronym

Here's a conversation that probably happened in some form or another many times in the Olden Days:

> Person 1: Hey, did you hear that Alfred bought a new horse?
> Person 2: Which Alfred? The son of John or the son of Jeffery?
> Person 1: Alfred, John's son.

I just made this up, of course, but it does suggest something about how some surnames (family names) originated—here, how the name *Johnson* came about. Names like this evolved as *patronymics*, which is a family name based on the name of a parent or ancestor. Although we are most familiar in English with *patronyms*, which are derived from a male relative, some cultures have also used *matronyms*, which are based on the name of a female relative.

When people lived in small groups, surnames weren't usually necessary; people were identified by a single name. As settlements grew and as people interacted with other groups, it became necessary—sometimes, anyway—to tell apart people who might be called the same thing. You might be known by where you came from (Alys of Bath), what you did for a living (Robin the Miller), or some distinguishing feature (James the

One-Eyed). Think about names from the Bible; most characters have single names—Abraham, Moses, Noah—but occasionally a name is qualified: Mary Magdalene ("Mary of Magadala"); Simon the Zealot; Jesus of Nazareth. Or, of course, you might be identified by who your father was.

Many names in English are patronymics. Most of these patronymic names have a recognizable *son* ending, like *Davidson, Edmundson, Gibson, Johnson, Robinson, Watson*, and *Wilson*. Sometimes the *on* ending is there, but it's not as obvious that it's a patronym, as in *Nixon*. Some patronyms don't have an explicit "son" part, as in *Gibbs, Rogers*, and *Willis*.

Other cultures also use patronymic names, many of which are familiar names to English speakers. The prefixes *Mac* or (*Mc*) and *O* are Celtic patronymics; *MacDonald* is "son of Donald," and *O'Neill* is "grandson of Neill."

In Welsh, "son of" was rendered using *ap* or *ab*, which gave us patronymic names like *Price* (from *ap Rhys*, "son of Rhys"), *Pugh* (from *ap Huw*, "son of Huw"), and *Pritchard* (from *ap Ritchard*, "son of Richard.") The prefix *Fitz* is a Norman patronym (*Fitzwilliam* is "son of William") that came to England after the Norman Conquest in 1066. The prefix *Fitz* was occasionally also used as a matronymic. For example, Henry II of England was also known as Henry FitzEmpress, the son of Geoffrey Plantagenet and Empress Matilda.

In Spanish, the *ez* or *es* suffix marks a patronym, indicating "descendant of." Among the 10 most common Spanish surnames, seven of them are patronymics, including *Fernandez, Gomez, Gonzalez, Lopez, Martinez, Perez, Rodriguez*, and *Sanchez*.[74] Spanish surnames—*apellidos*—often consist of a pair of family names, even if those names don't have a particle like *ez* that translates as "of." One part of the *apellido* represents the father's family and the other one represents the mother's family. For example, *Miguel Carlos García Martinez* might be read as Miguel Carlos, whose father's family is García and whose mother's family is Martinez.

Many cultures have patronymics for daughters as well. In patronymic cultures, though, names tend to reflect lineage through the father, so patronymics for daughters don't often end up as surnames. In Scottish, *Nic* is "daughter of"; in Irish, it was *Ny* or *Nyn*. If William's son was, say,

---

[74] http://www.lowchensaustralia.com/names/popular-spanish-names.htm

Robert McWilliam, that same William's daughter might be *Eleanor Ny William*. In Welsh, "daughter of" was *ferch*, and although it's not obvious, the name *Critchett* is derived from *ferch Richard* ("daughter of Richard").

Hebrew uses the word *ben* to mark a patronymic for sons, which shows up in a name like *Benjamin* ("son of the right side"). The equivalent "daughter of" is *bat*. In Arabic, the term for a son is *bin* or *ibn*, which is recognizable in a name like *bin Laden* ("son of Laden"). For daughters, it's *bint* or *ibat*. (Speaking of matronyms, when Jesus is mentioned in the Q'uran, he's *Isa ibn Maryam*, or "Jesus, son of Mary.")

The Nordic countries have historically followed a patronymic naming schema involving *son* or *sen* as a patronymic for boys (*Carlson* is "son of Carl"). Daughters used variants on *dotter* as a patronymic (*Carlsdotter*). The single most common surname in Sweden is *Anderson* or *Andersson*; in Denmark, it's *Jensen*.

But the Scandinavian countries ran into issues with patronymics. As the population increased, it became impractical to continue the tradition—hundreds of thousands of people had identical names, in part because the pool of *first* names wasn't that big. For example, in Denmark, 15 men's names account for 90 percent of the surnames.

Therefore, in Sweden in the 19th century, new patterns for surnames were developed that broke away from patronyms. Many new names used terms from nature as part of the name, which resulted in family names like *Ekberg, Lundgren, Dahlstrom, Sandstrom*, and *Bjorklund*. Norway and Denmark adopted similar protocols for the same reason. In 1901, Sweden passed a law that mandated "heritable" surnames, which effectively ended the traditional patronymic system. Daughters also started using the father-based patronymic with *son*, so the use of *dotter* surnames ended as well. However, there have been movements in the last few decades to allow individuals to adopt patronymic names again.

Unlike the other Nordic countries, Iceland continues the patronymic tradition. In fact, it's been enshrined in law since 1925, allowing a few exceptions for people who had previously adopted "family names." Patronymic naming extends even to people who become Icelandic citizens. Per the Icelandic Personal Names Act, "Foreign nationals shall adopt an Icelandic first name when they acquire Icelandic nationality and their descendants shall abide by the rule on patronymics."[75] But the law does allow people to adopt a matronymic (something like *Birgitdottir*) if they want to break ties with the father.

We could talk about patronyms all day, given how prevalent the custom is around the world. How about one more: in Russian, patronymics are part of a person's official name, serving as what English speakers might think of as a middle name. The ending is *ovich* for men and *ovna* for women. Patronymics also have a social role: they're used in interactions that show respect or rank, such as when students speak to teachers or colleagues talk at work. The custom is to use the first name followed by the patronymic: "Hello, Ivan Mikhailovich and Olga Vladimirovna. I enjoyed the presentation you gave at today's meeting." I find this use of patronymics charming. Not so much, though, that I'm willing to introduce it into our own workplace.

Related terms: aptronym, demonym, eponym, mononym, onomastics

pause filler (filler word, hesitation syllable)

If you've ever heard a recording of yourself giving a presentation or interview, you might have been unpleasantly surprised at how often you said "uh" or "um" or "y'know." For that matter, if you just tune in to ordinary conversation, you'll hear a lot of sounds like these, which are, reasonably enough, called *pause fillers*.

Pause fillers—also known as *filler words*, *hesitation syllables*, or if you like the fancy terms, *embolalia*—are sounds that a speaker uses to fill a pause before continuing. They don't have meaning in themselves (well, mostly); they're just little markers that help regulate the flow of conversation.

English has various pause fillers, including syllables like *um* and *uh* and words like *well* or *y'know*. Other languages have their own pause

---

[75] https://nat.is/proper-names/

fillers, which might be particularly noticeable to you if you're studying another language and listening intently to speakers in that language.[76]

Pause fillers are broadly characterized as *disfluencies*, which refer to any deviation from the normal flow of speech. The term *disfluency* has a negative cast to it, and the use of pause fillers like *um* or *uh* is sometimes looked down on as a sign of poor speaking skills. Who wants to hear someone giving a speech filled with *uh* and *y'know*? (People sometimes think that the word *like* is a filler, filler, which it can be, but it also has other uses, as described under quotative *like*.)

But pause fillers are extremely common. Michael Erard, who wrote an entire book about disfluencies (with the appropriate title *Um*), says that verbal blunders "are about as ubiquitous as ants at a picnic," and cites a study in which "uh" by itself accounted for four percent of the speech in a corpus of telephone conversations.

Pause fillers are also useful in discourse. One purpose for pause fillers is for the speaker to indicate that they haven't finished a thought yet. For example, you might stop to think for a moment while talking, so you throw in a pause filler:

I'll meet you in front of the library at … ***uh*** … let's say 6 o'clock.

The pause filler tells your interlocutor that you're not ready yet to yield the floor in your conversation.

Or let's say someone asks you a question. In conversation, people expect a response in about a fifth of a second (!), else the person who asks the question might think you didn't hear. To signal that you've heard the question but aren't quite prepared to answer, you start with "Um …" or "Uh …," which requires very little cognitive effort. If you're in a stressful situation—a job interview, say—the volume of pause fillers in your speaking goes way up while you think your way through an answer.

Another purpose for pause fillers is to indicate that you're repairing something, as in a sentence like this:

The meeting is in the south building, ***uh***, north building.

---

[76] A pause filler that's used in Mandarin—*nèige*, which means "that"—can sound a lot like the n-word in English, which has led to some misunderstandings when Chinese students live in English-speaking countries.

Here, the speaker uses "uh" to convey that they're hitting the conversational backspace key and that an update follows. And the listener can somehow manage to process this and mentally reinterpret the sentence, including which words have been corrected. That's an impressive amount of work for the simple "uh" to be doing in a sentence like this.

Pause fillers also have a social role in conversation, where they soften a response. Imagine that someone you don't particularly like invites you out to dinner. Compare the responses:

> Person 1: Do you want to get some dinner after work?
> Person 2: No.

versus

> Person 1: Do you want to get some dinner after work?
> Person 2: Well, …

This implicature can even be used in a conscious way, like this:

> Person 1: Isn't that a great idea?
> Person 2: Um.

The word *um* is the entire response, and the speaker knows that the listener knows exactly what "um" means here ("no")—a kind of meta use of a pause filler.

A related conscious usage of a pause filler is when you use *um* or *er* to alert the listener that they should pay particular attention to something you're *about* to say. Consider an example like this:

> The movie *Porky's* is not really the best exemplar of, um, the cinematic arts.

Here, "the cinematic arts" is meant ironically, which the speaker signals by preceding it with "um."

As with so many other "mistakes" in speech, linguists are interested in what pause fillers can tell us about how people produce and process language. Which pause fillers people use, and when, and how they're wielded can all provide insight into the language brain.

Learning about pause fillers has given me a new appreciation for the skills that are needed to be a professional broadcaster. When I watch sports, I sometimes find the color commentary to be inane. ("They need to step up their defense." Thanks for that insight, sportscaster.) But the broadcasters, who speak off the cuff and are charged with filling every moment with chatter, do a darn good job of keeping the pause fillers to a minimum.

Related terms: quotative *like*, tag question, uptalk

pedant's veto

A dilemma that writers and editors sometimes face is the question of whether to use a word or construct that can be controversial. For example, maybe a writer I'm editing has used a preposition at the end of a sentence. The writer is fine with it, obviously, and I know that the "no prepositions at the end of a sentence" rule is bogus. But if we go ahead and include a stranded preposition, will we get angry emails from readers who still consider this an issue?

If we decide to change the sentence and move the preposition, we've allowed ourselves to be subject to the *pedant's veto*. This is an objection to usage that's so strident that it causes people to avoid the usage. Because some people can get quite bent about certain usages, it creates a dilemma for those who dispense usage advice. As Ben Yagoda describes it in his book *How to Not Write Bad*, "Certain grammatical constructions are considered okay by some or most authorities but retain an offensive odor for many readers (and, crucially, for teachers and editors), and should be avoided." If you use these constructions, goes the argument, someone out there—a pedant—might be offended.

The term *pedant's veto* was used by Geoff Nunberg in an essay about the Wikipedia editor Bryan Henderson. Henderson was on a mission to stamp out the use of *comprised of*, which he views as incorrect. Henderson made 47,000 edits on Wikipedia toward that goal. Here's Nunberg's explanation:

> [Henderson's] jihad is only an exaggerated example of what I think of as the pedant's veto. It doesn't matter if you consider a word to be correct English. If some sticklers insist that it's an error, the dictionaries and style manuals are going to counsel you to steer clear of it to

avoid bringing down their wrath. That can be the prudent course, especially in an age when email and Web comment threads make things easy for what William Safire used to call the "gotcha gang." It's annoying to have to pass over a perfectly good word or expression just because somebody has a bone to pick with it, but who wants to start with these people?[77]

To avoid the pedants' ire, the style guide we use at work steers writers and editors away from *comprise* altogether, and suggests *consist of, contain,* or *include* instead. The word *comprise,* even if you don't use it in the phrase *comprised of,* has been vetoed.

In her piece on split infinitives, Grammar Girl says, "If you have to please others or avoid complaints, it's safer to avoid splitting infinitives."[78] In other words, don't annoy the "gotcha gang," even though the ban on split infinitives is a classic zombie rule. (To be fair to Mignon Fogarty, who is Grammar Girl, she has said that "it always feels awful to say, 'Don't use this word because an uninformed person will judge you.'"[79])

In its discussion of the distinction between *hanged* and *hung,* the *Merriam-Webster Dictionary of English Usage* says this:

> If you make a point of observing the distinction in your writing, you will not thereby become a better writer, but you will spare yourself the annoyance of being corrected for having done something that is not wrong.

Another question where a writer or editor might agonize about the pedant's veto is in deciding to use singular *they* (*The user should enter **their** password*).

The usages that are subject to the pedant's veto, like usage generally, change over time. (That is, these usages often involve skunked terms.) Sticklers used to complain about the incorrect use of *beg the question.* Originally, *beg the question* was the name of a logical fallacy in which the speaker assumes the truth of a conclusion, as in "That restaurant is very popular because so many people want to go there." In popular use,

---

[77] https://www.npr.org/2015/03/12/392568604/dont-you-dare-use-comprised-of-on-wikipedia-one-editor-will-take-it-out

[78] https://www.quickanddirtytips.com/articles/split-infinitives/

[79] https://tinyurl.com/466yw3nm

though, *beg the question* is now often used to mean "raise the question," as in "It begs the question of whether we want to go there." An editor might feel that the pedant's veto—someone might write in and complain!—is enough of a disincentive to use *beg the question* that they'll change it. This is true even though that expression is used so seldom in its nominally correct form that most people don't even realize that it didn't use to mean "raise the question."

The usage maven Bryan Garner tags entries in his book *Modern American Usage* using what he calls the Language-Change Index. In this system, stage 1 is an innovation used by few people and is not considered standard. The stages progress through levels of acceptability till stage 4, "virtually universal, but opposed on cogent grounds by a few die-hard stalwarts." Finally, stage 5 is "universally acceptable (not counting pseudo-snoot eccentrics)." It's up to writers and editors to determine whether they risk a pedant's veto "on cogent grounds … by stalwarts" or whether any objections are going to come from "pseudo-snoot eccentrics."

If you find yourself worrying that something you write might annoy pedants, you can fall back on a style guide, whose authors have already spent many hours thinking about whatever usage you're considering. If you go ahead and use whatever term you're worried about and someone writes in to complain about it, you can cite your authority with a clear conscience.

Related terms: skunked term, zombie rule

pejoration, euphemism treadmill

Centuries ago, the word *toilet* or *toilette* was a term for the items associated with getting oneself presentable to be in public—hairbrushes and whatnot. It then evolved to mean the general act of preparing oneself. (Alexander Pope: "The long Labours of the Toilette cease.")

Eventually *toilet* became a room in which one performed such labo(u)rs: a dressing room. When indoor plumbing was added to houses, dressing rooms got running water, and a *toilet room* became a room where one could not only dress but wash oneself. Naturally, when commodes moved indoors, that's where they ended up.

In some English-speaking areas, to "go to the toilet" still reflects the sense that *toilet* refers to the room itself. But *toilet* also came to mean the actual device (the commode). Americans in particular seem uncomfortable in even alluding to the act of relieving oneself, so the word *toilet* became sort of unsavory. An English person might run around the US asking people where the toilets are, but an American is almost certain to ask about the *bathroom* or *restroom* or the *ladies' room* or *the powder room* or *the gents'*.

All of this is to say that the word *toilet* has undergone the process of *pejoration*: a term that was once positive or neutral has become negative. (Compare *pejorative*.)

There are many examples, many of them ancient. An example that's often given is that the Old English word *cnafa* just meant "boy." But over the centuries it underwent pejoration and became the word *knave*. A man who worked on a villa was a *villain*, which originally was just a farmhand. But the word degraded to mean a wicked person.

More recently, you can also see a form of pejoration in the types of language used in advertising or marketing. For example, car dealers have learned that the term *used* has negative connotations. If you want to spend less for a car, especially in the luxury-car market, don't go looking for a used car. Look instead for a *pre-owned* one.

An interesting consequence of pejoration is what Steven Pinker refers to as the *euphemism treadmill*. As he explains in a 1994 editorial in the *New York Times*, a term becomes associated with an unpleasant idea, so people invent new terms—euphemisms. But the euphemistic words themselves become associated with the uncomfortable concept, so the new term likewise becomes tainted. We see this with a progression like *toilet* > *bathroom* > *restroom* > *ladies' room*. (In his editorial, Pinker is railing against what he considered political correctness at the *Los Angeles Times*, a stance that brought a strong response from a VP at that newspaper.)

The term *mental retardation* underwent the euphemism treadmill. *Retarded* and *retardation* derive from a Latin root meaning "slow" (compare *tardy*), and they're used in various fields to mean "slow down" or "decelerate." For example, musicians are used to seeing *rit.*, an abbreviation for the Italian word *ritardando*, at places where they're supposed to slow down.

In psychology, *mental retardation* was coined in the late 1800s as a technical term, designed to be a neutral way to refer to people who had intellectual disabilities. The term was specifically intended to be an improvement on terms like *idiocy*, *cretinism*, and *feeble-mindedness* that had been in use before. (Until 2007 there was an organization named the American Association of Mental Retardation.) Today, of course, we consider *retarded* to be an offensive way to refer to people; so offensive, in fact, that many people won't say the term and use a workaround like *the r-word*. (The expression *r-word* is an example of a minced oath, a way of working around a taboo term.) In psychology, practitioners have switched to talking about people with intellectual disabilities. (The association is now the American Association of Intellectual and Developmental Disabilities.)

In the November 1967 edition of *Ebony*, the scholar Lerone Bennett Jr. published the article "What's In A Name?"[80] This was an in-depth look at the history and ongoing discussion in the Black community about what name to use for Americans of African descent. It's fascinating among other reasons for how it describes how certain terms became pejorative, then were reclaimed, then pejorated again.

The process is continuous. An example is the word *liberal*. The root is *liber*, meaning "free," and in political contexts was used in the 18th century for someone favoring individual liberties and social reform. The word became associated with left-leaning politics, and with the notion of government involvement in economics and social initiatives. In the bruising political conflicts of the last 50 years, those with more right-leaning beliefs used the word *liberal* in such a way that it underwent pejoration (or to put it more colloquially, it was made into a dirty word), and many people on the left now prefer to label themselves as *progressive*.

A recent example came up in the realm of entomology (insect studies, not to be confused with etymology). For a long time, the common name of *Lymantria dispar* was *gypsy moth*. But the word *gypsy* is considered a slur by the Roma people to whom it was applied. In March 2022, the Entomological Society of America therefore adopted the name *spongy moth*

---

[80] https://tinyurl.com/49ptxuct

as a replacement for the earlier common name—"spongy" refers to the insect's egg masses. (The word *gypsy* is a good example of an exonym for the Roma people—a word that foreigners give to your people.)

A somewhat weird flex on pejoration has to do with periods in text messages. At some point in the development of text-message-based communications, the convention of ending a sentence with a period—a neutral enough habit in written communications—started taking on a negative connotation. It no longer just marked the end of the sentence; it added a sense of finality, the way an exclamation point marks excitement. As Ben Crair put it in *The New Republic*, "people use the period not simply to conclude a sentence, but to announce 'I am not happy about the sentence I just concluded.'"[81] Because the pejoration of periods has primarily occurred with younger people, it's led to some misunderstandings: a young person might wonder why their parent was sending text messages that sounded angry.

The next time you hesitate to use a word "in polite company," as the old expression has it, stop for a moment and think about why you're hesitating. Was the word once acceptable but no longer is? If so, you're probably looking at an example of pejoration.

Related terms: minced oath, semantic bleaching, zombie rule

personal dative

The following sentences are not remarkable:

> He got ***the kids*** a trampoline.

> They gave ***her*** flowers.

> She bought ***herself*** a car.

If you'll indulge some grammar talk for a moment, these sentences have a subject who's doing the action: *he*, *they*, and *she*. They each have a *direct object*: what did he get? A trampoline. What did they give? Flowers.

---

[81] https://newrepublic.com/article/115726/period-our-simplest-punctuation-mark-has-become-sign-anger

What did she buy? A car. And they each have an *indirect object*, someone who's the beneficiary. For whom did he get the trampoline? For the kids. To whom did they give flowers? Her. For whom did she buy the car? Herself.

So far, all very conventional. Interestingly, people also sometimes say things like the following:

> She ate ***her*** some lunch.

> He loves ***him*** some football.

> I need ***me*** a new shirt.

These sentences *look* like the previous ones—they each have a subject (*she, he, I*) and a direct object (*lunch, football, shirt*). But in standard written English, you can't put an indirect object into a sentence like *She ate some lunch* or *He loves football* or *I need a new shirt*.

Nonetheless, sentences like *She ate her some lunch* are common in some dialects of English, particularly in the American South and in Appalachia. Since the highlighted words in the second set of sentences are not indirect objects, linguists have devised the name *personal dative* for this nonstandard (but as I'll explain, useful) use of extra pronouns.

Why personal ***dative***? The word *dative* is a grammar term from back when grammar study meant the study of Latin. In many languages, nouns and pronouns have special forms, called *cases*, that mark their function in a sentence. For example, in English, the form *I* is used for the subject of a sentence, and the form *me* is used for the object. Many languages have more elaborate marking (cases): subjects have one form (*nominative case*); direct objects have another (*accusative case*); and indirect objects have yet another form (*dative case*).

Even though we don't have a special form in English for indirect objects, grammarians sometimes talk about *dative* when discussing the form of a pronoun that's the beneficiary in a sentence. (Fun fact: the word *dative* comes from the Latin word for "to give.")

That was a lot of grammar talk, and I hope you're still with me. To get back to the examples, in a sentence like *She ate **her** some lunch*, the word *her* is definitely not an indirect object.

You might be thinking that sometimes the extra pronoun *is* an indirect object. Consider a sentence like *I bought **myself** a car*. In this sentence, the word *myself* is the indirect object. What did I buy? A car (the direct object). Who did I buy it for? For myself (the indirect object). In standard English, when the object is a pronoun and it represents the same person as the subject, we use what's called the *reflexive* form of the pronoun for the object—the form that has *self* attached to it. In this case, *I* is the subject and the indirect object is also me, so the object pronoun is *myself*.

In some dialects, rather than using the reflexive form (*myself*), people can sometimes use just the dative pronoun: *I bought **me** a car*. In this example, *me* is used as the indirect object, but instead of the *myself* form, it's just *me*.

That looks similar to the personal dative, but notice that in the first examples earlier, the verbs (*ate, love, need*) don't take indirect objects. You don't eat someone some lunch, you don't love someone some football, and you don't need someone a new shirt.

So personal dative is not just a different way to show an indirect object.

And why is it the ***personal** dative*? Notice that in all the sentences earlier with personal dative, the extra pronoun refers back to the subject: ***She** ate **her** some lunch, **I** need **me** a new shirt*, and so on. The pronoun always has something to do with the person who's doing the verb.

If the personal dative isn't indicating an indirect object, what *is* it about? Linguists have been thinking about this for decades. One explanation is that the personal dative highlights the subject's involvement in the action. This might be why the personal dative always refers back to the subject. In the sentence *She ate her some lunch*, the extra *her* emphasizes the involvement of "she" in the act of eating lunch. As one linguist, Laurence Horn, put it, a personal dative like this is "satisfying the subject's perceived intention or goal."[82] Similarly, in *He loves him some football*, the extra *him* emphasizes his enjoyment; he's the one who's affected by football. Because of these uses, personal dative is sometimes described as *benefactive dative* (who benefits) or *affective dative* (who is affected).

Although the use of personal dative is considered nonstandard in modern English, something like it appears in other languages. French and Spanish have a way to include an extra ("pleonastic") pronoun that refers back to the subject and that has no explicit role in the sentence. Ancient

---

[82] http://www.cssp.cnrs.fr/eiss7/horn-eiss7.pdf

Hebrew apparently had it. And in Old English, manuscripts sometimes show extra pronouns like personal dative. The fact that a kind of personal dative existed in Old English *might* suggest (I'm not sure if this is entirely known) how it came to be in Southern and Appalachian dialects—they didn't add personal dative to their dialect; instead, they inherited it from an older form of English and just never lost it.

As an aside, personal dative illustrates something that isn't always obvious: nonstandard dialects can include features that provide expressiveness that isn't in the dialect that's taught in school. In both standard English and in Appalachian dialects, speakers can say *She ate some lunch*. But speakers of Appalachian dialects can also say *She ate **her** some lunch*, which adds nuance to the sentence that's hard to capture in a dialect that doesn't have this feature. Linguists try to puzzle out what personal dative is conveying. But speakers who have this feature in their dialect intuitively understand the rules (the grammar) for how and when to use personal dative. It shows that nonstandard dialects are not somehow "corrupted" versions of the standard dialect, or that they're less expressive. On the contrary, they are as rich—and sometimes richer—than more prestige dialects.

Related terms: conversational deletion, double modal

phatic communication

Imagine that you're at the grocery store and you run into someone you know casually. When you encounter one another, the other person smiles and asks, "How are you?" There are a couple of ways to answer this question:

Correct: "Fine, thanks! How about you?"

Incorrect: "Well, I had a headache last night, so I went to bed early. But I didn't sleep well, so this morning I'm just so tired."

Why is the incorrect answer incorrect? Because it misunderstands that when your acquaintance asked you how you were, they weren't actually asking how you were. Instead, they were engaged in *phatic communica-*

tion, which is talk that's primarily about being sociable rather than informative. In casual terms, we refer to this as *small talk*.

We use phatic communication all the time. Think about the times you've heard (or said) expressions like these:

How's it going?

What's up?

Hot enough for you?

How about those Seattle Seahawks?

These phatic "speech acts" aren't intended to solicit real information. They're just a way to establish a social bond. When you see someone you know, you want to acknowledge that you recognize them. Sometimes it's sufficient to just say "Hello," but the complicated rituals of social interaction often require more than just a verbal head nod. Hence these phatic expressions, which might *sound* like information-based conversation but have almost no literal meaning.

The Twitter user @mechanical_monk had a brilliant tweet that used the analogy of studying chess moves to understand how to respond to questions asked as phatic communication:

monk
@mechanical_monk

studying conversation the way you study chess openings

"if they go 'how are you', you play 'good, how are you'. now in this position the opponent has a few possible moves. for example after 'so how do you know [party organizer]', you can..."

10:11 AM · Aug 9, 2022

J.R.R. Tolkien, who was a scholar of languages, was well aware of phatic communication. In *The Hobbit*, Tolkien has Gandalf deconstructing the meaning behind a cheerful "Good morning" uttered by Bilbo (hat tip to Tom Scott on YouTube for this example):[83]

> "Good Morning!" said Bilbo, and he meant it. The sun was shining, and the grass was very green. But Gandalf looked at him from under long bushy eyebrows that stuck out further than the brim of his shady hat.
>
> "What do you mean?" he said. "Do you wish me a good morning, or mean that it is a good morning whether I want it or not; or that you feel good this morning; or that it is a morning to be good on?"
>
> "All of them at once," said Bilbo. "And a very fine morning for a pipe of tobacco out of doors, into the bargain."
>
> "What a lot of things you use 'Good morning' for," said Gandalf.

The topics for phatic communication like this tend to be formulaic. For English speakers, they're often questions about the other's health or about weather or sports. The responses to phatic questions are likewise formulaic; as I say, the correct answer to a phatic "How are you?" is pretty much always "Fine!"

To be clear, it's not the words themselves that make an utterance phatic; it's the context. If you visit someone in the hospital who's had an accident, asking "How are you?" is probably a sincere solicitation for information, and you wouldn't expect the patient to respond formulaically with "Fine!" And if someone says, "It looks like rain," that *might* be a phatic expression, depending on whether you're waiting together in line to get coffee or whether you're asking if it's a good day to go to a baseball game.

Although the examples I've included here are typical of greetings you might hear among strangers, phatic communication suffuses our conversation. We might use phatic communication to start a conversation ("How are you?"), in the middle of one ("That's terrible!"), or at the end of one ("Have a nice day!") It turns out that a significant amount of our conversation is phatic. The technology scholar danah boyd pointed this out on her blog:

---

[83] https://youtu.be/eGnH0KAXhCw

I challenge each and every one of you to record every utterance that comes out of your mouth (and that of everyone you interact with) for an entire day. And then record every facial expression and gesture. You will most likely find what communications scholars found long ago – people are social creatures and a whole lot of what they express is phatic communication. […] I think that you'll be lucky if only 40% of what you say constitutes "pointless babble" to a third party ear.[84]

As with all language, phatic communication changes over time. A couple of generations ago, when you were introduced to someone, you might say "How do you do?" These days, you might instead say "Nice to meet you." In fact, saying "How do you do" today might even sound a bit old-fashioned, at least among Americans.

Similarly, as Gretchen McCulloch describes in her book *Because Internet*, the conventions of how to greet someone in written communication are changing. Some people continue to use a greeting like "Dear <person>" to start an email, based on protocol inherited from letter-writing. Using *dear* like this is strictly a convention; for example, it's unlikely that a letter that was sent to a utility company and that began with "Dear sirs:" reflects any particular fondness of the writer toward the recipients. It's just how business correspondence was done. But for many younger people, the word *dear* has become, in effect, *un*-phatic. To them, you would only use *dear* to address someone who's actually dear to you, and starting an email with "Dear <person>" in any sort of professional context is weird and uncomfortable. As a result, they often use greetings like "Hi" or "Hey," which in turn seem oddly casual to older adults.

People sometimes are unclear on the phatic nature of stock expressions. For example, some people object when they say "Thank you" and get the response "No problem." To them, the correct response to "Thank you" is "You're welcome." But this misses the phatic nature of the interaction. They focus on the literal meaning of "no problem" and try to work out how a service or transaction can be "no problem" for someone. But it's just a change in the nature of phatic communication, like how people don't say "How do you do" as often anymore. If you think about it, "You're welcome," when you take it literally, isn't really a more sensible response to "Thank you" than "No problem" is.

---

[84] http://www.zephoria.org/thoughts/archives/2009/08/16/twitter_pointle.html

The lexicographer Katherine Barber even had a blog post about the history of responses to "Thank you," which include "Don't mention it" and "My pleasure."[85] She notes that "You're welcome" is, as far as she's been able to determine, only about 150 years old. And that "No problem" goes back to the 1970s and is therefore not the invention of those darn millennials.

An even more contentious example (in the US, anyway) is the furor about the expressions "Merry Christmas" versus "Happy Holidays." A slew of commentators, going back to at least the 1920s, wanted to convince people that there was a "war on Christmas," and one weapon in this struggle was the supposed attempt to stamp out the use of "Merry Christmas." It is true that commercial enterprises like retail stores have encouraged employees to use "Happy Holidays" when greeting customers. The idea is that this is the more inclusive term, both culturally and chronologically, since it could encompass all celebrations from Thanksgiving through New Year's Day. If you understand that both "Merry Christmas" and "Happy Holidays" are just phatic expressions—just seasonal versions of "Hello" or "Goodbye"—the controversy seems silly. However, at this point, societal forces have swamped what should be a minor issue of etiquette, and both expressions are edging toward being skunked—that is, if you use one or the other, *someone* will be offended.

Related terms: minced oath

phonesthemics (sound symbolism)

We have a lot of words in English that begin with *dr* and that pertain to liquids: *drain, dribble, drink, drip, drizzle, drool, drought, dry*. A fair number of words that begin with a *kl* sound (spelled *cl*) have something to do with connections: *clamp, clasp, clench, cling, clod, club, clump, cluster, clutch*. Some words that begin with *fl* are suggestive of movement: *flap, flit, flitter, float, flow, flush, flutter, fly*.

---

[85] https://katherinebarber.blogspot.com/2016/02/no-problem.html

A generally accepted principle in linguistics is that the relationship between sounds and meaning is arbitrary. The same concept is expressed in different, unrelated languages in wildly different ways. This is taken as evidence that in general there are no universal rules about what sounds mean. As John Locke said in *An Essay Concerning Human Understanding* in 1690:

> We may conceive how words [...] came to be made use of by men as the signs of their ideas; not by any natural connexion that there is between particular articulate sounds and certain ideas, for then there would be but one language amongst all men; but by a voluntary imposition, whereby such a word is made arbitrarily the mark of such an idea.

And yet there are these interesting collections of similar-sounding words that seem to share a general meaning. This correspondence between a sound and meaning is referred to as *phonesthemics*. The concept of phonesthemics is also called *sound symbolism*.

One form of correspondence between sound and meaning is *onomatopoeia*, in which a word imitates the thing it's supposed to represent—for example, the word *boom* sounds sort of boom-like, and *hiss* sounds hiss-like. Even then, the human ability to create words that mimic natural sounds is imperfect. Different languages have different words for the sounds made by dogs (*woof-woof* in English, *guau-guau* in Spanish, *hau-hau* in Polish) or roosters (*cock-a-doodle-do* in English, *kikeriki* in German, *chicchirichi* in Italian) and so on.

Onomatopoeia represents what seems to be an explicit attempt to match sound and concept. Phonesthemics, on the other hand, points to a more unconscious and possibly more universal set of associations.

Another well-known example in English is the long series of words that start with *sn* and that seem to have something to do with noses, like *sneeze, sniff, snore, snorkel, snot, snout,* and *snuff,* to list about half of them. In phonology, the *n* sound is a *nasal* because the sound is made through the nose, not through the mouth. (Try it.) So it makes sense that nose-related terms might have a nasal in them. In fact, phonesthemics seems notable across languages in words that pertain to body parts, in particular for words for the nose, for lips, and for teeth. One study found that in over a thousand languages, the word for "nose" has an *n* in it.[86]

A famous experiment in phonesthemics resulted in what's known as the *bouba/kiki effect*. In this experiment, subjects were asked which of the following shapes represented a "bouba" and which represented a "kiki":

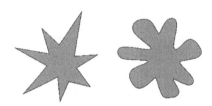

A surprising 95% of the people in the study choose the left shape as "kiki" and the right one as "bouba." Variations on the bouba/kiki study have been run multiple times with similar results, and the effect has been seen even with children.

People who study branding and marketing names have seen that people will associate front vowels (*i, e*) with small and thin things and back vowels (*o, u*) with big or thick products. The linguist Dan Jurafsky reports in his book *The Language of Food* that he ran a study to determine whether …

> […] we would see more back vowels in names of ice cream flavors, and conversely that thin, light foods like crackers would have more front vowels.

He did.

I've always been intrigued by the names that J. K. Rowling invented for the Harry Potter series. In particular, the houses at Hogwarts always seemed to me to be evocative in a way that's based on sound symbolism: Gryffindor, Hufflepuff, Ravenclaw, and Slytherin. (If you don't already know Harry Potter, guess which house the hero, Harry Potter, *doesn't* belong to.) It must be an interesting challenge for translators to render these names into other languages while retaining some of this feel.

---

[86] https://www.washingtonpost.com/news/speaking-of-science/wp/2016/09/12/a-nose-by-any-other-name-biology-may-affect-the-way-we-invent-words/

While there definitely seems to be something going on with phonesthemics, it's not entirely clear what. Are these sound-meaning associations evidence that all languages originated in a single ur-language? Probably not. But it does seem to mean that the association between sound and meaning might not be *entirely* arbitrary, as is generally accepted in linguistics.

One practical application, as noted, is that people who think up product names (and names in fiction) might be taking advantage of phonesthemics—or let's say that if they don't pay attention to phonesthemics, they might come up with a mismatch between sound and meaning and therefore a bad product name.

All of this notwithstanding, if phonesthemics were a strong principle in human language, you'd expect words in different languages to be similar if they referred to the same thing. Sometimes similar concepts do have similar words in different languages; for example, the human attempts to capture animal noises like dog barks are sort of similar in different languages. And sometimes words in unrelated languages do seem to have features in common. But mostly that seems to be coincidence. Maybe it would make it easier to study a foreign language if we knew that their words for nasal things also used a lot of *n*'s. But as with the many different words in many languages for *woof* (and for that matter, for *dog*), phonesthemics doesn't have a lot of application for languages or language learning. The linguist Mark Liberman says it this way:

> Some of these limitations [of sound symbolism] will become intuitively clear to you if you try to converse with monolingual speakers of a language you don't know, relying only on your shared inventory of "nonarbitrary associations" between speech sounds and meanings. The problem is that while such associations exist, they don't get you very far in creating a realistically shared vocabulary.[87]

Related words: aptronym, autological word

---

[87] http://languagelog.ldc.upenn.edu/nll/?p=28328

phonotactics

Suppose you have a child at home who's enthusiastic about dinosaurs. And suppose you're also teaching them to read. At some point while you're reading, you will probably encounter the word *pterodactyl*, the name of a flying dinosaur. If the young reader is sounding out words, you're faced with the conundrum of explaining that although *pterodactyl* starts with a *p*, you don't actually pronounce it.

Why not? The word *pterodactyl* comes from the Greek words for "wing" + "finger." The Greeks wouldn't have written the word *pteron* with *pt* at the beginning if they, too, just ignored that sound, would they? They didn't. In ancient Greek, the sounds *pt* at the beginning of a word is just fine.

But we don't do that in English. We have rules, so to speak, about how English sounds, and among those rules is that we don't use the consonant cluster *pt* at the beginning of a word or syllable. (The author Raj Haldar used this oddity of English for a funny twist on alphabet books—in fact, he used it in the title of his book, which is *P Is for Pterodactyl: The Worst Alphabet Book Ever*.)

If you look at the breadth of human languages as a whole, you find a large number of individual sounds, which in turn can be combined in an enormous number of ways. Nonetheless, any given language uses only a subset of all possible sounds. Moreover, any given language has rules about how those sounds can be combined. *Phonotactics* is the term for a language's sound rules.

We've certainly borrowed words that start with *pt*, like *pterodactyl* and *ptomaine*. It's not like English speakers can't say the combination *pt*; we do it all the time in words like *kept* and *slept*.

But because English phonotactics doesn't allow the cluster *pt* at the beginning of a word, these words give English speakers difficulty. The official pronunciations in dictionaries reflect how we deal with this: we simply drop the *p* in *pt*. Thus, Merriam-Webster lists the pronunciation of *ptomaine* as "tō-mān"—or in other words (other letters), as "toe-MAIN". Other Greek words we've borrowed that don't fit English phonotactical constraints are words that begin with *ps* (*psychology*), *pn* (*pneumonia*), and *mn* (*mnemonic*). As with *ptomaine*, we simply drop the part of the consonant cluster that doesn't fit English phonotactics.

In addition to simply deleting a sound, we have other ways of handling sounds that are not part of English phonotactics. We might insert an extra sound into a consonant cluster to make it pronounceable. For example, the word *knish*, which is a Yiddish word that came from Polish, is sometimes pronounced "kuh-NISH" because English phonotactics doesn't let us have the *kn* sound at the beginning of a word. (But it used to! We have some words today that start with *KN—knee, knight, knock*—that go back to Old English, and those were pronounced with an initial *kn* sound.)

We might also substitute a sound that's close. English doesn't have the *ch* sound that you find in the German name *Bach* or the word *Achtung* ("attention"), so we usually substitute a *k*, which is pretty close.

In Seattle, the local classical station has a program every weekday at noon during which they play 30 minutes of the music of J. S. Bach. The name of the program is *Bach's Lunch*, but it's a kind of phonological pun—because English speakers pronounce the *ch* at the end of *Bach* as a *k*, the name of the program sounds like *box lunch*.

It isn't just Greek that has given us words with phonotactical issues in English. We've "fixed up" many words that were borrowed from Nahuatl, the language of the Aztecs, so that the pronunciations fit English better. In the phonotactics of Nahuatl, the *tl* cluster is okay not just at the beginning of a syllable—hence a word like *chipotle*—but also at the end of a syllable (as you can tell from the name of the language). So their word *ocelotl* has become our *ocelot*, their word *chocolatl* became our *chocolate*, and their word *tomatl* became our *tomato*.

In some cases, English speakers will reanalyze a word to make it fit English phonotactics. One example is *helicopter*, from the Greek roots *heliko* ("spiral") and *pteron* ("wing"). We've changed that to *he-li-copter*, which splits *pt* across syllables and therefore avoids the phonotactical problem of *pt* at the beginning of a syllable. Some English speakers have trouble with the *tl* sound that starts the last syllable of *chipotle*. So they avoid the troublesome cluster by splitting it into "chee-POHT-lee" or "chee-POH-tull," which separates the *t* and *l* into separate syllables.

Other languages have different phonotactical rules. In Spanish, words can't start with *sk*, *st*, or *sp*, so they add a leading *e*, as in *escuela* ("school"), *estereo* ("stereo"), and *español* ("Spanish"). In Swahili, unlike English, words can start with clusters like *mb* (as in *mbuni*, meaning "ostrich") and *nd* (as in *ndege*, meaning "bird").

In Japanese, the name *McDonald's* doesn't fit the language's phonological rules. So when the name passed through the filter of Japanese phonotactics, the name of the restaurant becomes *makudonarudo*. And as Mark Liberman explains in detail in a fascinating post on the *Language Log* blog, when the expression *Merry Christmas* is pronounced in accordance with the phonotactics of the Hawaiian language, it comes out as "mele kalikimaka"—as many people know from a hit song from the 1950s.[88]

A practical—well, also frustrating—aspect of all this is that the phonotactics of the language or languages that you learned as a kid can limit how well you learn to pronounce a language that you learn as an adult. If we have a "foreign accent" in a new language, it's in part because the phonotactics of our primary language make it hard for us to master the sounds of a new language.

Related terms: folk etymology

pleonasm, tautology

Future plans. Tuna fish. Face mask. Personal opinion. Integrate with each other. Sudden explosion. 10:00 AM in the morning. The reason why. These expressions all have something in common, which you've probably guessed: they use more words than they need. After all, what else can you plan for *except* the future? What is tuna if not a fish? *All* AM times are in the morning. And so on.

The expressions are all examples of *pleonasms*, which refers to using more words than needed—that is, of redundancy. Because the expressions generally say the same thing twice, they're also categorized as *tautologies*.

For a brief and glorious period (till an editor found it), the user-created Wiktionary definition for *pleonasm* contained this self-describing definition:

---

[88] https://languagelog.ldc.upenn.edu/nll/?p=2862

pleonasm is the additional and extra use of added, spare, unnecessary, redundant (superfluous or surplus), unneeded, and uncalled-for words in addition to, and on top of, what is necessary or essential. Or required. Or obligatory or vital or requisite or crucial.

pleonasm - Wiktionary
https://en.wiktionary.org/wiki/**pleonasm**

Editorial convention says that redundancy should be avoided, in part because having more words gives the reader that much more to plow through. As it says in *The Elements of Style*, "omit needless words." Editors therefore routinely fix pleonasms like *advance planning, safe haven, mental anguish,* and *final result.*

But pleonasms have their uses. It's technically true, for example, that *Navy SEAL* is a pleonasm, since no other branch of the US military has SEALs. But not everyone knows that, so this redundancy can help the reader.

In any event, English (and language generally) has many inherent redundancies. For example, in standard English we use both a pronoun (such as *she*) *and* a verb conjugation (such as *she eats*) to mark third-person singular, but few people consider this an unnecessary redundancy. Redundancy in general helps make sure that a "signal" is clear. People sometimes object to the extra *at* in *Where is it at?* because it's redundant. But the extra *at* is a kind of signal redundancy that helps distinguish this particular instance of *where* from *where from* or *where to.*

Pleonasms can also create emphasis. Take an expression like *every single.* Sure, in *they do it every single time*, the phrase *every single* is redundant; this could just be *they do it every time.* But the pairing of *every* with the nominally redundant *single* expresses an emphasis that's missing if *single* is left out. Similarly, *laugh out loud* is a pleonasm (how else can you laugh except out loud?), but the fuller expression conveys a level of merriment higher than just *laugh.* Another example is *saw with my own eyes,* which has multiple redundancies (you see with eyes, of course, and *my own* could just be *my*). But again, the longer expression has an emphasis that's missing in just *I saw it.*

Many advertising copywriters know that *free gift* is a pleonasm. What kind of gift isn't free? But the dictates of their profession undoubtedly include the idea that sprinkling the word *free* in advertising copy, no matter how redundant, is never a bad way to attract the customer's attention. Why make the reader do the work of figuring out that if it's a gift, it must be free?

We occasionally end up with inadvertent pleonasms, so to speak, when we import words from other languages. The term *chai tea* is technically a redundancy; *chai* means "tea" in a number of languages. So is the term *naan bread*; *naan* is "bread" in Urdu. Referring to the *head chef* in the kitchen is redundant; *chef* means "chief" in French. Talking about the *Rio Grande river* is redundant, since *rio* means "river" in Spanish. For that matter, *loaf of bread* is etymologically a pleonasm, because *hlaf* in Old English meant "a portion of bread baked in one mass." These type of cross-language pleonasms are known as *bilingual tautological expressions*.

But we don't really think of these as pleonasms because the non-English word is opaque to us. In the case of terms like *chai tea* and *naan bread*, we've narrowed the meaning of the imported words to refer only to specific versions of those things. For example, although *naan* means "bread," we use the term only to refer to a specific type of flatbread.

Pleonasms can also have literary purposes, to make writing more pleasing or to convey social niceties. Mignon Fogarty (Grammar Girl) points out that polite speech is often redundant. She uses the example of *I'm just writing to tell you that you didn't get the job* as an example of a wordy sentence whose redundancies help soften the writer's bad news.[89]

Many stock phrases in English are pleonastic. Think of *alas and alack, hale and hearty, hearth and home, one and only, part and parcel*, and *time and tide*. You might not even think of these as pleonasms because they've become idioms in their own right. They're also satisfying to use, since we like alliteration (*hale and hearty*) in English. (These expressions might be considered clichés, but that's a different problem.)

The wedding ceremony in the Anglican *Book of Common Prayer* includes the redundant expressions *dearly beloved* and *joining together* in the well-known sentence *Dearly beloved: We have come together in the presence of God to witness and bless the joining together of this man and*

---

[89] https://www.quickanddirtytips.com/education/grammar/when-is-it-ok-to-be-redundant

this woman in Holy Matrimony. But it would be a grave disservice to edit this beautiful and familiar prose to omit needless words.

As an editor, I keep an eye out for pleonasms. But it's helpful to take a step back and think about the context in which they appear. As the editor Stan Carey has said about pleonasms:

> Rather than assume that wordy redundancy should always be eliminated, language users can judge its effect on communication in a given context. Sometimes even in formal writing, there's no harm in a delay or detour if it makes the message more meaningful or memorable.[90]

Maybe after reading this, the next time you hear a pleonasm, you'll just *shrug your shoulders.*

Related terms: double genitive, redundant acronym phrase, singular *they*

plurale tantum (lexical plural)

When you get dressed, you might put on some pants (trousers) or perhaps some jeans. You generally won't put on is *a* pant or *a* trouser or *a* jean. That's because the words *pants* and *trousers* and *jeans* are each a *plurale tantum,* also known as a *lexical plural*: they're words that are typically used only in the plural. The term *plurale tantum,* as you might guess, is Latin, meaning "always plural." The plural is *pluralia tantum.*

(It's true that the singular version *pant* for *pants* is sometimes used in the fashion industry, part of the industry's interesting use of the *fashion singular,* along with singular *trouser, jean,* and *tight.* But I'll propose that that's part of the argot for a specific industry.)

Many pluralia tantum represent objects that have a kind of plurality; that is, they represent things that are bipartite. For example, pants, trousers, and jeans have two legs. Another plurale tantum is the word *(eye)glasses,* which typically come with two lenses. When you want to cut some paper or string, you use *scissors,* a lexical plural for a tool that

---

[90] https://stancarey.wordpress.com/2011/01/04/omit-needless-criticisms-of-redundancy/

is in effect two knives. Other examples are *shears*, *pajamas*, and *twee-zers*. It's easy to see the plurality of these items because you can use *pair of* with them: *pair of trousers, pair of glasses, pair of scissors*, and so on.

But not all pluralia tantum are so clearly based on pairs. As a post on the *Language Log* blog examined,[91] we seem to be of two minds about the word *diapers*. A baby can wear *diapers* or a *pair of diapers* but can just as easily wear *a diaper*. It might not be surprising that a pants-like garment for a baby is a plurale tantum, but it's a little surprising that it can live comfortably alongside a singular version.

Once you get past *pluralia tantum* that have an obvious pair-like quality, things are not so clear. When someone does you a favor, you offer them *thanks*, not *a thank*. From our perspective, there's nothing particularly plural-y about *thanks*, yet we treat it as a plural noun and use a plural form of the verb ("thanks are due").

An interesting case is the word *premises* to mean land plus the buildings on it, as you might see in "No food or drink allowed on the premises." There is a singular version of the word—*premise*—but it means something different, like "proposition, assumption." So *premises* to mean "property" is a plurale tantum even though there is a singular-looking version of the word. (Etymologically, *premises* to mean "land, property" did evolve from the singular *premise* via legal language, but that relationship is not clear—and is irrelevant—for purposes of how we use the words.)

A horror movie might give you *the willies* or *the heebie-jeebies*, but I've yet to hear of one that gave you just a single *willy* or *heebie-jeebie*. If you're not getting much done, you might be in the *doldrums*. Or maybe if you got your *druthers*, you'd be doing something else. Perhaps you're in *cahoots* with someone. Those young people engage in *shenani-gans* and *hijinks*, but never in the singular. Your junk drawer might be a *shambles*. You might be in the *throes* of agony. And as my wife points out, no one gets just one *blue*, they always get *the blues*.

A couple of these once did have singular form. Historically, there was a noun *thank* that meant "thought," but we've lost that sense now and are left only with the plurale tantum *thanks*. The singular form *doldrum*, which showed up in English about the same time as the plural *doldrums*,

---

[91] http://itre.cis.upenn.edu/~myl/languagelog/archives/004200.html

didn't survive the mid-19th century. There is a singular version of *throe* attested, but *throes* has mostly been used in the plural. *Hijinks* is also *high jinks*; a *jink* is an old word for a prank. The word *cahoots* once had a singular form, *cahute*.

But others just sort of sprung into being as pluralia tantum. The word *heebie-jeebies* was made up by an American cartoonist in the 1920s. The word *druthers*, which today is a noun and a plurale tantum, originated in the verb phrase *would rather not*, which became *[they] druther not*, which became *druthers*. And sometimes we just don't know: no one is quite sure where *the willies* or *shenanigans* come from.

Fun fact: *Kudos* and *biceps* look plural, but they're not, at least, not in a formal sense. For more on that, see back-formation.

Related terms: hapax legomenon, unpaired word

polysemy

Consider the following sets of statements:

> She gets **milk** from her goats, a fact that she **milks** on her blog about back-to-the-land living.

> They discovered a **mole** in the garden. They discovered a **mole** in the agency.

> He set out to **master** the craft of violinmaking. He became the **master** of a famous workshop in Italy.

Here's an observation that will not surprise you at all: words can have multiple meanings. In language circles, this is known as *polysemy*. This word comes from Greek *poly* ("many") and *sema* ("sign, mark"), which we also see in the word *semantic*. And not just words: polysemy can occur with phrases or really with anything that has more than one meaning.

In its broadest sense, the term *polysemy* simply indicates that a word has several meanings. You've seen this when you look up a word in a dictionary; you discover that there are multiple definitions for the word you're looking at. If you look up *milk* in the Merriam-Webster online dictionary, you find four entries for *milk*—one each as a noun, verb, adjective, and geographical name—with multiple definitions for some of the entries. In the dictionary where I looked, the word *mole* has six entries (and a total of ten definitions), including one for the Mexican chili sauce. I recently looked up the word *draft* in the OED, which includes all historical senses, including obsolete ones, and found that it has about *50* distinct definitions.

A narrower definition of *polysemy* holds that words are polysemous if there are multiple meanings but they share some sort of common concept or common root. In this narrower sense, the definitions for *milk* are polysemous because they all are related in one way or another: the noun senses of *milk* all refer to a milky fluid, and the verb senses derive from literally extracting the fluid (*he milked the cow*) or metaphorically extracting value (*he milked that story for years*).

The word *mole*, on the other hand, has multiple meanings, some related, some not. For example, you can talk about *mole*, the burrowing animal, and about *mole*, the spy. The spy sense is a metaphoric variant of the animal, because the spy "burrows into" an organization. So these two definitions of *mole* are polysemous.

But the mole on someone's cheek and a mole as a chemical quantity and mole, the Mexican chili sauce, are all from entirely different roots and have no relationship to the burrowing animal. (The Mexican sauce isn't even pronounced like the animal; the sauce is "MOLE-eh.") Per the narrow definition of polysemy, these are not polysemes, or variants on the same word. Instead, they're homophones or homographs instead— words that sound the same or are spelled the same but have different meanings.

As I noted, many words in the dictionary have multiple entries for a word, and there are often multiple definitions for one entry. One of the choices that lexicographers have to make is whether to give a word its own entry or whether to list its definition as another sense of an existing word. In general, dictionaries list the polysemes together in one entry. That's why when you look up *mole* in the Merriam-Webster dictionary, the senses for the animal and the spy are included in a single entry. (Dictionaries list nouns and verbs separately even if they're related, so *milk* (the fluid) and *milk* (the verb) have separate entries.)

A funny and clever take on polysemy is a video by Zach Sherwin in which he creates a rap that rhymes the word *set* dozens of times, but each time the word has a different meaning. Example: "The stage is set/for definitions like a high-def television set."[92]

But the distinction between polysemes and homonyms isn't always perfectly clear, since some words that derive from a common root can evolve into very different ideas. For example, the noun *fleet* ("a fleet of ships") and the adjective *fleet* ("quick") both (probably) derive from a common root. But most people probably don't think of these terms as having a common element. The verb *to buff* ("polish") and the noun *buff* ("fan of," as in *film buff*) ultimately come from the same source ("buff[alo] leather," believe it or not), but this connection is so obscure today that we think of these distinct senses as separate words.

The development of a word's polysemy can take surprising turns, as with contronyms, which are words that can have two opposite meanings. For example, the word *seed* can mean either "add seeds to" or "remove seeds from." Talk about polysemy. A more recent example is *literally*, which is widely used both to mean "literally" *or* "figuratively," to the annoyance of some people. (For more on *literally*, see semantic bleaching.)

In some cases, polysemy can engender controversy, generally when one sense of the word has powerful associations. One such word is *master*, which has generated a lot of discussion in the last couple of decades. In 2015, Harvard University was asked to change the term *House Master*, which had been used for a long time as a title for faculty members who supervise residential houses at the institution. This usage derives from the sense of *master* to mean "teacher," as in *headmaster*. But a group of students noted the strong negative connotations of *master* as in *slave master*, and they agitated for change. A few people who were opposed to this change argued that *master* is polysemous and one sense should not crowd out the other—for example, Steven Pinker, who teaches at Harvard, tweeted that "All words have > 1 meaning." Harvard decided to go ahead and make the change.

Some people might think that this is just political correctness. But the same phenomenon of unsavory connotations—polysemy notwithstanding—has caused certain polysemous terms with perfectly fine historical

---

[92] https://youtu.be/DxAnK02BC2k

pedigrees to fall out of favor, like *cock* for "rooster," *pussy* for "cat," and *ass* for "donkey."

The opposite of polysemy is *monosemy*: the property of having only one meaning. Aside from technical terms, monosemous terms are harder to find than you might think. For fun someday, try flipping through a dictionary someday and finding words that have exactly one meaning.

Related terms: homonym, hypernym

portmanteau word (blend)

There's an endless need for new words to describe novel things or concepts. How do we get these new words? Sometimes we borrow them from other languages as loanwords (*karaoke, sushi*) or as calques (*beer garden, earworm*). Sometimes we construct them out of existing roots, using classical roots (*television*) or good old Germanic roots (*keyboard*) or a combination (*microwave*). Sometimes they're made up seemingly out of thin air (*raunchy*).

Fun fact: Words that are made up of roots from different languages are sometimes referred to as *hybrid words* or, better yet, *frankenwords*. For more about *franken* as a prefix, see the entry on libfixes.

And sometimes we mix existing words. These are known as *blends*, of course, or more interestingly as *portmanteau words*, or just *portmanteaus*.

You know many portmanteau words, like these:

- *bit* ("binary" + "digit")
- *brunch* ("breakfast" + "lunch")
- *electrocute* ("electricity" + "execute")
- *emoticon* ("emotion" + "icon")
- *Frappuccino* ("frappé" + "cappuccino")
- *sexpert* ("sex" + "expert")
- *smog* ("smoke" + "fog")
- *telethon* ("television" + "marathon")
- *turducken* ("turkey" + "duck" + "chicken")

Portmanteaus are compounded from other words but are not themselves compounds. Compounds combine complete words—for example, *schoolboy*, *raindrop*, *football*, and *smartphone*. Portmanteaus, on the other hand, combine *parts* of other words.

The linguist John Algeo described a number of ways that we can form portmanteaus.[93] We can "overlap" complete words (*sex* + *expert* = *sexpert*). We can clip words and then combine the clipped parts (*br[eakfast]* + *[l]unch* = *brunch*). Or we can both clip *and* overlap words (*mot[or]* + *[h]otel* = *motel*). A rare version of this last approach, is a *sandwich blend*, in which words are clipped and one word is inserted inside another (*blog* + *law* = *blawg*).

Most blends are made up of two words. But there are some examples of multi-part portmanteaus, like *turducken*. A special case of portmanteaus are syllable acronyms like *sci-fi* and *Nabisco*.

News-making episodes can trigger a wave of portmanteau creations. The COVID-19 pandemic has spawned many: *covidiot*, *coronacation*, *coronapocalypse*, *elbump*, *maskulinity*, and more. Britain's vote to leave the EU likewise spawned some portmanteaus, including the word *Brexit* itself ("Britain" + "exit"). Most of these will come and go as our need to discuss these ideas comes and goes. But a few might survive.

Portmanteaus have existed in English for a long time, but the name is not that old. The word *portmanteau* refers to a type of suitcase that opens into two equal parts. (Notice that *portmanteau* is a loanword from French: "carry" + "cloak.") Lewis Carroll repurposed this term to refer to a word that combines the meanings of two other words. In *Through the Looking Glass*, Humpty Dumpty explains to Alice what the word *slithy* from the poem "Jabberwocky" means:

> 'Well, "slithy" means "lithe and slimy." "Lithe" is the same as "active." You see it's like a portmanteau—there are two meanings packed up into one word.'

Some portmanteaus work better than others. A couple of graduate students at the University of Pennsylvania did some research into this. They surveyed people to rate 88 blends; high ratings went to certain blends

---

[93] http://itre.cis.upenn.edu/~myl/languagelog/archives/002780.html

like *mathlete* and *sexpert*. Low ratings went to other blends like *fozzle* (fog drizzle) and *wonut* (waffle donut).

Lane Greene, who writes about language for the *Economist*, suggests that a bad portmanteau is one where you can't figure out what the constituent parts are, which seems true for the examples that are rated low. (On Twitter, people occasionally mock bad portmanteaus, especially ones used in marketing, with the hashtags *#shitmanteau* or *#portmanNO*.) Still, sometimes even a questionable portmanteau will get traction, as seems to be happening for the word *smize* ("smile" + "eyes").

Once in a while you'll find a portmanteau that includes a word that is itself a portmanteau. An example is the word *Regrexit*, a term coined for people in the UK who seemed to regret voting for Brexit. *Regrexit* combines *regret* + *Brexit*; *Brexit* is itself a portmanteau, as noted earlier. Another example is the word *diavlog*, invented by the lexicographer Ben Zimmer. *Diavlog* blends *dialog* and *vlog*, where *vlog* is a portmanteau of *video* and *blog*, and where *blog* blends *web* and *log*. There doesn't seem to be a formal term for these types of multi-portmanteau portmanteaus. Some people have proposed *recursive blend* or *recursive portmanteau*; Ben Zimmer referred to his creation as a *second-order blend*. ("Or make that third-order" he says in the blog post where he talked about *diavlog*, since it combines three levels of blends.) I kind of like *telescoping blend*, but this paragraph might be the only place you'll ever encounter that word.

A jocular subspecies of *portmanteau* is *portmonthteau*, which describes blends based on the names of months: *Rocktober*, *Sharktober*, *Febrewary*, *Decembeard*, *Deal-cember*, etc. You might agree that *October* seems to be particularly popular for portmonthteaus. Whether you enjoy the cleverness of these made-up words is, of course, another question.

Related terms: infix, libfix, nonce word, syllable acronym

prescriptivism, prescriptivist

You just bought a new house that has a big yard. Your cousin Alex is a botanist, so you invite them over to identify all the plants in your garden and where they came from. On another day you invite over your cousin Pat, who's a landscape architect. You want Pat to tell you what to plant and how to arrange plantings to give your yard that eye-popping appeal.

Both of your cousins are experts in plants. But you're asking them different things. Alex can tell you what your plants are called and how plants work. Pat can tell you how best to arrange plants to get a specific effect.

Of course, this is a simplified view of the world of plant experts, but it provides an analogy (also simplified) of two types of language experts: *descriptivists* and *prescriptivists*. I have a separate entry for descriptivism, so here I'll focus on just prescriptivism.

Prescriptivism is an approach to language studies whose goal is to recommend (prescribe) specific usage. People seek prescriptive guidance all the time to sort out questions like whether to write *eat healthy* or *eat healthily*, where to put the comma, when to capitalize words, whether it's okay to use singular *they*, how to organize a sentence elegantly, and many other questions of style and usage.

Editors and writers rely on the authority of various formal usage guides, like the *Chicago Manual of Style* (for commercial publishing), the *AP Stylebook* (journalism), the *MLA Handbook* (humanities), the *Publication Manual of the American Psychological Association* (social and behavioral sciences), and *Garner's Modern English Usage* (general), to name only some of the best-known resources. There are also many places on the web where people can find usage advice, from the *Grammar Girl* site ("Quick and Dirty Tips")[94] to blogs like *Grammarly* and *GrammarBook*.

Writers find these prescriptive guides useful precisely because they provide definitive guidance. Following the guidance can help the writer create text that's consistent and that conforms to conventions that the audience is accustomed to. It also means that the writer doesn't have to try to make decisions on their own about dozens of little usage questions.

---

[94] http://www.quickanddirtytips.com/grammar-girl

And, importantly, it can help the writer avoid usages that many people would consider mistakes. All of this is simply in the service of writing clearly and with minimal distraction to the user.

In some language communities, there are formal organizations that act as prescriptivist authorities. In France, the Académie Française lays down guidelines on what it considers correct vocabulary and grammar for French. In Spain, the Real Academia Española (RAE) plays a similar role: "to ensure that the Spanish language, in its continuous adaptation to the needs of its speakers, does not break its essential unity." (From the RAE site: "... velar por que la lengua española, en su continua adaptación a las necesidades de los hablantes, no quiebre su esencial unidad."[95])

Although there have been proposals over the centuries to create an English-language academy, that never happened. As a result, in English, the kinds of advice that prescriptivism provides—the best way to write something, the official way to spell or punctuate something—have emerged more organically, the work of many people across a variety of resources, with no central authority. (Of course, there's a difference between having a central, recognized authority and following its guidelines.)

But prescriptivism tends to irk linguists when it's done poorly. "Done poorly" here can mean presenting opinions or personal preferences as authoritative guidance. You're also getting poor prescriptivist advice when the authority seems not to be well versed in historical or contemporary grammar studies. As the linguist Mark Liberman once advised, "If someone proposes a grammatical principle that is violated by the titles of two or more classic novels or stories, you should think twice before paying them money for further advice on grammar and usage."[96]

Some people also consider that prescriptivism can put a value judgment on how people use language, and that it encourages the idea that using language in non-endorsed ways is a personal failing. In effect, prescriptivism can end up stigmatizing nonstandard usage. This can be true if a prescriptivist implies that there is only one true or correct version of English and that anything other than standard English is a "corruption" of the language. The editor Steve Dodson sums up the objection to this

---

[95] https://www.rae.es/la-institucion/la-rae
[96] http://itre.cis.upenn.edu/~myl/languagelog/archives/001442.html

view: "'Prescriptivism' is nothing more than linguistic elitism, and like any elitism it's used as a club to harm the people least able to fight back."[97]

Some prescriptivists subscribe to this viewpoint, sure. But at its best, prescriptivism is about helping people be effective in their communication, which involves making judgments and doling out thoughtful advice. Telling people how to do something well inevitably means deciding that one usage works better than another. The craft of editing is primarily a prescriptive one ("use this word, not that one" or "it's clearer if you write it this way"). An experienced editor will understand that much of the advice they're providing is based not on language absolutes, but on conventions that apply for the text that they're looking at, the audience it's for, and the context in which they're editing.

People often think of dictionaries as prescriptive guides to the language and that they catalog the *correct* definitions and pronunciations for all the approved words. This isn't true. Contemporary dictionaries are generally created based on descriptivist principles—that is, they record the way people actually use words.

This confusion occasionally causes people to complain when they look in a dictionary and find words or definitions that they don't agree with. For example, in the Merriam-Webster dictionary, the definition for *literally* is listed both as "in a literal sense or manner" *and* as "in effect; virtually." People who complain might think this means that dictionaries are endorsing "bad usage." But lexicographers see their job as providing information that helps people decode what they read and hear, not to serve as gatekeepers for what words *should* mean. Still, to help readers understand the context of words, dictionary editors often indicate whether a word is slang or substandard, or they'll sometimes provide usage notes for terms that are frequently confused or are controversial.

Similarly, people sometimes interpret the advice of grammar-checking programs as authoritative. (The grammar checker in Microsoft Word has had a *lot* of advice for me as I've drafted these entries.) But people might not realize that, as with usage guides, the advice from a grammar checker is a judgment call. (It's possible that some people feel that the advice is authoritative because it comes from a computer.) Moreover, a lot of

---

[97] https://languagehat.com/david-foster-wallace-demolished/

grammar checkers can be tuned to dial up or down the formality they police—for example, whether they'll flag contractions or flag every instance of the passive voice.

Obviously, the whole enterprise of dispensing language advice can be a tricky one. Awareness of what prescriptivism is about, and of the controversies about it, and of the agendas of the people commenting on it, is always helpful.

In the meantime, though, make sure you keep straight which advice you're hearing from your cousins Alex and Pat.

Related terms: descriptivism, recency illusion

quotative *like*

The word *like* is a multi-purpose tool in English. You can *like* something, and you can look *like* someone, and can stamp a *like* on someone's Facebook post, and you eat, *like*, a ton of chocolate for lunch. Another use of *like* is to introduce what someone said:

I'm, ***like***, "Yeah!"

And then she was, ***like***, "I'm not going to school today."

Words that introduce quotations like this are called *quotatives*, so using *like* this way is, naturally enough, called *quotative like*.

English has quite a few quotative terms—standard ones include *say*, *ask*, *report*, and so on:

He ***said***, "No way."

"Are you coming home early?" they ***asked***.

We also have a collection of quotatives that are considered less standard. These include the words *go* and *all*:

Then she ***went***, "Ha! Your turn"

He was ***all***, "No way!"

The newest entry in this list of (currently) nonstandard quotatives is *like*.

Although quotative *like* might seem like it's just a nonstandard variation of something like *say*, linguists suggest that there's a qualitative difference among quotatives. In other words, it's not just because those kids today are ruining the language or whatever.

One theory is that quotative *like* started out as a way to convey feelings, as in *I was, like, sooo embarrassed*. From there it evolved for recounting not just dialog, but an attitude toward that dialog. A speaker's choice to use *like* instead of *say* therefore conveys something about the speaker's disposition toward the quoted material. As one article says, "[...] the speaker vocalizes the contents of participants' utterances, but also her *attitudes* toward those utterances."[98] Compare:

> She said, "You crashed the car!"

> She was, like, "You crashed the car!"

The second sentence includes a suggestion of emotion that the use of *said* does not.

The use of quotative *like* is pretty recent; it seems to have emerged in the 1980s. It spread fast and is very prevalent among young speakers—about 80% of college students use it. Therefore, there's a chance that this usage will become more standard in the future as the generations turn over.

Related terms: pause filler, tag question

rebracketing

You might not know that the word *apron* wasn't originally *apron*; it was *napron*, related to the word *napkin*. But a funny thing happened along the way. People would say *a napron*, which other people heard as *an apron*. (Try it.) This was long before there were dictionaries to consult on such

---

[98] https://theamericanscholar.org/and-im-like-read-this/

matters, so there was no authority to ask. In due time (like, starting in the 1500s), we settled on *an apron*, and here we are.

The change of *a napron* to *an apron* is known as *rebracketing*, because it changes the brackets, so to speak, around where the word boundaries are. For example, is it *[a][napron]* or *[an][apron]*? There are other names for this phenomenon, including *metanalysis*, *reanalysis*, and *misdivision*, the last of which seems a little judgmental, don't you think?

The change of *a napron* to *an apron* wasn't a fluke. We've done the same thing multiple times. The tool we now know as *an auger* was a *nafogar* or *nauger* in Old English, but by the 1400s had started showing up as *augur*. Perhaps you know *Vipera berus*, a snake common in Western Europe? Before it was *an adder*, it was *a nadder*, as in this excellent citation from about 1425: "Þei maken a maner of hissynge as a nedder doth." (The Þ character is for what we now know as a *th* sound.) The word *nonce* as in *for the nonce* came about through rebracketing of the expression *for Þan anes* in Old English, which meant "for that particular purpose."

You can see how it would be relatively easy for the *n* at the beginning of a noun to wander over and attach itself to the preceding indefinite article, turning *a* to *an*.

Rebracketing works in the other direction as well, moving the *n* from the end of *an* to the beginning of the noun that follows it. We did this with *a newt*, the animal, which was originally *an ewt*. (Well, it was originally *efeta*, but developed a form *ewt*.) In medieval English, the word *eke* meant "additional." *An eke name* referred to an additional name for someone. But after rebracketing, *an eke name* became *a nickname*. (If you happen to speak German, you might recognize that *eke* is related to the German word *auch*, which means "also.")

A fascinating example that came about due to rebracketing is the expression *a whole nother*, as in *that's a whole nother thing*. It's a little weird that the word *whole* should end up in the middle of the word *another* like that. But it turns out that, sure enough, *another* was originally *an other [thing]*, and this was sometimes analyzed as *a nother*. The space between *a* and *nother* that came about by rebracketing made it possible (so to speak) to insert a word in between them. Even though today we think of *another* as a single word, the expression *a whole nother* shows a vestige of this earlier rebracketing.

We might expect rebracketing to be a curious historical phenomenon, something that happened before dictionaries and whatnot. But language is an aural phenomenon, and our understanding of language is primarily a function of what we hear. And people continue to hear things in idiosyncratic ways. The children's rhyme "I scream, you scream, we all scream for ice cream" is a play on this, but who among us has not misheard something like this?

Rebracketing can be the source of some eggcorns. As listed in an NPR article, people have rebracketed *chest of drawers* as *chesterdraws*, *best thing since sliced bread* as *best thing since life's bread*, and *prima donna* as *pre-Madonna*.[99]

Rebracketing can also be played for laughs. An ongoing bit on the TV program *Saturday Night Live* involves a supposed round of celebrity *Jeopardy!* The comedic premise is that "Sean Connery" (actually the comedian Darrell Hammond) reads the categories as misles, such as *S words* as "swords." That's an innocuous one; most are rude, like imaginative and vulgar rebracketings of *Let It Snow* and *An Album Cover*. (There's a video on YouTube that gathers up all of these bits from over the years.[100])

In December 2021, a prominent legislator posted a tweet that showed a great example of rebracketing, writing *there enlies* instead of *therein lies*:

You haven't heard a word from the media about it.

There enlies the problem.

5:49 PM · Dec 11, 2021 · Twitter for iPhone

If you just hear the phrase *therein lies* and aren't already familiar with it, it's easy to imagine how it can be parsed as *there enlies*.

---

[99] https://www.npr.org/sections/thetwo-way/2015/06/01/411231029/here-are-100-eggcorns-that-we-say-pass-mustard
[100] https://youtu.be/mMOjRCuMmsw

I'm often tempted to see if I can sneak some rebracketing into everyday conversation. "Would you like a napple?" I want to ask. "Or maybe two napples?" Just to see if people will notice.

Related terms: libfix, misle, mondegreen, phonotactics

recency illusion

On GrammarMonster.com, there's a note about the word *can* that goes like this:

Can I play outside, Grandma?
You can, dear, but you're not allowed.[101]

The site has this explanation: "The grandchild used *can* in its more recently developed, additional meaning of *may* or *to have permission to.*"

What's interesting here is the suggestion that using *can* with the meaning "to have permission" is a recent development—so recent, in fact, that a grandmother and her grandchild have different meanings for the word.

This is … not true. In 1828, Noah Webster had this definition for *can*: "To have just or legal competent power, that is, right; to be free from any restraint of moral, civil or political obligation, or from any positive prohibition. We *can* use a highway for travel, for this is permitted by law." There are many other examples of using *can* to mean "to have permission" going back to the 1400s. For example, the OED has a cite for the word *can* from 1567 that says, "They that be vnder their fathers rule, by ciuill Lawe can not marrye withowt their Fathers consent."

Grammar Monster's theory that using *can* to mean "to have permission" is a new thing is therefore an example of the *recency illusion*: the idea that a word or usage originated recently, when it's actually been around much longer.

Some people think that singular *they* (*Everyone should bring **their** own lunch*) was invented not long ago, perhaps out of some nod to political

---

[101] https://www.grammar-monster.com/glossary/literal_meaning.htm

correctness. But Jane Austen was using singular *they* in her novels at the turn of the 19th century. Some people think that using apostrophes to mark plurals is a recent development, probably due to declining education standards. But the reality is that people have been confused about how to use apostrophes since we started using them (see greengrocer's apostrophe). Using *literally* to mean "figuratively" is not some latter-day corruption of English, as some people think, but goes back to the 1700s.

The term *recency illusion* was invented by the linguist Arnold Zwicky. He was miffed that someone was writing about a particular usage (*between you and I*) and was making this claim: "This oddity, which seems to have emerged only in the last twenty or so years, [...]." He was miffed in particular because a claim like this is not hard to verify—or in this case, debunk. Even a pretty casual search would have turned up that *between you and I* appears in Shakespeare, and there are plenty of examples over the last couple of centuries, including occasionally in the writings of Benjamin Franklin.

Zwicky describes some other, similar types of illusions:

- The *adolescent illusion*, where people think that young people are particularly likely to engage in some term or usage. This is a variant on the *out-group illusion*, where you notice the behavior of other people, but you don't notice the same behavior in your own group. A good example of this is vocal fry, a kind of creaking of the voice, which is stereotypically associated with young women. But in reality it's used by men and women in a wide age range.

- The *antiquity illusion*, where people incorrectly think that some feature that seems normal to them has been in the language forever. For example, it's taken me a long time to accept that sentence-modifying *hopefully* (*Hopefully they'll get here on time*) didn't really become widespread until just before I was born.

- The *frequency illusion*, where people believe something is much more widespread than it really is. Do kids these days use quotative *like* constantly? (*She was, like, "I'll be right there."*) Careful counts of words used in speech suggests that the frequency is, well, an illusion.

To be clear, the recency illusion is only an illusion when you're wrong. Many novel-to-you usages probably are older than you think, but many usages that you're just now noticing really *are* recent. For example, maybe you've recently noticed young people using the verb *adulting* ("to assume adult responsibilities"). If you sense that this is a new term, you're right. Similarly, if it seems to you that people are using *because* in a new way (*because reasons*), again you'd be right. How do I know this? I looked those terms up.

The larger lesson with the recency illusion and the rest of these illusions is that any claims that are made about language need to be checked. If you're just noticing something, is it really new, or is it only new to *you*? If it *seems* like you're hearing something all the time, is it really more frequent, or are you just paying closer attention? And so on.

As Zwicky says of all these, "the point is that you actually have to look at the facts; your impressions are unreliable."

Related terms: prescriptivism

redundant acronym phrase

Your friend tells you "I stopped by the ATM machine, but I realized I'd forgotten my PIN number." You resist the urge to say "ATM machine? PIN number?" (At least, I hope you're resisting.)

What you recognize is that your friend is using some *redundant acronym phrases*. The initialism *ATM* stands for "automatic teller machine," so adding *machine* to the end (*ATM **machine***) is redundant. Similarly, *PIN* stands for "personal identification number," so *PIN **number*** is likewise a redundant acronym phrase. A redundant acronym phrase is therefore a special case of a pleonasm.

People who want to write or speak carefully try to avoid these types of redundant acronym phrases. After all, it's both correct and clear to say *I have to stop by the ATM* or *I forgot my PIN*.

Still, there is a tendency with some acronyms to add that last element as a word. It's easy to find examples online of *PIN number*, including in newspaper headlines, like this example from the *Guardian*:

The most common pin numbers: is your bank account vulnerable?

Data blogger and technology consultant Nick Berry has been crunching pins to see which are easiest to guess

The Corpus of Contemporary American English (COCA) lists nearly 200 instances of *ATM machine*.

ATM machine and *PIN number* are well-known examples and are easy to spot. But it's not hard to find others that are less obvious, like these:

- *DC current*. *DC* stands for "direct current."
- *GUI interface*. *GUI* stands for "graphical user interface."
- *GIF format*. *GIF* stands for "Graphics Interchange Format."
- *HIV virus*. *HIV* stands for "human immunodeficiency virus."
- *HTTP protocol*. *HTTP* stands for "hypertext transfer protocol." (The expressions *HTTP protocol* and *GIF format* both appear on the website of the World Wide Web Consortium (W3C), which is responsible for, among other things, the HTTP standard.)
- *ISBN number*. *ISBN* stands for "International Standard Book Number."
- *Please RSVP*. *RSVP* stands for "répondez s'il vous plait," a French phrase that means "please respond."
- *SAT test*. *SAT* originally stood for "scholastic aptitude test." (Although the company that owns the test decided fairly recently that *SAT* doesn't stand for anything; that is, it's an orphan acronym.)
- *UPC code*. *UPC* stands for "universal product code."

In some of these cases, it might seem a little odd *not* to use the redundancy. People seem not to want to say *the drawing is in GIF* (rather than *GIF format*) or *scientists have isolated the HIV* (rather than *the HIV virus*). The abbreviation *FAQ* stands for "frequently asked questions," plural, but people nonetheless write *FAQs*.

What seems to be happening with redundant acronym phrases is that the abbreviation (*ATM, PIN, GIF, HIV*) has become independent from its constituent elements. When people use the abbreviations, they're not thinking of what the letters stand for. Instead, the acronyms or initialisms are becoming *lexicalized*—that is, they're evolving from abbreviations into words in their own right.

Lexicalization has happened before, including with words that you know but don't think about. The word *laser* was originally an acronym for "light amplification by stimulated emission of radiation," and the word *radar* was originally "radio detection and ranging." A word that's most of the way through the process of lexicalization is *scuba*. This stands for "self-contained underwater breathing apparatus." Some people still write it as *SCUBA*, using all capital letters to indicate its origin, but dictionaries routinely list it as *scuba*, all lowercase, without indicating that it's an acronym.

Among the examples listed earlier, *RSVP* is fully lexicalized. It's used as a noun (*several RSVPs*) and verb (*they RSVPed*), and its status as an initialism is almost completely defunct. This is in spite of its spelling— all capital letters—and its pronunciation as R-S-V-P. It helps, of course, a lot of people don't know what RSVP stands for, since it refers to an expression in French. Other opaque initials come from the tech world or from a specialized field, like *GIF*, *UPC*, and even *ISBN*, so people learn the terms without knowing what they stand for.

Words like *ATM*, *PIN*, and *GIF* are also used as nouns in themselves, meaning that people can pluralize them (*ATMs*, *PINs*, *GIFs*) and use a possessive form (*the ATM's location*, *my PIN's numbers*, *the GIF's size*). These are all evidence that people think of terms like *ATM* and *PIN* and *GIF* and *UPC* not as abbreviations but as words in themselves. No wonder people end up tacking on what look like redundant words to these words, er, abbreviations.

When discussing redundant acronyms, I would be remiss if I did not mention *RAS syndrome*. This is an expression that describes the tendency toward redundancy that you've seen in this entry. You will no doubt be pleased to learn that *RAS syndrome* stands for *redundant acronym syndrome syndrome*.

Related terms: backronym, pleonasm, syllable acronym

reduplication

In Malay, the word for "house" is *rumah*. If you want to talk about more than one house—that is, you want to say *houses*—you say *rumah-rumah*. You just repeat the word. It's as if you were saying *I own one house, they own two house-house.*

The process of repeating a word or a part of a word is known as *reduplication*. In Malay, reduplication is a part of the language's grammar—it's the grammatical way to form the plural of some words. Many languages use reduplication for various grammatical purposes, including Farsi, Indonesian, Nepali, Swahili, Tagalog, Turkish, Hawaiian, and American Sign Language (ASL).

By the way, you might wonder why it's *reduplication* instead of just *duplication*. Basically, we imported it as an academic term that way from Latin, where the *re* prefix might have been an intensifier.

If you're learning English, your textbook won't talk about reduplication as a formal part of English grammar. But we use reduplication all the time. Sometimes we use it to form words. Other times we use it to emphasize words or shade their meaning.

Consider the following examples, all of which show some form of reduplication:

- *bye-bye, hubba-hubba, night-night, pooh-pooh, so-so*
- *fender-bender, hoity-toity, hokey-pokey, okey-dokey, Oompa Loompa, walkie-talkie*
- *chit-chat, flim-flam, hip hop, kitty cat*
- *artist-schmartist, fancy-schmancy*
- *very, very good*
- *faster and faster*

First, let's talk about the different types of reduplication. In *exact reduplication* we repeat a word—*bonbon, boo-boo, bye-bye, hubba-hubba, tutu, yo-yo*. Repeating a word like *very* (*very, very good*) is also a form of exact reduplication. Words based on exact reduplication are also referred to as *tautonyms* (Greek for "same" + "word").

In zoology, the scientific names for some animals are tautonyms. These include the moose (*Alces alces*), the American buffalo (*Bison bi-*

son), the Western gorilla (*Gorilla gorilla*), and the black rat (*Rattus rattus*). Interestingly, in the naming conventions of botany, tautonyms are forbidden.

We've imported some words from other languages that use exact duplication. These include *beriberi* (from Sinhalese) and *mahi-mahi* (from Hawaiian). An example of exact duplication that hides out in English is the word *barbarian*, which is from ancient Greek *barbaros*; they used *bar-bar* to dismissively describe the speech of foreigners (like our *blah-blah*).

In *rhyming reduplication*, the second term is a rhyme of the first one— *artsy-fartsy*, *claptrap*, *easy-peasy*, *hocus-pocus*, *hokey-pokey*, *helter-skelter*. These are also sometimes just called *rhyming compounds*.

In *ablaut reduplication* (also called *vowel-shift reduplication*), we repeat the word but change the main vowel—*chit-chat*, *criss-cross*, *flim-flam*, *tell-tale*. (*Ablaut* is normally used to describe a change in the vowel for a grammatical function, such as to form the past tense, as in *sing-sang-sung*.) Ablaut reduplication has an interesting property in that it follows a sound rule. If you look closely, you'll see that the first word uses a vowel like *i* (sometimes *e*), and the second word uses a vowel like *a* or *o*. It seems that for English speakers, we want to start with a front vowel (*i* or *e*) in the first word, and a back vowel (*a, o, u*) in the second word.

Finally, in *schm-reduplication*, we add *schm* to the beginning of the second word: *artist-schmartist*, *bagel-schmagel*, *sale-schmale*. This is a variant on rhyming reduplication, but it adds *schm-* at the beginning of the second term.

So those are the *types* of reduplication we have. Then there are the various ways in which we *use* reduplication.

Historically we've used exact reduplication, ablaut reduplication, and rhyming reduplication to create words like *hubba-hubba*, *nitty-gritty*, and *zig-zag*. Using one of these forms of reduplication is not very "productive," as linguists say—that is, it's not a common way to create new words.

But we do still do it occasionally. For example, the name *King Kong* was coined in the 1930s, and the word *walkie-talkie* was created during the 1940s. Some more recent examples are *bling-bling*, the word *po-po* as a shortened form of *police*, and the expression *cray-cray*, which is a variant of *crazy*. Marketing people sometimes like to use reduplication for brand names, as in *Ding-Dong* (snack cakes), *Kit-Kat* (candy bar), *Spic and Span* (cleaning product), and *Tic-Tac* (mints). A recent example is *TikTok* (video app).

We seem to naturally use exact reduplication when we use baby talk (more formally referred to as *infant-directed speech*). We say things like *bye-bye*, *choo-choo*, and *doo-doo* to children who are just learning language. There's some evidence that the exact reduplication in baby talk helps infants learn words.

We use schm-reduplication to indicate derision or dismissiveness. *Rules, schmules! I do what I like!* As the linguist Arika Orent says, "It's a handy way of downplaying or dismissing something without being too aggressive or unfriendly."[102] The origins seem to be in Yiddish, a language that has many derisive words that begin with the *sh* sound (*schlemiel*, *schmuck*, and so on). This type of reduplication is more productive than other types; you can conjure up new instances at will (*dictionary-schmictionary!*), but the words it produces are almost always nonce words.

My favorite use of exact reduplication is for contrast, which is referred to as *contrastive focus reduplication*. Consider these examples:

> Are you reading the e-book? No, I'm reading the ***book***-book.

> Is that almond milk? No, it's ***milk***-milk.

> Do you like him, or do you ***like***-like him?

In this type of reduplication, we use both repetition and vocal emphasis to show the contrast. In the ***book***-*book* and ***milk***-*milk* examples, emphasizing the first element establishes the contrast with e-book or with almond milk. In the ***like***-*like* example, the repeated element acts as an intensifier: do you (just) like him, or do you (really) like him?

We also can use exact reduplication to indicate degree. How did you like that restaurant? Maybe it's better than *very good*; perhaps it's *very, very good*. We can also do this with the word *so*: that new flavor of ice cream is not just *so yummy*, it's *so, so yummy*. We can add more *very*s or

---

[102] http://mentalfloss.com/article/51600/rules-shmules-5-phonetic-pitfalls-shm-reduplication

sos to indicate an even greater degree: *very, very, very good* or *so, so, so yummy.* Weirdly, although we can add degrees of emphasis by repeating *so* (*so, so yummy*), something that's *so-so* is mediocre ("How was the movie? It was so-so.")

Or think about your ancestors. Your grandmother's mother is your *great*-grandmother. If you want to refer to *her* mother, you can use exact reduplication—she's your *great-great*-grandmother. Although in practice this gets awkward beyond two or three degrees, it's legit to keep adding instances of *great* to talk about ever more distant generations, like your *great-great-great-great-grandmother*.

One more. Another way we use reduplication is when we say something like *They were running **faster and faster**.* This is called *comparative reduplication* because it repeats the comparative form of a modifier. But it isn't exactly like the *great-great-grandmother* example. When we say someone is running *faster and faster*, it is true that they're running faster. But the *-er and -er* reduplication indicates that they're running *progressively* faster: they're accelerating. Comparative reduplication captures a change over time.

As I said earlier, English isn't generally considered to have a formal role for reduplication. But when you look at all these examples of how we use reduplication in English, you might wonder whether we're not really that different from repeating *house* to mean "more than one." As the linguist Rory Turnbull said on Twitter, "Yeah I guess technically English has reduplication but it's not reduplication reduplication."

 **Rory Turnbull**
@_roryturnbull   ...

Yeah I guess technically English has reduplication but it's not reduplication reduplication

8:33 AM · Apr 23, 2021 · Twitter Web App

Related terms: retronym

retronym

When my wife and I had our wills drawn up recently, we had to make an appointment and visit the lawyer's office in person to sign them. It seems that wills are among the documents that still require a *wet signature*—a signature made using a pen and ink. You might stop right here and ask, "Aren't all signatures wet?"

All signatures *used* to be wet. But since the advent of digital signatures, we've needed a word to describe the old-fashioned, pen-and-ink type. Hence *wet signature*. This is a beautiful example of a *retronym*, or a term that's invented to distinguish an old thing from a newer version of that thing.

You know many retronyms:

- *acoustic guitar*
- *brick-and-mortar store*
- *snail mail*

The fundamental characteristic of a retronym is that it wasn't necessary at some earlier stage of the language. Before the invention of electric guitars, the only kind of guitar that existed was an acoustic guitar, so the only meaning of *guitar* was an acoustic guitar. At some point in history, people had to start referring to *dirt roads* to distinguish those from the paved roads that become the default. Before we shopped online, we went downtown or to the mall and physically entered *brick-and-mortar stores* (or more probably concrete stores, but that's not nearly as good a retronym). And once we had email, we needed a way to talk about that other kind of mail, the kind that you put a stamp on. In the documentary *The Booksellers*, Fran Lebowitz makes this retronymic observation: "You know what they used to call independent bookstores? Bookstores."

The term *retronym* was invented in 1980 by Frank Mankiewicz, who at the time was president of National Public Radio. He enjoyed collecting examples of these neologisms. Among his finds was *hardback book*, which was an early retronym that contrasted with the newer-fangled paperback books. (What retronym do you use for a book that isn't an e-book?) Another of Mankiewicz's examples was *analog watch*, which became necessary when digital watches were invented.

The definition for *retronym* in FreeDictionary.com notes that we have a few retronyms in English generally (*whole milk*, *snow skiing*), but that "hacker jargon," i.e., technological vocabulary, is rich in retronyms. (Their exact words are "hacker jargon is necessarily (at points capriciously) rich in retronyms"; I found the word "capriciously" amusing.) Among their examples are *natural language* (contrasting with programming languages) and *biological virus* (contrasting with a computer virus). Now that everyone has digital cameras, when you want to refer to the old type, you have to talk about a *film camera*. Gamers now use the term *tabletop game* or *board game* for a non-digital game. Perhaps you bought a special digital antenna so that you could get *broadcast TV*. An emerging retronym is *ICE car*, where *ICE* stands for "internal-combustion engine," since electric vehicles are becoming more and more common. An excellent recent retronym—one that winks knowingly at the whole idea of retronyms—is *acoustic bicycle* to contrast with an e-bike.

But retronyms can come up in many contexts. In the social realm, for example, the word *marriage* is developing retronyms like *traditional marriage* and *straight marriage* to contrast with terms like *same-sex marriage*.

There are many words that we can affix to a word to indicate that we mean it as a retronym. A good example is the word *classic*. The use of *classic* in this sense originated with Coke Classic, which the Coca-Cola company used as the name for its original formula after the disastrous introduction of so-called New Coke in 1985. Since then, other products have had *classic* added to their names to indicate that they represented an older generation—a good example is the Macintosh Classic.

Other examples of retronymic prefixes are *manual* (*manual transmission*), *regular* (*regular coffee*), *wired* (*wired headphones*), and *plain* (*plain M&Ms*). With the popularity of almond milk, goat milk, coconut milk, oat milk, and so on, we sometimes need a word to describe the kind of milk that comes from cows. So you'll sometimes see the term *dairy milk* for what was once just *milk*. In the realm of food, *organic* is a kind of retronym, harking back to a time when all food could be assumed to be organic, and contrasting with the default.

And as our most elderly relatives might remember, there was a time before disposable diapers. These days, of course, if you use the older kind of diaper, you might have to refer to it as a *cloth diaper*.

I was delighted to learn about retronymic terms that we use all the time in the world of editing. Although we usually edit electronically, some editors still prefer to work on *hardcopy*—that is, copy that's printed on paper. When desktop publishing become widespread and we all became familiar with some details of typography, we had to start distinguishing typographic quotation marks (*curly quotes* or *smart quotes*) from the older style that were based on the limited character set available on typewriters. Those became known as *straight quotes*, as you can see in this dialog box from the Microsoft Word options:

AutoCorrect		? ✕
AutoFormat		Actions
AutoCorrect	Math AutoCorrect	AutoFormat As You Type

Replace as you type

☐ "Straight quotes" with "smart quotes" ☐ Ordinals (1st) with superscript
☐ Fractions (1/2) with fraction character (½) ☑ Hyphens (--) with dash (—)
☐ *Bold* and _italic_ with real formatting

The introduction of the backslash character (\) on computer keyboards also meant that we now sometimes have to be careful to use the term *forward slash* when we mean a virgule (/).

And speaking of language things, the development over the centuries of different national versions of English—American English, Australian English, Canadian English, South African English, and many more—has meant that what was originally just *English* now has to have a retronym of its own: *British English*. My understanding is that not everyone is happy about that.

Related terms: back-formation

rhotic accent, non-rhotic accent

If you ask Americans how people in Boston talk, you'll often hear a variation of "Bostonians say *I pahk the cah in the yahd* instead of *I park the car in the yard*." In other words, Americans think of the stereotypical Boston accent as one where people drop their *r*'s.

And this is true—it is a feature of the Boston accent that the *r* is dropped in certain circumstances. In language terms, this means that Bostonians have a *non-rhotic accent*. This contrasts with a *rhotic accent*, which is one where people *do* pronounce the *r* in the equivalent circumstance. Or to put it another way, rhotic speakers pronounce *r*'s as they are written.

(Full disclosure: I grew up in the American west, and I have a rhotic accent. My wife grew up in Massachusetts, and as a younger person she had a non-rhotic accent.)

Even if you don't think much about Boston accents, you're probably familiar with this distinction, and you'd recognize these rhotic versus non-rhotic differences:

- "butter" (rhotic) versus "buttah" (non-rhotic)
- "farm" (rhotic) versus "fahm" (non-rhotic)
- "southern" (rhotic) versus "south'n" (non-rhotic)

Rhotic is a scholarly sort of way to refer to *r*-related things; *rho* is the Greek name for the letter (ρ) that we pronounce as *r*. (If you were in a fraternity or sorority in college, you probably know a bunch of Greek letters, including rho.) So a rhotic accent is an *R*-ful accent, so to speak, and a non-rhotic accent is an *R*-less one.

Rhotic accents are typical in the US, Canada, Scotland, and Ireland. Non-rhotic accents are found in England, Australia, Africa, and some other places that are associated with British English. Although the US is mostly rhotic, non-rhotic accents are found in the Northeast (Boston, New York, Maine) and in parts of the South. Non-rhotic pronunciations are also a feature of African American English (AAE).

The description that non-rhotic speakers "drop their r's" is somewhat imprecise. For one thing, non-rhotic accents are not uniform. Non-rhotic speakers in New England, in the American South, and in England can have variations in how *r*'s are handled. Even so, we can make a few generalizations about non-rhotic accents, with the proviso, as noted, that this varies a bit between accents.

One point is that non-rhotic speakers don't drop *all* their *r*'s—they still use *r*'s at the beginning of words, as in *really* and *rhotic* (ha). Generally speaking, the *r* is dropped after vowels, which means that non-rhotic speakers drop *r*'s in the middle of words. That's why the pronunciation comes out as *pahk* and *fahm* and *buttah*—these are all examples where the *r* is dropped after a vowel.

But wait, it's not that simple. To complicate things, speakers of some non-rhotic dialects pronounce an *r* if it's *followed* by a vowel. Although you might hear *cah* for *car*, you'll also hear *carry* with an *r*, because in *carry* the *r* is followed by a vowel. The vowel doesn't have to be part of the word itself. You'll also hear an *r* in *far away*, where the vowel that follows is in a separate word.

Some non-rhotic speakers even *add* an *r* when it technically shouldn't be there, as in *I sawr it* ("I saw it") or *pastar and sauce* ("pasta and sauce"). This extra *r* is called an *intrusive R* or *linking R*, the latter name because it links two vowel sounds.

Because non-rhotic speakers don't pronounce (some) written *r*'s, there's occasional confusion between the spelling and the sound of words. People have found examples of signs in non-rhotic areas where the writer added an extra written *r*—examples include signs that say "canverser" for "canvasser" and "fetter cheese" for "feta cheese."

Conversely, non-rhotic speakers will make rhymes from words that are not pronounced the same in rhotic accents, which can throw off rhotic speakers. For example, an English nursery rhyme starts with "Ride a cock-horse/To Banbury Cross." This rhymes fine if you pronounce *horse* non-rhotically, as *hoss*. Another example is the character Eeyore the donkey in the Pooh books by A. A. Milne. The name is supposed to represent the sound a donkey makes. For rhotic speakers, this might be *hee-haw*, but Milne was English, so for him, *Eeyore* is *hee-haw* without the *h*'s and of course with the *r* not pronounced.

It might occur to you that it's odd that many speakers pronounce words without an *r* even though the *r*'s are there when the words are written out. This is because non-rhoticity is a feature that developed in some dialects of English *after* we started getting a handle on our spelling system.

Historically, English was rhotic—people pronounced the *r*'s, which is why the words are spelled as they are. The loss of *r* started in England in the 1500s and spread slowly over the course of the following centuries. When colonizers left England bound for North America starting in the 1500s, they took their accents with them. The fact that most of North America is largely rhotic is a clue that most of those settlers were still pronouncing *r*'s. Other colonies like Australia, New Zealand, and South Africa were settled by English speakers later than North America, after dialects in England had started becoming non-rhotic. So those settlers took their non-rhotic accents with them.

Why do some parts of the US have non-rhotic accents? Some areas that were settled later might have had a greater influx of non-rhotic speakers. And although the US and Britain split after 1783, many Americans, particularly in the dominant cities of the Northeast, continued to look to London for cultural trends. One theory, therefore, is that the developing non-rhoticity in England was mimicked by status-conscious speakers in the US and copied by others.

In England, non-rhotic pronunciation is considered standard because it's part of the prestige dialect—the Queen's accent is non-rhotic. Non-rhotic accents had some prestige in the US—think FDR and the Kennedys—but they're also associated in places like Boston and New York with working-class speakers. And it seems like non-rhotic accents are more prevalent with older speakers in the US, meaning that in the US, non-rhotic accents might be fading. But they're still going strong in Australia and other places, so we'll still be able to talk about rhoticity for quite a while.

Related terms: epenthesis

Scunthorpe problem

In 1996, a user in the British town of Scunthorpe tried to register an account with the internet provider AOL. But he couldn't; it wouldn't accept the form he filled out that stated his name and address. He talked to the technical support people, who suggested to him that the problem was the name of the town.

It seemed that AOL's filtering software detected what it thought was profanity in the name *Scunthorpe*. (I'll leave it to you to sort out what word the filtering software found.) Tech support advised the user to enter the town name as *Sconthorpe*, changing the *u* to an *o*.

Although the user had a frustrating experience, English at large got the benefit of a new term: the *Scunthorpe problem*. This refers to the type of heavy-handed filtering for profanity that ends up blocking what are perfectly fine words.

It makes sense that a provider might want to block names, email addresses, URLs, and other strings that might contain profanity. For example, imagine that you're in charge of the website for a prominent newspaper. You don't want a commenter to register a name like FuckCapitalism and then post a series of comments that are visible to everyone. You therefore scrutinize the usernames of people who are registering so they can comment. You can't possibly do this by hand, so to speak—there are simply too many names to review—so you delegate the job to some software that works from a very long list of potentially offensive terms. A lot of software like this just looks for terms without any context, and it therefore rejects names that contain a potentially offensive term anywhere in them. Like *Scunthorpe*. (There are filters that take into account the context in which a potentially offensive string appears, but these are not as easy to create.)

During the pandemic, this happened during a conference being held by the Society of Vertebrate Paleontology. The conference had moved online, and after presentations there were Q&A sessions conducted as chats. Participants discovered that questions that included the words *pubic*, *Hell*, and even *bone* were being thwarted. As one participant noted, "Words like 'bone,' 'pubic,' and 'stream' are frankly ridiculous to ban in a field where we regularly find pubic bones in streams."[103] The conference organizers put together a spreadsheet of banned words and got the company that created the conference software to un-ban the ones that they needed. (A side note is that the filtering software blocked the surname *Wang*, which affected a number of people who were participating, but it didn't ban the name *Johnson*. This did not go unnoticed, and it points out that software can reflect the biases of the people who create it.)

Over time, the Scunthorpe problem has manifested itself in a variety of ways. According to a blog post on the topic, people with names like Cockburn and Libshitz were initially refused email addresses by their

---

[103] https://www.vice.com/en/article/dyzamj/a-profanity-filter-banned-the-word-bone-at-a-paleontology-conference

providers, and a mushroom enthusiast was unable to register the domain shitakemushrooms.com.[104] One of my colleagues at work reported that when he worked at a previous company, he was unable to do searches that involved the word *analysis*. A Twitter user reported that her university had filtered an email that included the name *Sussex*:

Dr Sandra Jansen 🔒
@sj2915

Our uni spam filter is so good that it filtered an Email that included the word 'Sussex' in the subject line.

10:17 AM · May 7, 2020 · Twitter Web App

Sometimes it's not initially clear why a term has been blocked. An online community devoted to Doctor Who supposedly blocked the word *TARDIS*. The reason turned out to be that the word contains the string *tard*. For a time the provider Yahoo! blocked email names like *Callahan*, which turned out to be because they included the string *allah*. Early in 2020, Twitter's filters blocked news of Dominic Cummings, a British political strategist, from appearing in its trending topics list, as well as blocking the hashtag *#dominiccummings*. It might take a moment to understand that the filter found the word *cumming* in the name and blocked it.

At times the problem manifests in a different way—instead of rejecting a term, the filtering software substitutes a less offensive term for the one it thinks it's found. Some filters just substitute asterisks (avoidance characters) for the offensive string. That works if the goal is to turn the word *ass* to ***, but it's an instance of the Scunthorpe problem if the filter turns *class* to *cl**** or turns *manuscript* to *m****cript*.

Other filters try to swap out the offensive string for something else. For example, the string *tit* is sometimes replaced with *breast*, resulting in words like *breastle* and *Consbreastution*. The string *butt* is so commonly swapped in for *ass* that this type of global-replacement-gone-wrong is sometimes known as a *clbuttic mistake* (*classic* > *clbuttic*):

---

[104] https://www.sporcle.com/blog/2017/04/the-scunthorpe-problem/

The Scunthorpe problem has even moved to voice interfaces. An episode of the podcast *More or Less: Behind the Stats* from the BBC was titled "Delta cases, blue tits and that one-in-two cancer claim." People who listened to the podcast using Amazon's Alexa discovered that Alexa bleeped out *tits* when reading the title.

As I noted, the Scunthorpe problem arises when filters for obscene words aren't very sophisticated. Knowing that obviously obscene words will be filtered, people find ways to work around the restrictions, using euphemisms, avoidance characters, and emoji such as peach and eggplant.

And there are some real challenges. I'm always entertained by stories of people who try to sneak vanity license plates that have innuendo past the censors at the DMV. An article on Jalopnik.com lists 100 license plates that were banned by the licensing agency in the state of California.[105] Given how many commenters on the article are mystified by why the plates might be offensive, it's clear why software alone can never save us from people's determination to say something naughty.

Related terms: minced oath

---

[105] https://jalopnik.com/100-license-plates-banned-by-the-california-dmv-5830513

semantic bleaching

When I was a young person, we were guarded about saying the word *suck*. Whatever the origins were of saying that something *sucked*, it sounded sort of dirty to us, and it was not for polite company.[106] But during the course of my lifetime, the word *suck* in the expression *that sucks* went from being vulgar to a word that appears on bumper stickers ("Mean People Suck").

This is an example of *semantic bleaching*, a process by which a once-powerful word loses its oomph. Another example is *bitch* in a phrase like *Bitch, please* to mean something like "Are you kidding?" Hearing "Bitch, please" can be startling to those who are not used to this bleached sense when it's produced by, say, 11-year-olds. The word *dick* likewise seems to be undergoing some bleaching, from a pronouncedly vulgar word for "penis" to something more akin to "annoying or contemptible person," with the useful adjectival form *dickish*.

These examples of semantic bleaching are relatively recent, within the last generation or so. But we have plenty of historical instances of semantic bleaching in English. A good example is the word *terrible*, which means "very bad," as in "That performance was terrible." But the original sense of the word is still sort of visible: *terrible* originally meant something that inspired terror. You can see this meaning in the line "He hath loosed the fatal lightning of his terrible swift sword" from the 19th-century poem "Battle Hymn of the Republic." That's a sword that inspires terror, not one that's very bad. Today, the word *terrible* is bleached enough that you can say something like "That meeting was terribly boring."

In "terribly boring," *terribly* works as an intensifier. A number of other qualifiers also show the effect of semantic bleaching. The word *very* comes from Latin "true" (*verus*), but we just use it to mean "more." Another example is *really*, which we likewise use only as an intensifier and don't usually mean as "in a true way." A particularly good example is the

---

[106] Although we kids might have suspected that *that sucks* alluded to something sexual, it's also possible that *suck* to mean "bad, objectionable" came from *suck eggs* or *suck hind teat*. No matter; we considered it in the realm of taboo words, and the sense of *suck* to mean "to be no good" is still listed in Merriam-Webster as "slang, sometimes vulgar."

word *pretty*. In a sentence like "That couch is pretty ugly," *pretty* means "somewhat," not "beautiful." That sure is some bleaching.

Semantic bleaching is also how we got what seems like a contradictory sense of *literally*, as in a sentence like "I laughed so hard I was literally dying." In a usage like this, literally is just another bleached intensifier, like **terribly** *boring*, **pretty** *ugly*, and **awful** *nice*. As with these other usages, there's no real danger that the bleached sense is ambiguous and that the person speaking is literally—as in, for real—dying.

As you saw in the earlier example, semantic bleaching can soften taboo words. The word *shit*, a sturdy Anglo-Saxon word for feces, still has that meaning. But in other uses it's been bleached to mean something like "stuff" ("I left my shit at his house") or "disapproval" ("She gave me shit about the stain on my shirt"). It can even function as a contronym ("Pancakes is the shit," an example on Urban Dictionary.)

Even more recently, the term *WTF* or *wtf* has started becoming bleached. This started as an abbreviation for *what the fuck*. I was interested to note that I've seen instances of the abbreviated *wtf* creep into chat-room exchanges at work. You'd probably be pretty surprised to see someone write *what the fuck* at work, but the corresponding *wtf* abbreviation has become bleached enough to be making tentative appearances in informal work forums like chat. In a Twitter poll by the linguist Laura Bailey, 49.6% of the respondents reported that for them, *wtf* and *what the fuck* are "meaningfully different."

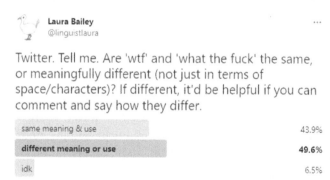

Laura Bailey
@linguistlaura

Twitter. Tell me. Are 'wtf' and 'what the fuck' the same, or meaningfully different (not just in terms of space/characters)? If different, it'd be helpful if you can comment and say how they differ.

same meaning & use	43.9%
different meaning or use	49.6%
idk	6.5%

230 votes · Final results

8:46 AM · Oct 29, 2020

Another recent bleaching is the term *AF* (or *af*), which stands for *as fuck*. A good example is a tweet by @Schreids that reads "Today I learned that a) Lake Superior had a Twitter account and b) it's salty AF":

Michaela Schreiter
@Schreids

Today I learned that a) Lake Superior had a Twitter account and b) it's salty AF.

Theoretically speaking anyways, it's obviously fresh water.

⟶ **Lake Superior** @LakeSuperior · Dec 21, 2022
This impending storm better be as good as they say it is. I'm going for thirty footers.

9:56 AM · Dec 22, 2022 from Mississippi Mills, Ontario

The term *AF* has become bleached enough that the Coca-Cola company can play slyly with its meaning in an advertisement for their Aguas Frescas brand of soft drinks:

Because semantic bleaching weakens strong terms, people have to continually come up with new terms to get their (strong) point across. This is sometimes referred to as the *hyperbole treadmill*. The insult that would have shocked your grandparents barely registers today. On page 83 of his book *Three Scientists and Their Gods* (1988), the writer Robert Wright described the process of semantic bleaching (which he calls *overextension*) this way:

Forty years ago, if a person said "damn," you could safely infer that something had gone really wrong. The word was reserved for things like stubbed toes, missed trains, and the discovery that a spouse had somehow accumulated matchbooks from several dozen local motels. Then people started using it for lesser occasions: running out of milk, missing the first five minutes of *Perry Mason*. As *damn* was thus diluted, its original function was assumed by *shit*. Damn became the equivalent of *darn*, which then faded out of the picture altogether. By the end of the 1970s, though, *shit*, too, had fallen prey to overuse. In its place came various crude references to sex, and eventually even these expletives became commonplace. The search for alternatives is well underway and has yielded great bursts of creativity. But meanwhile, in mainstream America, far from the cutting edge of profanity, the crisis grows: it is getting harder and harder to vent deep anguish.

At work here is a general principle: any word or phrase used too loosely loses its meaning. Thus, *wonderful, fantastic,* and *awesome*—which at one time had specific and separate meanings—now mean merely "very good."

The bleaching of formerly shocking terms presented an interesting challenge to the writers of the TV series *Deadwood*. The writers wanted to convey the roughness of the residents of a town in the US frontier in the 1880s. They wrote a lot of swearing into the character's speech, but the vulgarity is modern—that is, the swearwords used in the series are anachronistic. As the linguist Geoff Nunberg pointed out, 19th-century swearing would have involved blasphemy, not sex. But words like *hell* and *goddam* have been so bleached in the 21st century that the writers had to substitute more up-to-date swearing in order to convey the level of vulgarity that they were aiming for.

The opposite of semantic bleaching happens as well—when words become taboo. For more on that, see the entry for pejoration.

Related terms: genericization, minced oath, pejoration

semantic broadening, semantic narrowing

The meanings of words tend to feel stable to us; we learn the meanings of words, and those largely stay the same on the timescale of our lives. But meanings are not fixed, and a surprising number of word meanings have slipped around over the course of the centuries.

The word *barn* once referred specifically to a place to store barley; it comes from an Old English term *bere-ern*, meaning "barley place." Obviously, today we use the word *barn* to refer to a building that stores many types of things, including bales of hay, cows, and tractors. Along those lines, the word *kidnap* originally referred to snatching (nabbing) a child (kid)—in the 17th century, children used to be snatched and then shipped off to work in the colonies ("foreign plantations"), yikes. Today you can use *kidnap* for adults.

Both *barn* and *kidnap* have undergone a process called *semantic broadening*, where their meaning expands. Because the word becomes more general, this is also called *semantic generalization*.

The semantic broadening of the words *barn* and *kidnap* took place a long time ago, but semantic broadening has occurred more recently as well. One more contemporary example is the word *cool* to mean "in vogue" instead of just referring to temperature. The word *tea* referred originally to the infusion made from tea leaves. In modern English, *tea* has broadened to mean an infusion of almost anything, as in *mint tea*. And in some parts of the UK, *tea* has broadened even further to mean a complete evening meal, as this tweet from a UK-based editor shows:

Kia Thomas | Fiction Editor
@KiaThomasEdits

Someone else please make tea (dinner, for Americans and posh people) for me. There are no words for how much I do not want to do it.

Another kind of semantic broadening occurs when brand names are genericized, such as how *coke* is sometimes used (especially in the American South) as a generalized term to mean "soft drink."

There's also an opposite effect called *semantic narrowing*, where the meaning becomes more specific over time. The word *meat* once referred generally to food. For example, Old English had the word *morgen-mete*, which translates as "morning food"—in other words, breakfast. This original meaning of *meat* (or *mete*) as "food" explains the idiom "One man's meat is another man's poison." Now, of course, *meat* refers just to the flesh of animals. The word *deer* originally referred just to animals, but over time its meaning narrowed to refer only to certain types of ruminants. (The word *deer* is cognate with the German word *tier*, which just means "animal." In German, the word didn't undergo semantic narrowing.) The word *girl* once referred to a child of either sex or to a young person, but starting in medieval times the word started narrowing to refer to, well, girls.

A more current example is the word *crafting*. A traditional definition of *to craft* is to "make or manufacture." But today we have branched off a narrowed sense that describes a hobby: "making decorative articles by hand," as one definition puts it.[107] Another example is *gaming*, which has narrowed senses of "gambling" (as in the Nevada Gaming Commission, which oversees gambling regulations) and more recently refers to "the playing of computer or video games."

It's never clear why or when a term will broaden or narrow. In the case of *deer*, it's possible that other terms became available (*animal*) that allowed *deer* to take on a more specialized meaning. But the range of possible reasons for semantic change is quite lengthy, and includes "social reasons," fuzziness, and taboos.

Related terms: contronym, genericization, semantic bleaching

shibboleth

There's a city in the state of Washington named Sequim. An almost sure way to tell if someone is from the state of Washington is how they pronounce the name. Locals know it as "squim," a startingly unintuitive pronunciation. Anything else—"see-quim" is a common first try for non-locals—immediately shows that one is an outsider.

---

[107] https://www.lexico.com/en/definition/crafting

The name *Sequim* therefore functions as a *shibboleth*: a pronunciation, a word choice, or some other usage that identifies a person as a member (or not) of a group. Around the Seattle area, other shibboleths are the pronunciation of the city of Puyallup ("pew-AL-up"), the name of the big farmer's market downtown ("Pike Place Market" or just "the market"), and how to refer to Mt. Rainier ("The mountain is out" for "Mt. Rainier is visible"). Say anything else and you just won't sound like you're from around these parts.

The word *shibboleth* comes from ancient Hebrew, where it refers to a stream (or ear of corn, depending on whom you ask). This word became interesting because in Biblical times, due to dialectical differences between tribes of the Israelites, some groups couldn't pronounce the initial *sh*, instead saying "sibboleth." (The story sure makes it sound like the phonotactics of the Ephraimites didn't allow them to put a *sh* sound at the beginning of a word.)

At one point there was a battle between the Gileadites ("shibboleth"-sayers) and the Ephraimites ("sibboleth"-sayers, no *sh-*). The Gileadites won the battle and afterward guarded the fords across the River Jordan. In the Old Testament, Judges 12:5-6 tells the sad story:

5 And the Gileadites took the passages of Jordan before the Ephraim-ites: and it was so, that when those Ephraimites which were escaped said, Let me go over; that the men of Gilead said unto him, Art thou an Ephraimite? If he said, Nay;

6 Then said they unto him, Say now Shibboleth: and he said Sibbo-leth: for he could not frame to pronounce it right. Then they took him, and slew him at the passages of Jordan: and there fell at that time of the Ephraimites forty and two thousand.

This violent origin story has, sadly, been repeated many times in history. A relatively recent example was the so-called Parsley Massacre that took place in 1937 in the Dominican Republic. In that case, people who could not properly pronounce *perejil* (the Spanish word for "parsley") were killed.

Most shibboleths are more benign. A familiar shibboleth in North America is the pronunciation of the letter *Z*. Americans say "zee"; Cana-dians say "zed." There's a story, one that's hard to verify, from the era of the Vietnam War. American border patrol personnel might suspect that someone entering the US from Canada was a draft dodger who'd escaped to Canada but was hoping to make a surreptitious visit back home. The story goes that these border personnel would ask the visitor to say the alphabet as fast as he could. If a man said "zee" instead of "zed," he would be unmasked as an American. Or anyway, that's how I heard the story. Whether the story is true or not, it's a good example of how a shibboleth works.

As I was showing earlier, local names for landmarks are often shibboleths. People who are not from the state of Oregon often pronounce the name as "ORE-eh-gone," which is not how the locals say it ("ORE-eh-gun"). For example, in the Steely Dan song "Don't Take Me Alive," you can tell that Donald Fagen, who's singing in the first person about a boy from Oregon, is not from that state by the way he pronounces the name.

Southern Californians have La Jolla ("la HOY-ya"). Many names in California are of Spanish origin, but for many of them, the shibboleth is that locals pronounce the names using English vowels, like "San PEE-dro" for San Pedro or "Los FEE-liss" for Los Feliz.

In New York City, Houston Street is pronounced "HOW-stun," which differs from the name of the city of Houston in Texas ("HEW-stun"). Apparently people from Milwaukee pronounce the name with two syllables ("Mwockee"), and if you use three, you're obviously an outsider. And as anyone who's traveled around the UK knows, the British Isles are a minefield of shibboleths based on the pronunciations of local place names.

Shibboleths can also involve word choices. People in western Pennsylvania (and famously in Pittsburgh) use the word *yinz* for the plural of *you* (equivalent to *y'all* or *youse* in other dialects). This is such a clear shibboleth that Pittsburgh natives are sometimes referred to as *yinzers*. Another example is the habit of Southern Californians of adding *the* to the names of freeways ("the 405"), a habit that distinguishes them even from people in the northern part of the state.

The Gershwin song "Let's Call the Whole Thing Off" plays on shibboleths involving the pronunciation of the word *tomato* (to-MAY-to/to-MAH-to). In the song, the different pronunciations of a catalog of words, including *tomato, laughter, either, oysters, after*, and *pajamas*, are shibboleths that tell us that the couple in the song are incompatible because they belong to different social groups. (There's a happy ending, though.)

Shibboleths don't just mark tribal associations or identify groups by where they live. They can also act as class markers. A Tumblr post has a long list of names that you'd better pronounce correctly if you want to sound well educated, at least in some circles—names like Roland Barthes, J. M. Coetzee, Chuck Palahniuk, and Thomas Piketty.[108]

Shibboleths are also ways for young people to exclude older people. It's a truism that by the time parents have started adopting the linguistic habits of their kids—everything from vocabulary to whether to put a period at the end of a text message—the kids have moved on to new and exclusionary ways of communicating. (For more on periods in text messages, see the entry for pejoration.) Basically, any group that develops its own way of speaking (which is pretty much every group) will have shibboleths that help members of the group identify each other and, importantly, to identify who doesn't belong.

An editor once made a shibboleth-y observation about the use of the en dash, which is a kind of dash (–) that's sized between a hyphen (-) and a full dash (—). This relatively rare piece of punctuation has certain uses that most people wouldn't recognize or bother with ... but editors do. As the editor said:

> Of course, the only practical use of the en dash is as subtle code to communicate, from one publishing professional to another, the abstract concept, "I am copy editor. Hear me roar." Recognizing the en dash can be like a secret handshake to our club.

Related terms: familect

singular *they*

Fill in the missing pronoun in the following sentences:

Someone called, but _____ didn't leave a message.

Hey, look, someone dropped _____ notebook.

---

[108] https://lazenby.tumblr.com/post/109628210407/list-of-shibboleth-names

Everyone should bring _____ own lunch.

If a person is treated that way, who can blame _____ for complaining?

This can be a little tricky. You could use *he*:

Someone called, but **he** didn't leave a message.

Hey, look, someone dropped **his** notebook.

However, using *he* in these sentences would strongly suggest that you think the unknown person is a man. You could try accommodating everyone:

Everyone should bring **his or her** own lunch

If a person is treated that way, who can blame **him or her** for complaining?

This is an equitable solution, in the sense that it tries to cover all possibilities. But no one actually talks like that, and even in the sometimes starchy world of professional editing, the *his or her* option is considered awkward.

The problem is that Modern English doesn't have an *epicene pronoun*—a pronoun that can refer in a gender-free way to someone in the sentence. If we know the sex of the person we're referring to, we can choose *he* or *she*. (*A woman called, but **she** didn't leave a message.*) But if you just don't know, it's hard to make that choice.

We work around this limitation in a couple of ways. One solution historically has been to use generic *he*—that is, to use the masculine (*he, him, his*) to refer to persons of unknown gender: *A fool and his money are soon parted.* (This is an example where the masculine form—*he, him, his*—is being used as a hypernym.) Biblical text was originally written (translated) this way, as in this passage (John 14:21) from the King James Version: "He that loveth me shall be loved of my Father, and I will love him, and will manifest myself to him." Many laws use *he* as the default pronoun, including the US Constitution: "[no person] shall be compelled in any criminal case to be a witness against himself."

But this is often unsatisfactory. The *he*-ness of generic *he* proved to be slippery, as when 19th-century suffragettes in the US discovered that legislatures sometimes insisted that laws had been written with generic *man* and *he* in mind (taxes) but other times insisted that the law meant gendered *man* and *he* (voting).

In contemporary use, generic *he* often doesn't work well either. This becomes evident in a sentence like *Every teacher must bring **his** own laptop computer*, or even better, *A nurse is expected to provide **his** own stethoscope*. As noted, one solution is to include both pronouns (*his or her own laptop*), but this approach is clunky and artificial.

A solution that's sometimes proposed for longer, formal written text is to alternate pronouns. A style guide that I have on the shelf (published in 2012) suggests this: "If you need to make third-party references to more than one person in the same document, use *he* for some individuals and *she* for others." This approach has a few downsides, though. It puts a burden on the writer to make sure they have an equitable distribution of pronouns. And there's a subtle problem that the distribution of *he* and *she* can end up distributed into traditional gender roles, like *he* for programmers and *she* for support roles. Switching between *he* and *she* can also be noticeable to readers, bringing something to the foreground that might distract the reader from the goal of the text.

But there is a solution that we use in vernacular English all the time—namely, singular *they*:

Someone called, but ***they*** didn't leave a message.

Hey, look, someone dropped ***their*** notebook.

This solution has a long history in English. It was and is extremely common in spoken English. In earlier periods, it wasn't particularly remarkable even in written works; Jane Austen used it many times in her novels, as did Henry Fielding in *Tom Jones*.

However, the usage came to be considered inelegant or incorrect for formal English in the 19th and 20th centuries. The sticking point is the logic of grammar—*they* is usually plural. In its textbook usage, *they* references a plural noun and takes a plural verb. Per this thinking, using *they* to refer to a singular thing is ungrammatical. (*Some**one** called and said that **they are** going to call back later.*)

But a problem with this line of argument is that we have this situation also with the pronoun *you*, and we (mostly) manage fine. You can use *you* when you're addressing one person or several, and it always takes a plural verb (*you are*). There are times when it's unclear in context whether *you* refers to more than one person, and in spoken English we therefore often use words like *youse* or *y'all* or *yinz* or *you guys* when we want to clarify that we mean plural *you*. But in standard written English, it's *you* for both the singular and plural second person. (I'll observe that the use of *you guys* for the second-person plural is not without controversy. For most people, the word *guy* is marked for masculine, but *guys* in the plural is, for many people, bleached enough to work for any collection of people.)

To come to grips with the issue of the missing epicene pronoun, many suggestions have been floated over the last few centuries for invented gender-neutral pronouns. Ideas have included *E* (capitalized to match *I*), *zie, hir, hiser, hesh, ne, um, tey, heer*, and *thon*, a blend of *that* and *one*. The linguist Dennis Baron wrote an entire book about the history of epicene pronouns in English (*What's Your Pronoun? Beyond He & She*).

How well did these efforts work? A couple of the suggestions—especially *thon*—got a lot of discussion. And a few of the proposals did make it into dictionaries, albeit labeled as "suggested" words. Some individual suggestions were championed by writers who did their best to promote a new pronoun by using it in their works. Swedish has had some success in introducing a new epicene pronoun (*hen*). But so far none of the proposed epicene pronouns have been accepted by style guides for formal writing or have made it into everyday speech as an improvement on singular *they*. (However, hold that thought.)

In recent years, editorial opinion has shifted (if at times grudgingly) to acknowledge that singular *they* is widely used and is acceptable. In 2017, the Associated Press style guide updated its guidance to allow singular *they* "when alternative wording is overly awkward or clumsy." The *Chicago Manual of Style* accepts singular *they* in informal writing in the types of constructions that I'm using here as examples.

Which brings up another issue associated with singular *they*. In all of the preceding examples, singular *they* has referred to an unnamed person whose sex isn't known or to impersonal antecedents like *someone* or *everyone*. In the last few years, another use for singular *they* has emerged—namely, as a pronoun to refer to someone who does not identify as either male or female. For a person like that, neither *he* nor *she* is an appropriate pronoun, and many people in this situation request that they be referred to using *they*: *April sent me **their** draft document*. People often have the option to specify their preferred pronouns, and for many people, that pronoun is *they*.

Among the style guides I mentioned earlier, Chicago is clear about using singular *they* as someone's preferred pronoun: "a person's stated preference for a specific pronoun should be respected." They add: "This usage is still not widespread either in speech or in writing, but Chicago accepts it even in formal writing."

The question of a pronoun for nonbinary people has generated interest again in the possibility of an invented pronoun. When asked to list their preferred pronouns, some people have offered pronouns (or *neopronouns*) like *ze*, *zie*, *e*, and *ey*, among others. A difference from earlier discussions is that these proposals are often personal: the question is "What's *your* pronoun?", not necessarily what the pronoun should be for everyone.

In effect, the need to recognize the grammatical needs of nonbinary people cracked open the discussion of whether and when we can use singular *they*. The feminist movements that started in the 19th century eventually forced us to admit that generic *he* was not a good solution. And the contemporary discussions of how to refer to people who identify as nonbinary obliged us to come up with a pronoun that was neither *he* nor *she*. As it turns out, one solution to our need for an epicene pronoun has been there all along—namely, singular *they*.

Related terms: hypernym

skunked term

Think about the word *nonplussed* in the following sentence:

> When I answered the door in my underwear, the delivery person was nonplussed.

Some people who hear this will think that *nonplussed* means that the delivery person was taken aback. Others will think that the delivery person was unfazed.

You can look up *nonplussed* in a dictionary, where you'll find that the primary meaning is "unsure about what to say, think, or do: perplexed" (Merriam-Webster). But enough people use *nonplussed* to mean "unfazed" that a few dictionaries also list a meaning like "not bothered, surprised, or impressed by something" (same dictionary).

It appears that the meaning of *nonplussed* is in the process of shifting in such a way that different people have almost opposite interpretations of what it means. This puts a writer into a quandary. You might want to use the word *nonplussed* in something you're writing, and you're confident that you know that it means "perplexed." (After all, you just looked it up.) But lots of people might misinterpret the term to mean "unfazed," which means they'll take away the wrong meaning from what you're writing.

This makes *nonplussed* a *skunked term*: a term that people avoid because its meaning or use is disputed. You don't know how people will interpret a term or react to it, so you just stay away from it. ("Much as people are afraid to approach a dog that has been 'skunked' because it stinks," my editor contributes.) Skunked terms have become lexical pariahs.

A word or expression becomes skunked when it's in the process of undergoing "a marked change from one use to another," as Bryan Garner describes it in his style guide *Garner's Modern English Usage*. That is, the word is undergoing *semantic drift*—its meaning is changing enough that the old and new meanings are significantly different.

Some people will know and insist on the old meaning; other people will use the term with a different meaning. (*Nonplussed* is not just changing meaning; it's becoming a contronym.) In formal situations, you might therefore want to steer around it. "To the writer or speaker for whom credibility is important, it's a good idea to avoid distracting any readers or listeners," says Garner.

As an example, Garner talks about the word *hopefully* as used in a sentence like the following:

Hopefully we'll get there before the store closes.

Although this usage is widespread today, some people (Group 1) maintain that it is incorrect to use *hopefully* as a sentence-level modifier, and that *hopefully* means only "in a hopeful manner." Others are perfectly fine with this usage and might not even understand what the issue is (Group 2). People who are aware of this split decision on *hopefully* might decide to avoid using *hopefully* altogether, and thus *hopefully* becomes a skunked term. Here's Garner's description:

> "[H]opefully" is now unusable: some members of Group 1 continue to stigmatize the newer meaning, and any member of Group 2 would find the old meaning peculiar.

I think a lot of people would be surprised to hear someone suggest that *hopefully* is "unusable."

Garner lists some other words that he considers skunked terms: *data* (singular or plural?), *decimate, effete, enormity, fulsome, impassionate, intrigue,* and *transpire.* (Where you are with these words, and whether you even know what the controversy is about them, is probably a good indicator of how much you worry about using skunked terms.)

Other terms that are undergoing semantic drift and might be considered skunked are *aggravate, bemused, disinterested,* and *notorious.* A term that I personally hesitate to use is *hoi polloi,* because although the dictionary definition is "the common people," I suspect that a lot of people think it means the high-class people, perhaps because it sounds like *hoity-toity.*

The term *bi-monthly* is probably skunked. The word has an established meaning of "every other month," but lots of use it to mean "twice per month" (i.e., they interpret it as "semi-monthly"). So if you want to be sure that your readers understand that you mean "every other month," you should avoid *bi-monthly* and use a different term instead.

The editor Max Weiss posted a poll on Twitter asking people about the expression *deceptively simple.* Do people think it means "Seems simple, is complex," or does it mean "Seems complex, is simple"?

Max Weiss ✓
@maxthegirl

···

Time for a poll I've done more than once, but I never tire of!
Deceptively simple means:

Seems simple, is complex	46.8%
Seems complex, is simple	**53.2%**

741 votes · Final results

1:06 PM · Nov 20, 2020 · Twitter Web App

The results were almost even (47% and 53%, respectively). That seems to be about as clear an indicator as you can get that *deceptively simple* is a skunked term and should be avoided by anyone who wants to avoid misinterpretation.

A skunked term can be the source of the pedant's veto, where writers avoid a term or a usage because they don't want to annoy sticklers and pedants. That's the case with many of the terms listed earlier from Garner, like the sentence-scope *hopefully* question, and with terms like *beg the question*. But not always; sometimes it's just a matter of not wanting to be misinterpreted by readers. Heaven knows it's hard enough to write clearly even without using words that readers might read differently from what we intend.

But at some point, new usages *do* get accepted. The author and educator Ben Yagoda once wrote, "For a new usage to become accepted, somewhere along the way CUI [changing usage impulse] must infect some proportion of the populace; then it spreads until resistance would be equally difficult and futile."[109] You could argue that expressions like *beg the question* to mean "raise the question" and sentence-modifying *hopefully* are so widely accepted now that they have passed through their phases of being skunked terms and that arguing to the contrary is just being, well, contrary.

Related terms: etymological fallacy, pedant's veto, zombie rule

---

[109] https://www.chronicle.com/blogs/linguafranca/cui

snowclone

In the original Star Wars movie (*Episode IV: A New Hope*), the character Obi-Wan Kenobi, the hero Luke Skywalker, and two droids are stopped at a roadblock by some imperial stormtroopers. The troopers are on the lookout for droids carrying secret plans. Obi-Wan, using his Jedi mind tricks, waves his hand at the trooper in command and says, "These aren't the droids you're looking for." The trooper turns to the other soldiers, says, "These aren't the droids we're looking for," and then lets the party proceed.

The expression *These aren't the droids you're looking for* caught people's attention as a way to say that someone was barking up the wrong tree. Soon enough people started substituting other words for *droids* to convey other ways in which you might be being fooled (all of these are from real source):

> These aren't the security updates you're looking for (instead, it's malware)

> These aren't the smartwatches you're looking for (they're disappointing)

> These aren't the data files you're looking for (has your organization been breached?)

> These aren't the feminists you're looking for (they're just celebrity spokespersons)

What happened was that the original expression *These aren't the droids you're looking for* became a *snowclone*: an expression that's based on the pattern of a well-known phrase. You know many snowclones, like these:

> Got Aloha?

> Orange is the new black

> To vaccinate or not to vaccinate

> Yes, Virginia, there is life after retirement

The term *snowclone* came about because the linguist Geoff Pullum had been writing about the shopworn notion that Inuit-speaking people have many words for snow, as in this sentence from an article in the *Economist*: "If Eskimos have dozens of words for snow, Germans have as many for bureaucracy." When it was pointed out to Pullum that this type of comparison to "words for snow" was made often, he observed that …

[W]e need a name for … a multi-use, customizable, instantly recognizable, time-worn, quoted or misquoted phrase or sentence that can be used in an entirely open array of different jokey variants by lazy journalists and writers.[110]

The term *snowclone* was suggested in 2004 by Glen Whitman, an economist, and was soon blessed by Pullum.

For snowclones to be effective, they require the reader or listener to understand the pattern on which they're based. That way, the snowclone can borrow some of the meaning of the original and play with it. For example, examples that use the snowclone *Yes, Virginia* … require the reader to understand the original story of "Yes, Virginia, there is a Santa Claus" (originally a newspaper editorial). The snowclone then plays with the theme of the original—the affirmation of a belief that might have been called into doubt.

Similarly, *Orange is the new black* is based on the snowclone "(some color) is the new black," a fashion cliché.[111] The expression is the title of a book (later TV series) about a middle-class woman who goes to jail, so orange refers to the color of her prison garb.

Expressions that include "the new black" are not the only variant on the *X is the new Y* snowclone. It also works for ages ("60 is the new 40"), hair color ("gray is the new blonde"), vacation destinations ("Sicily is the new Tuscany"), and many more.

You probably recognize *To vaccinate or not to vaccinate* as a snowclone based on the famous line from *Hamlet* ("To be or not to be"). And if you're from the US, you probably recognize that the expression *Got Aloha?* is based on the snowclone "Got X?" This originated as the "Got Milk?" advertising campaign for a California-based dairy board. The snowclone works as a way to promote practically anything—that is, you can substitute whatever you want for *X* in *Got X?*

---

[110] http://itre.cis.upenn.edu/~myl/languagelog/archives/000061.html
[111] Ultimately attributed to the fashion editor Diana Vreeland, but also misquoted; she was referring to the use of pink in India as equivalent not to black, but to navy blue. This is not the first time that a quotation got garbled on its path to popularity.

An emergent snowclone, so to speak, is the pattern *It's not ___ unless it comes from the __ region of France, otherwise it's sparkling ___*. This is based originally on an assertion about wine: It's not champagne unless it comes from the Champagne region of France; otherwise it's sparkling wine. (The use of the word *champagne* to refer only to wine from the Champagne region is the law in many countries, but not in the US.[112])

There have been a lot of variants on this snowclone, like these that I found on Twitter:

> A friend emailed to remind me that it's not a Quarantine unless it comes from the Quarantine region of France. Otherwise, it's just Sparkling Isolation. (Nancy Pearl)

> it's not a podcast unless it comes from the podcast region of france, otherwise it's just a sparkling radio show. (a pale slim ghost)

> It's not a real Kraken unless it comes from the Kraken region of France. Otherwise it's just sparkling calamari. (Simon Little)

At one point (no longer, it appears), the ThinkGeek site sold the following snowcloney t-shirt, based on the gamer phrase "im in ur base killin ur doods":

---

[112] https://www.champagne.fr/en/about-champagne/a-great-blended-wine/champagne-designation

The brand consultant Nancy Friedman uses the term *sloganclone* for ad campaigns that use snowclones in their slogans. For example, she's found a whole series of ads in which the tagline ends with "one X at a time," where *X* has been *story, plank, student, truth,* and *handbag,* to name just a few recent examples.

The linguist Erin O'Connor created a kind of database of snowclones, inspired by the Eggcorn Database. ("Snowclones are the new eggcorns," as she says on the About page.[113]) It's fun to browse through her examples—I guarantee that you'll find many familiar expressions and that you had no idea that there were so many snowclones out there.

Related terms: malaphor

spelling alphabet

Probably you've had to spell your name out loud to a clerk over the phone or in a government office. If so, you might have noticed that a number of the letters in our alphabet sound the same. For example, *B* and *D* and *P* and *V* can be hard to distinguish, particularly if you're talking on a cellphone or through a pandemic mask.

People often use the "as in" approach to make clear what letter they mean by saying something like B *as in* boy, D *as in* dog, and so on. Some people might have worked out a complete alphabet with a word for each letter. For example, the linguist Arnold Zwicky created an alphabet for himself that's based entirely on the names of ungulates: "Z as in zebra, W as in water buffalo, I as in ibex, …". But most people probably have just a few of these letter-word associations that they use for particularly troublesome letters, perhaps spelling a name like this: "P as in puppy, O, P as in puppy again, E." (This example is inspired by true events.)

This casual approach works fine for occasional interactions. But if you're running an organization of millions that routinely needs to communicate by voice under suboptimal conditions, you want to work out a system. This was a problem that the military faced when they started us-

---

[113] https://snowclones.org/about

ing radio communications. So they invented what's called a *spelling alphabet*: a set of words that represent letters of the alphabet when reading aloud. Spelling alphabets are sometimes referred to (though technically not correctly) as *phonetic alphabets*. (For more on phonetic alphabets, see the entry for International Phonetic Alphabet.)

Here's an example of a spelling alphabet that's used internationally:

A=Alfa	J=Juliett	S=Sierra
B=Bravo	K=Kilo	T=Tango
C=Charlie	L=Lima	U=Uniform
D=Delta	M=Mike	V=Victor
E=Echo	N=November	W=Whiskey
F=Foxtrot	O=Oscar	X=Xray
G=Golf	P=Papa	Y=Yankee
H=Hotel	Q=Quebec	Z=Zulu
I=India	R=Romeo	

Early spelling alphabets, such as those used by the British military in World War I, did the same thing that you and I might do while talking on the phone: they had words just for the sounds that are especially hard to distinguish. Over time, spelling alphabets were developed that had words for each letter. Different spelling alphabets developed in different branches of the military and in different countries. Commercial enterprises such as Western Union also had their own variants.

After World War II, international NATO forces settled on the spelling alphabet listed above. Countries that have additional letters, such as the umlauts in German, have additional entries for this otherwise standard list of words. The alphabet is also used in commercial aviation so that pilots can spell out flight numbers clearly across the world.

Spelling alphabets have to be carefully designed. After all, you don't want a spelling alphabet where the words for different letters are hard to distinguish—you wouldn't want to use *bear* for *B* and *care* for *C*, since these would be easily confused. In addition, if the alphabet is used internationally, as with NATO forces and with commercial airline pilots, the alphabet must include words that radio operators from different nationalities would be able to pronounce and hear clearly.

A few terms (letters?) from spelling alphabets have moved into mainstream English. If someone says "Roger" in reply to a request, they're echoing an older spelling alphabet, where *Roger* stood for *R* and was used for "received." During the Vietnam War, American soldiers referred to enemy combatants as Charlie, which was half of "Victor Charlie"—in other words, VC, or Viet Cong.

My daughter recently said she was trying to come up with a spelling alphabet for her work that was "less militaristic." From this discussion I learned that for a while, people could upload their versions to the My Phonetic Alphabets site (now sadly dormant), which has some funny and inventive takes on spelling out loud, such as an alphabet based on Disney movies.

A few years ago, I memorized the NATO spelling alphabet just for fun. (I would practice by reading license plates out loud while stuck in traffic.) When I need to spell my name out loud these days, I can reel off Papa-Oscar-Papa-Echo without even thinking about it. Ironically, this doesn't always improve the situation; some people just look at me blankly. As with all communications, both the sender and the receiver have to be on the same channel.

Related terms: International Phonetic Alphabet (IPA)

squinting modifier (two-way modifier)

I love finding ambiguity, so I'm fond of something called *squinting modifiers*, also called *two-way modifiers*. Here's an example:

The man we talked to **recently** won a contest.

In the example, *recently* can modify *talked*, so that the sentence means that we talked to the man recently. Or it can modify *won*, meaning that the man won a contest recently.

Squinting modifiers cause ambiguity because they can modify either what precedes or what follows. They can be explained as a form of attachment ambiguity—namely, as a matter of where in a sentence's "tree" the modifier is attached.

Here are some more examples:

Eating fatty foods *frequently* is bad for your health.

Writing *clearly* is hard.

I told my boss *this morning* I was sick.

In the first sentence, *frequently* can refer to how often you eat fatty foods, or it can refer to how often it's bad for your health to do so. The second sentence can be interpreted either as "It's hard to write clearly" or as "Obviously, writing is hard." (It might not be clear which meaning is intended, but both interpretations are true, if you ask me.) In the last sentence, it's not clear whether you told your boss this morning, or you're sick this morning, or perhaps both.

The word *often* is a nice way to make squinting modifiers because its placement in a sentence is pretty free. The following is a good example from *Merriam-Webster's Dictionary of English Usage*:

Laughing *often* can be embarrassing.

Why are they called *squinting* modifiers? When I think of the word *squint*, I don't think of it as a different way to say "two-way"; I only use the word to mean a narrowing of the eyes. The linguist Neal Whitman tracked this question down in an entertaining blog post.[114] It turns out that this construction was first described in French as *construction louche* and was then translated literally (that is, calqued) into English. One of the meanings of the word *louche* is "cross-eyed." A technical meaning in English of *squint* is "to have the axes of the eyes not coincident" or "to cause to look obliquely." It's this "cross-wise" sense of *squint* that explains the name.

As with many cases of ambiguity, it's usually obvious to the speaker or writer what the intention is of the squinting modifier. But it might not be so clear to listeners and especially to readers. Editors often spot and fix instances of squinting modifiers, thereby reducing ambiguity, though sadly this is at the expense of amusement for those of us who love ambiguity.

Related terms: attachment ambiguity

---

[114] https://literalminded.wordpress.com/2011/03/02/squint/

syllable acronym

An acronym, as we know, is an abbreviation made up of the first letters of a series of words: *AWOL* (for "absent without official leave"), *NATO* (for "North Atlantic Treaty Organization"), and *scuba* (for "self-contained underwater breathing apparatus"), to name just a few.[115]

So what do we make of a word like *sci-fi*, as in a *sci-fi book*? This is an abbreviated form of "science fiction." It isn't quite an acronym, though, because it includes more than just the initial letters of the words. In fact, it includes the initial *syllables* of the words. So *sci-fi* is an example of what is, reasonably enough, called a *syllable acronym*. (To the best of my knowledge, syllable acronyms are not also known as *syl-acs*. But it seems a little like they should be, don't you think?) Syllable acronyms are a specific type of portmanteau word.

There are a lot of syllable acronyms, including a few that are so well established that you might not realize they're abbreviations:

- You might enjoy watching *sitcoms* ("situation comedies") on TV.
- Your camera might let you take movies in *slo-mo* ("slow motion") with *hi-fi* ("high fidelity") sound.
- You probably connect to the internet using a *modem* ("modulator-demodulator").
- If you're an aspiring fiction writer, you might be familiar with or even have participated in *NaNoWriMo*, which is a syllable acronym for "National Novel Writing Month."

A number of brand names are based on syllable acronyms, including *Texaco* (for "Texas Company"), *Conoco* (for "Continental Oil Company"), *Alcoa* (for "Aluminum Company of America"), and *Nabisco* (for "National Biscuit Company"). In fact, Nabisco might have been the first company name that was based on a syllable acronym. The word *canola*, as in *canola oil*, might have originally been a trademark made from "Canadian oil, low acid." (An alternative theory is that *canola* comes from "Canada" + "oil.")

---

[115] Some people make a strict distinction between *acronyms*, where the resulting abbreviation can be pronounced as a word (*NATO*), and *initialisms*, where the resulting word is sounded out as letters (*FBI*).

We even have some syllable acronyms that we get from other languages. One that can be hard to miss is *Pokémon*, the game and character universe. The name *Pokémon* is a shortened form of "pocket monsters," or in Japanese, *Poketto Monsutā*. From German we got *Nazi* (from *Nationalsozialist* or "National Socialist") and *Gestapo* (from *Geheime Staatspolizei* or "secret state police"). The name LEGO for toy bricks is a syllable acronym for *leg godt*, Danish for "play well," or that's what the company says.

Syllable acronyms occasionally are used as the names of geographic areas:

- *SoCal* and *NoCal* for southern and northern California.
- *TriBeCa* ("triangle below Canal") and *SoHo* ("south of Houston") in New York City.
- *SODO* in Seattle. This was originally "south of the Kingdome" (the Kingdome was an indoor stadium in downtown Seattle), but after the Kingdome was torn down, it was reinterpreted as just "south of downtown."

Syllable acronyms also seem to be popular for the names of events, especially conventions. I used to regularly attend COMDEX ("Computer Dealers' Exhibition"). These days, people I know attend ComiCons (comic book conventions), AppSec (an application security conference), InfoSec (an information security conference), and DefCon (another security conference, the name borrowed from the DEFCON, a US military syllable acronym that stands for "defense readiness condition").

Celebrities sometimes get nicknames that seem like syllable acronyms. Examples include *A-Rod* (Alex Rodriguez), *Flo-Jo* (Florence Joyner), *J.Lo* (Jennifer Lopez), and *ScarJo* (Scarlett Johansson). The lexicographer Ben Zimmer notes in a post on the *Language Log* blog that the letter *O* seems particularly common in syllable acronyms.

Even celebrity couples can attract nicknames based on syllabic acronyms, like *J-Rod* for the once-affianced couple J.Lo and A-Rod, and *Kimye* for Kim Kardashian and Kanye West. (Given the, er, dynamic nature of celebrity coupledom, these examples are likely to be outdated by the time you read this. But there will probably be new ones!) Whether the people in question enjoy having these nicknames is, of course, a different issue.

Related terms: backronym, numeronym, portmanteau word, redundant acronym phrase

tag question

Your friend Pat is having a frustrating Monday. They spent all Sunday washing and polishing their car, but this morning it's pouring down rain. After telling you this, Pat says, "It always rains after I wash my car, you know?"

That "you know?" at the end of Pat's anguished sentence makes it seem like they're asking a question about your meteorological knowledge. But they're not; the part at the end of Pat's sentence is called a *tag question.*

A tag question is a clause or word that's added to the end of a declaration to make it into a question—or something that *looks* like a question. You hear tag questions all the time, like these:

He's a handsome fellow, *isn't he*?

You don't get it, *do you*?

So that's what you think, *is it*?

It's a lot of work, *innit*.

Tag questions generally follow a pattern. The first part of the sentence is an assertion of some sort. The tag question is at the end and is framed as a yes/no question. If the tag question is a proper clause, it only ever uses pronouns that refer back to something earlier in the sentence ("They're not coming, are *they*?"). If the tag question includes an explicit verb, it usually has the opposite polarity (negative or positive) from the main verb—for example, if the statement is "That was a dumb move," a tag question would be "wasn't it?"

Tag questions can act as real questions, where the speaker expects a response. For example, a speaker might say, "I bet you're French, right?"

or "She's not dating that guy, is she?" Speakers use tag questions like these to signal what type of response is expected. For example, in "I bet you're French, right?", the speaker is signaling that they're pretty sure that they're talking to a French person and are asking for confirmation. In a similar vein, in a sentence like, "She's not dating that guy, is she?", the speaker signals incredulity and that they're hoping for a negative response ("Oh, no way").

But many tag questions are rhetorical, as in questions that end with *you know?* or *right?* With the tag question, "It always rains after I wash the car, you know?", Pat isn't really expecting an answer and is certainly not expecting you to confirm or deny the assertion. If a proud grandparent shows you a photo of their new grandchild and says, "He's a handsome fellow, isn't he?", they're not expecting you to weigh their statement. (It would be a serious faux pas to respond with "Not really.")

Whether a question that follows a statement is a tag question can depend on the intonation of the sentence—or if the tag question is written out, on how it's punctuated. Compare these sentences:

We're having pizza for dinner, ***aren't we***?

We're having pizza for dinner, ***aren't we***.

In the first example, the speaker uses an intonation that makes *aren't we?* into a real question, not just a signal for confirmation. The interpretation is probably that the speaker wants confirmation of an unclear situation or is maybe communicating that they're looking forward to dinner. In the second example, the intonation of *aren't we* is flat, which marks it as a tag question. In that case, the tag question gives the impression that the speaker is resigned to a disappointing situation.

We have quite a few ways in English to form tag questions. We can use verbal constructions (*... isn't it?* or *... aren't they?*), or select from a whole host of markers, including these:

- ..., *right?*
- ..., *you know?*
- ..., *no?*
- ..., *okay?*
- ..., *eh?*
- ..., *amirite?*

In some British dialects, people use *innit* as a tag question ("It's a funny world, innit"), which is a reduced form of *isn't it*. A few years ago, the linguist Gretchen McCulloch noted that people had started using *y/y* (short for "yes or yes?") as what she identified as a tag question. (Example: "So I should wear my matching shirt at some point, y/y?") You might notice that these tag particles, let's call them, aren't as constrained as the more clause-like tag questions from earlier. But they all still function in the same way, which is that in the end, they make a statement in the form of a question.

Related terms: biscuit conditional, pause filler, quotative *like*, uptalk

toponym

Place names can show interesting history. If the name of a city in England ends in *chester*, like Winchester and Lancaster, it was likely once a Roman camp (*castrum*). Names ending in *burg* or *bury* or *borough*, like Edinburgh, Canterbury, and Scarborough, indicate towns that were once fortified; the root *burg* means "fortress," as in the German word *Burg*. The name or ending *thorpe* means "village," which is the origin of names like Scunthorpe.

The study of place names is called *toponymy*. It's a subset of onomastics, the study of naming. The word *toponomy* comes from the Greek for "place" + "name." Learning about how people have named places in the world around them provides lessons in history (who settled a place, and when?) and sociology (what have people considered important, and why?). On top of that, place names often become the origins of everyday words, like *bikini*, *cognac*, and *tuxedo*.

When people have had the task to name a place, they've used a lot of inspirations. One source is geographical or landscape features. For example, many towns in England have names that end in *don* or *dun* or *tun*, like Abingdon and Croydon. This ending (related to *dune*) is a remnant of an Anglo-Saxon word (possibly borrowed from Celtic) for "hill." Similarly, the prefix *pen-*, as in Penzance, can reflect a Welsh word for hill. The town of Plymouth in England is at the mouth of the Plym river.

There's a town up the river a ways named Plympton. (The *p* in the middle of the name *Plympton* is probably an example of epenthesis—inserting a sound to make it easier to pronounce the word.)

Another source of naming inspiration is human-made artifacts, like the examples earlier of *Winchester* (based on a Roman camp) or *Scarborough* (a fortified place). Names ending in *wich* or *wick* (*Warwick, Ipswich*) often referred to settlements. The ending *ham* (Nottingham, Durham) could refer to a homestead or farm. The *kirk* ending (*Dunkirk*) can derive from a church.

I should pause here and note that we can make some good guesses about the origins of names that go back to prerecorded history, as people have done about the names I've mentioned so far. But the origins can be a bit hazy—many of them originated before written records. Dave Wilton, who has a PhD in medieval English literature and who writes about word origins, notes in a blog post, "take any origins of place names with grain of salt unless they are accompanied with a chain of citations to supporting evidence."[116] It's generally easier to ascertain the origins of more recent names—like those in the United States.

Onward. People have sometimes named places for other people. The city of Cincinnati in Ohio is named for the Roman military leader Cincinnatus. A famous battle was fought during World War II in the city of Stalingrad, named (actually, renamed) for a then-hero of the Soviet Union, Joseph Stalin. Closer to where I live, Puget Sound was named for Peter Puget, an English explorer. And Kirkland, Washington, was named for Peter Kirk, one of the founders of the city—which I mention because Kirkland, Washington, is the source of the Kirkland Signature store brand for Costco, whose headquarters were originally in that city.

For that matter, the continent of America is named for the Italian merchant and explorer Amerigo Vespucci. He's generally credited as being the first to recognize that the New World was a new continent and not the easternmost edge of Asia.

Many places in the US and Canada and other former colonies are named for existing places in the old world. There are cities named Athens, Harlem, Cambridge in the United States (sometimes more than one). It's a good guess that places in North America that begin with *New*, like

---

[116] https://www.wordorigins.org/harmless-drudge/a-note-on-toponyms

New Jersey, *New Hampshire*, *New Orleans*, and *Nova Scotia* (Latin for "New Scotland") are named for places in Europe.

Places are often named for the people who live there. England got its name because it was the land of the Angles, a Germanic tribe that settled there starting about 450 CE, along with the Saxons. (Hence Old English is also known as Anglo-Saxon.) The name *Germany* comes from a name that the Romans used (*Germanus*) for the collection of Germanic tribes on the empire's northwestern frontier. The name *Russia* was named for the Rus' people who lived in the area of the Baltic Sea and the Black Sea in early medieval times.

Some places are even named for ideas. Los Angeles was originally *El Pueblo de Nuestra Señora la Reina de los Ángeles*, or "The town of our lady the queen of the angels." Santa Cruz, California, is Spanish for "holy cross."

In many parts of the world, current place names were adapted from indigenous languages. In the United States, names like *Minnesota, Wisconsin, Illinois, Mississippi, Niagara, Chicago, Wyoming, Walla Walla* (Washington), *Seattle*, and hundreds more are based on native names.

Not surprisingly, toponyms can reflect political changes. The city once known as Byzantium under the Greeks was conquered by the Romans. It was briefly renamed New Rome before being renamed Constantinople in honor of Emperor Constantine. After the Ottomans conquered the city in 1453, and the city became Istanbul.

This is of course a simplified history of the names; the city has had names not only for different periods of its history, but in different languages like Greek, Latin, and Turkish.[117]

The city of Saint Petersburg in Russia—originally named for Peter the Great—became Petrograd in 1914 to have a more Russian name. In 1924, the city was renamed Leningrad, only to be renamed back to Saint Petersburg in 1991. In Vietnam, the city once known as Saigon is now officially known as Ho Chi Minh City.

Using the correct (or at least, a specific) toponym can be a sensitive issue. The government in Taiwan (earlier, Formosa) refers to the island as

---

[117] Also, I should note that several people who read this entry thought it should contain a link to the song "Istanbul (Not Constantinople)" by the band They Might Be Giants, so here it is: https://youtu.be/xo0X77OBJUg

the Republic of China (ROC). This status is not recognized by the People's Republic of China (PRC), that is, by mainland China. The PRC asserts that Taiwan is the "Taiwan Authority." Companies that do business in PRC can get into commercial or even political trouble if they use the name Taiwan in a way that does not align with the Chinese government's view of the island.

A controversy erupted in 2015 in the United States about the name of the peak in Alaska that's known to the local natives as Denali. The peak had been officially designated as Mt. McKinley in 1917. When the Obama administration restored Denali as the official name, some legislators—especially in Ohio, McKinley's home state—objected. In the state of Washington, there has been a movement to rename Mount Rainier back to its indigenous name of Mount Tahoma.

As I said earlier, the word *toponym* can refer not just to place names, but to words that derive from those names. Many common words have toponymic origins. Here's a short list, but there are many, many more:

- *bikini*, named for the Bikini Atoll in the Pacific, where an atomic-bomb test was performed, and which (somehow) inspired a new fashion in women's swimwear.
- *buffalo wings*. The origin of this otherwise gryphon-sounding sports bar favorite is that the dish was invented at a bar in Buffalo, New York.
- *canary*, the bird, named for the Canary Islands, where it originated. The islands themselves are named for the dogs—*canus* in Latin—that lived there.
- *chartreuse*, the name of a liquor and of a color, which derives from *La Grande Chartreuse*, a Carthusian monastery in France where the liquor originated.
- *cognac*, named for the city of Cognac in France, which is the center of the cognac industry.
- *magnet*, derived from *magnitis lithos*, a Greek term meaning "Magnesian stone"; Magnesia is an area in Greece.
- *marathon*, named for the city in Greece from which Pheidippides made his 26-mile run to Athens in 490 BC to announce a Greek victory over Persia.
- *mayonnaise*, named for the town of Mahon in Spain.

- *rugby* (Rugby football), named for a school in the town of Rugby, England, where the game was invented.
- *tangerine*, named for the city of Tangier in Morocco.
- *Trojan horse*, named for the city of Troy.
- *tuxedo*, named for Tuxedo Park, a town in New York, where the tail-less formal jacket debuted in the United States.

A surprising number of words for fabrics are toponyms, usually because that's where the fabric came from. For example, the word *jeans* comes from the Italian city Genoa, where they made a type of twilled cloth. Other examples of toponymic fabrics are *calico* (the Indian city Kozhikode, also known in English as Calicut), *cashmere* (Kashmir), *damask* (Damascus), *denim* ("serge de Nîmes"), *muslin* (Mosul), and *suede* ("de Suede," meaning "of Sweden").

Toponyms can sometimes hide in words that we use all the time. A great example is the word *debunk*, which means to "expose as false or incorrect." This term was invented in 1923 to mean "take the bunk out of." *Bunk* here is short for *bunkum*, meaning "nonsense," and it originates from a speech made in Congress in 1820 by the representative from Buncombe, North Carolina.

The OED has this note about how we got *bunk* (*bunkum*) from *Buncombe*: "The use of the word originated near the close of the debate on the 'Missouri Question' in the 16th congress, when the member from this district rose to speak, while the house was impatiently calling for the 'Question'. Several members gathered round him, begging him to desist; he persevered, however, for a while, declaring that the people of his district expected it, and that he was bound to make a speech for Buncombe."

I tell you, toponyms are everywhere.

Related terms: demonym, eponym, onomastics, patronym

umlaut, diaeresis (dieresis)

Mention the word *umlaut* to someone, and there's a good chance that they'll say something about a rock band like Mötley Crüe or a brand name like Häagen-Dazs. That's because many people think of umlauts as the pair of dots that appear above a letter.

And that is definitely one way we use the word. But *umlaut* means a number of things, and examining its various meanings provides a surprisingly broad tour of language things.

Let's start with the dots. If you're not a copy editor or typography wonk, you probably use *umlaut* to refer to a *diaeresis* (or alternatively a *dieresis*), which is the technical-slash-typographical name for the dots above a letter. In certain copy-editing circles (famously at the *New Yorker*), the diaeresis is used to indicate that the second vowel in a two-vowel sequence should be explicitly pronounced. In the pages of that magazine you'll find spellings like *Chloë, naïve, coöperate* (compare *coop* and *coöp*), *reëlection,* and *zoölogy.* (The practice of using a diaeresis for these vowel combinations is so closely associated with the *New Yorker* that the editor Benjamin Dreyer was once moved to observe, "One's house style oughtn't to be visible from outer space.")

Benjamin Dreyer ✓
@BCDreyer   ...

One's house style oughtn't to be visible from outer space.

#totallynotasubtweet

12:27 PM · Apr 10, 2018

Some other languages also use diaeresis as an orthographic device. For example, in the Spanish writing system, a diaeresis is a hint to the pronunciation of the letter *u.* If a reader sees *güe* or *güi,* the reader knows the *u* is pronounced. The word *guitarra,* no diaeresis, is pronounced similarly to how it is in English (hard *g,* no *w* sound). But the word *lingüística,* with a diaeresis over the *u,* sounds like "ling-gwis-tica," with written *ü* representing a *w* sound.

As you can see, this usage of the diaeresis is strictly practical—it helps people understand how to read or pronounce words. Then there are other, less functional uses of the symbol.

For example, some metal bands adopted the dots as a graphical element in their names, like Blue Öyster Cult, Queensrÿche, Motörhead, and Mötley Crüe. Using an umlaut in this way has nothing to do with pronunciation, of course; it's strictly for effect. As a result, this type of decorative touch got the name *heavy-metal umlaut* or sometimes *röck döts*. The movie *This is Spinal Tap*, which mocked heavy-metal bands, mocked this affectation as well. The poster for the movie includes an umlaut over the *n* in "Spinal," which is a brilliant little touch of satire, since umlauts only make sense over vowels, as I'll explain momentarily.

And it's not just heavy-metal bands. Nancy Friedman, a professional brand-naming consultant, has an article called "The Ündeniable Ümlaut," in which she traces the popularity of the umlaut in brand names such as Häagen-Dazs, Frusen Glädjé, and YogaMöm.[118] Using an umlaut character like this for effect is an example of *sensational spelling*, in which a word or phrase is deliberately spelled in an unusual way for effect—for example, *Krispy Kreme* (the donut company) *Led Zeppelin* and *Linkin Park* (the bands), and *Ludacris* (the rapper).

So that's *umlaut* as an orthographic convention and occasional ornamental element.

The term *umlaut* also describes certain vowel sounds. For example, people who study German learn that among its vowels, the language has the separate letters *U* and *U-umlaut*; the sound of the letter *U-umlaut* is represented in writing by *Ü*. These are distinct vowels, and they're not interchangeable in German words; for example *Mutter* means "mother" and *Mütter* means "mothers," plural. In German, the *u* sound is pro-

---

[118] https://www.vocabulary.com/articles/candlepwr/the-undeniable-umlaut/

nounced "ooooh." If you start saying "eee" but then round your lips as if you were saying "ooooh," you get the sound represented in writing as *Ü*—what's described in phonological terms as a *rounded front vowel*. There are also the letters *O* and *O-umlaut* (*Ö*), as well as *A* and *A-umlaut* (*Ä*), which are also distinct pairs.

Other languages also have vowel sounds that are written as vowels with umlauts. Finnish has the letter *Ä*, which is distinct from *A*, and the letter *Ö*, which likewise is distinct from *O*. Turkish has distinct vowels that are represented in writing as *O* and *Ö*, and *U* and *Ü*.

In standard dialects of English, the collection of vowels doesn't include the sounds that are represented in other languages by umlauted letters like *Ü* and *Ö*. But some dialects do include the sounds, though not necessarily as different vowels, just as a variant pronunciation. For example, some speakers of Scots English use the *ü* sound in place of *u*.

Although we don't have the *ä*, *ü*, and *ö* sounds in most English dialects and therefore no letters for those sounds, now and then we need to write non-English words that include the letters. Sometimes when we write out German words or names that include an umlaut, we add an *e* after the vowel, like writing *Schroedinger* for the German physicist *Schrödinger* or writing the name of the Wayne Newton hit as "Danke Schoen" (for German *danke schön*, "thank you"). But often we just use the vowel without the diaeresis. For example, we've imported the German word *über* ("over") as the word *uber*, which we use as a synonym for *super* (*uber-cautious*). And of course there's the ride-sharing company Uber. Similarly, the name of the German composer Händel is often just written as *Handel*. (Händel himself dropped the umlaut. Although he was German, he spent a long time in England, where he composed for the British court.)

Finally, the term *umlaut* also refers to a phonological *process* in which one vowel in a word affects how another vowel in the word is pronounced. In fact, that's the origin of the word *umlaut*: it's German for "near" + "sound." (This is another lexical remnant, as with the word *ablaut*, of the early influence of German scholars in the study of language.) In Germanic languages, which include Old English, the umlaut process is also known as *i-mutation*, because the presence of an *i* sound at the end of a word could "mutate" the vowel in the stem of the word.

This umlaut/i-mutation is the source of some of our irregular plurals, like *goose* > *geese*. It worked like this: in Old English, the word *goose* was *gos*. In the earliest days of Old English, the plural of *gos* was *gosiz*. But due to umlaut, the *i* in the second syllable caused the *o* to mutate, which produced a sound like *e*. Over time, the *i* in the plural disappeared, but the mutation that it had caused remained, and the plural of *gos* settled as *ges*. Something similar happened with *mouse* (the plural of *mus* became *mys*), *foot* (*fot* > *fet*), and *louse* (*lus* > *lys*), *tooth* (*toth* > *teth*), and *man* (*mann* > *menn*).

We don't form plurals by adding *i* to nouns anymore. And even when we do have words that end in *i* sounds (*agree, committee, aioli*) or *is* sounds (*trustees, honeybees*), the *i* in the final syllable doesn't have any effect on the main vowel.

I should note that although English doesn't have umlaut/i-mutation today, versions of the phenomenon exist in other languages. For example, Turkish and Finnish have *vowel harmony*, in which the vowels of a word are affected by suffixes (particles) that are added to the word.

Let's review. *Umlaut* can refer to the following:

- The dots above a letter, also known as *diaeresis*. This type of umlaut is just orthographical: it either tells a reader how to pronounce a letter (*naïve, coöp*) or it's purely decorative (*Mötley Crüe*).
- Certain vowels that exist in other languages like German or Finnish, but that we don't have in standard English (*über, Schrödinger*). In those cases, the letter that has the dots is a distinct vowel, different from the other vowels in the language.
- A process that mutates a vowel if it's followed by an *i* sound. This process occurred in the early days of Old English but doesn't anymore in modern English. Still, it's fun to know that umlaut is why we ended up with some odd plurals like *geese* and *lice*.

It's not impossible that this was more than you wanted to know about the term *umlaut*. I will entirely understand if you're happy just to spot and occasionally use some decörative döts in your wörds.

Related terms: International Phonetic Alphabet (IPA), spelling alphabet

unpaired word

Your favorite sports team loses the championship match, so you're dismayed. But if they had won, would you be … mayed? Or consider that movie you watched recently, the one with the ruthless villain. At the end he has a change of heart, so he becomes … ruthful?

As we know, you can't un-*dis* the word *dismayed*, and for the opposite of *ruthless* people don't use the word *ruthful*. The words *dismayed* and *ruthless* are both examples of something called an *unpaired word*, which is a word that seems like it should have an opposite but doesn't.

In a blog post, the Irish editor Stan Carey pondered what he called "the strange case of 'ambiguate'."[119] Everyone knows the word *disambiguate*, meaning "to remove uncertainty." But when have you ever heard the word *ambiguate*? You haven't, because *disambiguate* is likewise an unpaired word.

Some other unpaired words you know are *awful, disappoint, disconsolate, disheveled, feckless, hapless, impeccable, inadvertent, unkempt, unruly,* and *unwieldy.* In most cases, the unpaired word includes some sort of negating particle (*dis, un, less*), and we lack the corresponding non-negated form. These negative unpaired words are also sometimes called *lonely negatives.*

Unpaired words can occur when one of the embedded parts is a term that's otherwise extinct or has become so uncommon that people don't know it. That's the case with *ruthless; ruth* was a term that meant "the quality of being compassionate," but in that sense the word is archaic. Similarly, *unruly* once had the antonym *ruly*, meaning someone who was amenable to rule, but obviously we lost that term. There is a word *wieldy,* but I'd bet that you only use the word *unwieldy.* These faded antonyms to negative words are sometimes referred to as *lost positives.*

Unpaired words can also arise when an embedded part is an older or variant version of an existing word. In *unkempt,* for example, *kempt* is an older term that is related to the existing word *combed.* In *feckless* (meaning "ineffective, incompetent"), *feck* is a dialectical variant on *effect*, so *feckless* describes someone who has no effect. In *disappoint,* the *appoint* part has a mostly obscure definition meaning "to provide what is neces-

---

[119] https://stancarey.wordpress.com/2021/08/22/the-strange-absence-of-ambiguate/

sary." (We see this in the phrase *well-appointed*, like a well-appointed office.) Thus *disappoint* refers to *not* providing something necessary. In the word *impeccable*, *peccable* is a rare but not unknown word meaning "capable of sin."

In yet other cases, we imported a word that already had a negative particle but either didn't import or lost the paired non-negative term. That was the case for *dismayed* and *disheveled*, which we imported from French with their *dis-* prefix already in place.

In some cases, a word's status as unpaired is evident only when you think about it. One example is *innocent*. The *in-* prefix is a negation (compare *intolerant* or *inarticulate*), but what is *innocent* a negation of? It turns out that the *nocent* part is from a Latin stem that means "to harm," which we see also in *noxious*. A similar word is *innocuous*, which has the same roots.

There are a few cases of unpaired words where it's the negated version that we lack. One example is *awful* (whose original meaning was "awe" +" full," i.e., inspiring awe). There's no *awless* or *aweless*, though this could certainly be a useful word at times. In this vein, one of my colleagues attended a presentation once, and when I asked him how it was, he said, "I was whelmed." In that case, we have pairs (*overwhelmed*, *underwhelmed*), but we no longer use the root *whelm*.

A masterpiece of playing with unpaired words is the piece "How I Met My Wife" by Jack Winter, which appeared in the *New Yorker* in the July 25, 1994, issue. The piece is a brilliant collection of sentences like this:

> She was a descript person, a woman in a state of total array. Her hair was kempt, her clothing shevelled, and she moved in a gainly way.

Here's some fun with unpaired words: I challenge you, the next time you go to a dinner party, to tell the cook that the meal was absolutely "gusting." (No, don't do that.)

Related terms: hapax legomenon, mountweazel, negative polarity item (NPI), plurale tantum

uptalk (high rising terminal)

James Gorman, writing in the *New York Times Magazine*, once wrote about a phenomenon he'd noticed:

> I used to speak in a regular voice. I was able to assert, demand, question. Then I started teaching. At a university? And my students had this rising intonation thing? It was particularly noticeable on telephone messages. "Hello? Professor Gorman? This is Albert? From feature writing?"[120]

What Gorman had noticed was something called *uptalk*: a way of saying a declarative sentence so that it sounds like a question.

This phenomenon has several other names, including *upward inflection* and *high rising terminal* (often abbreviated as *HRT*). It was Gorman who coined the term *uptalk* in 1993 in his article. But the phenomenon was identified at least as early as the mid-1970s and actually goes back way into the past.

Uptalk is stereotypically associated with young women—so much so, in fact, that it's not hard to find articles advising young women to change this feature of their speech because of the adverse impression it's supposedly going to give potential employers and others. Example: "Uptalk - What it is and Why You Don't Ever Want to Do it!"[121] (The lexicographer Steve Kleinedler has some thoughts about articles that purport to give linguistic advice like this: "Clickbait listicles that describe what you're communicating as 'incorrect,' 'damaging to your career,' 'offputting' etc. are generally complete bullshit with no basis in linguistics.")

However, uptalk is attested among other speakers as well, including men and older speakers. In those demographics, uptalk is either not well noticed or not considered a speech habit to be eradicated. This of course suggests that the impact that uptalk has on listeners has much to do with who's producing it.

The origins of uptalk are not known. It's been variously proposed to have come from California ("Valley Girl" talk), Australia, New Zealand,

---

[120] http://www.nytimes.com/1993/08/15/magazine/on-language-like-uptalk.html
[121] https://tinyurl.com/22pwjtks

the northern portions of Britain (those historically influenced by Scandinavian), or Northern Ireland. A fun theory suggested by Mark Liberman is that uptalk migrated with the so-called Okies (traditionally of Scots-Irish descent) to California during the Dust Bowl years (1930s). But in a kind of antedating, linguist Matt Gordon posted on Twitter about a dialectical note he'd found from 1890 that said that people in Charleston, South Carolina "constantly end the sentences with the rising inflection, so that they appear to be asking questions at first."

Matt Gordon
@AnotherLinguist

Cool observation of "uptalk": In Charleston SC, "they constantly end the sentences with the rising inflection, so that they appear to be asking questions at first" (fr. Dialect Notes 1, 1890) #KidsToday. .

People who study uptalk seem to agree that it's probably becoming more common, although there's no good way to determine how prevalent it was before the advent of audio recording.

There's also discussion about what the purpose of uptalk is—that is, what its discourse functions are. People advising young women to shed uptalk will claim, for example, that it signals lack of confidence. But uptalk can be heard from people who are anything but unconfident; Mark Liberman has a fascinating blog post that identifies instances of uptalk in a speech by George W. Bush.[122]

In the 1980s, the linguist Cynthia McLemore studied uptalk in a Texas sorority. In the paper discussing her findings,[123] she reports various purposes that she identified for uptalk: to signal a relationship between textual units, create suspense, invite inclusion, elicit agreement (like a tag question), and regulate turn-taking between speakers.

The point is that there is considerably more subtlety to the use of uptalk than just lack of confidence. Because uptalk has a variety of conversational uses among those who use it, it's likely to persist in those speech

---

[122] http://itre.cis.upenn.edu/~myl/languagelog/archives/002708.html
[123] http://itre.cis.upenn.edu/myl/llog/CAM_Interpretation.pdf

communities for as long as it serves those purposes. Even if articles sternly tell young people to quit it.

Related terms: pause filler, quotative *like*, tag question

word aversion

Many people simply dislike certain words—they can't stand to see or hear these words. Encountering the words makes them cringe or shudder.

The words aren't necessarily unusual and aren't commonly accepted as offensive. We're not talking here about curse words or ethnic slurs, or words that refer to controversial topics like politics. No, the words here are perfectly ordinary words, except that some people experience *word aversion* when confronted with one of these words.

The words that trigger word aversion in people vary, and they're often unique to individuals. Among the terms that people report disliking are *pugilist*, *vigil*, and even *egg*. You might wonder what people find revolting about these words. (Then again, perhaps you experience word aversion to one or more of these words yourself.) But that's the thing: word aversion is idiosyncratic.

That said, certain words do come up a lot when you survey people about their word aversions. The word that seems to bother the most people is *moist*. An article in *Scientific American* with the brilliant title "Probing the Moist Crevices of Word Aversion" reports that 20% of a test group says they have an aversion to *moist*. In a poll by the *New Yorker* that asked people which word they'd like to see eliminated from English, *moist* took the prize (that is, it was "the runaway un-favorite"). Other terms that engender unusual levels of word aversion are *ointment, panties, slacks*, and *vomit*.

The question is why people develop word aversion. The paper from which *Scientific American* got its data suggests two hypotheses. The first idea is that the sequence of sounds in a word might be inherently unpleasant. In *moist*, perhaps the *oy* sound next to the *s* and *t* is just naturally unlikable. But in their experiments, the researchers found one person (but only one) who said that they felt the same way about the words *foist* and *hoist*.

An intriguing but unresearched version of this idea is the "facial feedback" theory, which says that people dislike words that use the same muscles that we use when making a disgusted face. We don't like *moist*, according to this idea, because to say it, we have to emulate the expression of a negative emotion. This could suggest that word aversion would be cross-cultural—people around the world might be equally averse to some of the same sound combinations—and to theories of phonesthemics.

The second idea about the origins of word aversion is that it has to do with the word's meaning. The word reminds people of a thing or concept that they have aversion to—or they dislike it, as the researchers wrote, "because of negative semantic connotations." The researchers found some evidence that they could prime the people in the study in a way to affect people's perception. If the word *moist* was preceded in the study by (for example) sexual terms, people had a stronger aversion to it than if *moist* was preceded by a baking term like *cake*. (Someone on Twitter spotted a recipe that used the word *damp* to describe a cake, presumably to avoid the word *moist*.)

And interestingly, there might have been some social component to the study: one participant reported that they initially didn't mind *moist*, but after hearing other people talk about it, the word started bothering that subject also. The more that people report being averse to the word *moist*, the more other people likewise find it icky.

The researchers tentatively concluded that word aversion for common words is probably that they remind people of something they don't like. Their data suggests that some people were more subject to word aversion than others. If you don't like *moist*, you might be likelier than other people to have an aversion to the word *phlegm* as well.

So although people have different word aversions, and you might be puzzled why your co-worker has banned the word *hardscrabble*, there are some commonalities. Perhaps you, too, have joined a couple of thousand people in a Facebook group named "I HATE the word MOIST!" Whatever your personal word aversions, you can at least know that other people have equally arbitrary—but equally strong—aversions to their own set of words.

Related terms: pedant's veto

zombie rule

Many people would tell you that this sentence has something wrong with it:

He refused to tell us where he was from.

The issue, as these people see it, is that the sentence ends with a preposition (*from*). Here's another sentence that a lot of people—perhaps the same people—would say also has something wrong with it:

The five-year mission of the starship Enterprise is to boldly go where no man has gone before.

In this example, the claim is that you're not supposed to split infinitives—that is, you're not supposed to put a word like *boldly* between *to* and *go*.

The problem with asserting that these constructions are wrong is that that isn't true. It isn't true from the perspective of usage: prepositions at the end of a sentence (*terminal* or *stranded* prepositions) as well as split infinitives are perfectly normal in everyday English and have been forever, basically. And it isn't true from the perspective of authority: you'd be hard-pressed to find a usage guide written in the last 100 years that agrees with these claims. Even the venerable *Elements of Style* says that a stranded preposition "sometimes […] is more effective in that spot than anywhere else" and that "some infinitives seem to improve on being split."

And yet it doesn't seem to matter what linguists or editors or style guides say about the split-infinitive rule and the stranded-preposition rule. People continue to believe that these are real rules of English. Because it seems impossible to kill a belief like the no-split-infinitive rule, the linguist Arnold Zwicky invented a term for it: *zombie rule*. As he describes it:

... no matter how many times, and how thoroughly, it is executed by authorities, it continues its wretched life-in-death in style sheets and grammar checkers and the like.[124]

Although Zwicky's term is the most colorful way to describe these rules that refuse to go away, he was not the first to write about them. In 1926, H. W. Fowler called them *fetishes*, which he described as "conventions misapplied or unduly revered" and *superstitions*, whose enforcement he called "unintelligent applications of an unintelligent dogma." The editor Benjamin Dreyer refers to them as *nonrules* and labels them as "largely unhelpful, pointlessly constricting, feckless, and useless."

Many zombie rules were invented out of thin air. For example, the idea that you can't split an infinitive originated when Enlightenment-era grammarians were attempting to model English grammar on Latin. In Latin, infinitives do not have a marker like *to* (*to praise* is just *laudare*), so they could not be "split." These grammarians were writing some of the first grammars that described English, and since they had no models for English, they turned to grammars that they did know: those for Latin. So they invented rules that would make English act more like their beloved Latin, even if the English they heard and read didn't meet this standard.

John Dryden, the prolific 17th-century English writer, criticized his contemporary Ben Johnson for using prepositions at the end of a sentence: "The preposition in the end of the sentence; a common fault with him, and which I have but lately observed in my own writing." It takes some kind of grammatical confidence to declare something wrong that *you yourself do.*

Dryden's opinion became canon, and for a few centuries, usage manuals parroted this rule and similar ones—which, to repeat, were often based on opinions about how English should work like another language entirely.

In the 20th century, usage manuals shifted to basing their guidance on how well-known writers actually wrote. And a lot of respected writers wrote by how they heard English in the ear, not on how Latin grammar works. Nonetheless, a number of the rules persisted, and here we are, still talking about these zombie rules.

---

[124] http://itre.cis.upenn.edu/~myl/languagelog/archives/002189.html

The cite earlier from Arnold Zwicky gives us a hint about why. As he suggests, zombie rules are enforced (or can be) by grammar checkers. In Microsoft Word, you can set the grammar checker to help you find stranded prepositions:

Grammar Settings

Writing style:

Grammar & Refinements

Options:

- [ ] Progressive Use
- [x] Wordiness
- [ ] Words Expressing Uncertainty

Formality

- [ ] Colloquial Verb Phrase
- [ ] Contractions
- [ ] Informal Language
- [ ] Missing Auxiliary in Question
- [ ] Number Formatting
- [ ] Opinion Markers
- [ ] Preposition at End of Clause
- [ ] Slang
- [ ] Subjunctive Mood

Why would Microsoft Word care about what is in effect a zombie rule? Because even if *you* know the rule is discredited, other people don't. Sometimes those people might be offended by your usage, and sometimes it's important not to offend them. (This is known as the pedant's veto.)

To complicate matters, there's not necessarily agreement on which usage guidelines are zombie rules. Some people believe that you should never start a sentence with a conjunction like *and* or *but*. (Fowler: "The supposed rule is without foundation in grammar, logic, or art.") Some people insist that the word *none* must always take a singular verb. *The Elements of Style* uses the example "None of us *is* perfect," but then notes that the verb should be plural if none refers to more than one person or thing: "None *are* so fallible as those who are sure they're right."

One rule that many people believe but that has an origin as arbitrary as the stranded-preposition rule pertains to using *that* and *which*. American usage guidelines generally recommend using *that* for restrictive clauses and *which* only for non-restrictive ones, as in these examples:

The book *that* I read belongs to her. (restrictive, okay)

The book *which* I read belongs to her. (restrictive, not okay per American style conventions)

The book, *which* I read, belongs to her. (non-restrictive, okay; note the commas)

Some linguists (for example, Arnold Zwicky and Geoff Pullum) argue that this is a pseudo-rule because the use of restrictive *which* (the second example) is common in spoken English and in casual writing. Enforcing a ban on restrictive *which* is "which-hunting," as it says in *The Elements of Style*.

The force of the *that/which* rule seems to be attributable to H. W. Fowler (him again!), who was trying to come up with consistent guidelines for using relative *that*, *which*, and *who*. He noted that these related terms …

> … have come to us from our forefathers as an odd jumble, & plainly show that the language has not been neatly constructed by a master-builder who could create each part to do the exact work required of it; neither overlapped nor overlapping.

He then proceeded to articulate that "perhaps the line of improvement lies in clearer differentiation between *that & which*." (In effect, he was repeating a mistake made by earlier grammarians, namely trying to prescribe how English *should* work.) American usage mavens took up this suggestion with vigor and wrote it into their manuals. Many American writers and editors today believe that the distinction between relative *that* and *which* is a natural rule in English grammar. But as with the rules discussed earlier, it's not. It's a rule that was made up as a kind of wishful thinking about how English *should* work.

In any event, if the rules about split infinitives and stranded prepositions are a guide, the *that/which* rule is likely to be … undead … for a long time.

Related terms: etymological fallacy, pedant's veto, skunked term

Quick reference

This section is a summary of all the words. My hope is that if you encounter some interesting phenomenon, the tables in this section will make it easy to find the name for the thing you've encountered.

I've organized the terms into sections:

- Words
- Sentences and phrases
- Sounds
- Punctuation and spelling
- Ideas

Words

absolute adjective
> An adjective that technically doesn't have degrees.
> Example: *perfect, unique*

anthimeria
> Using a word as a different part of speech.
> Example: *an ask, to adult*

aptronym
> A name that's particularly suitable to a person.
> Example: Steve *Wynn* (one-time casino owner)

back-formation
> A word derived from a different part of speech.
> Example: *Taser > to tase*

backronym
> An acronym created in order to form a word.
> Example: *SAD (seasonal affective disorder)*

calque
> A concept-for-concept translation from another language.
> Example: *Übermensch* (German) translated as *superman*

capitonym
> Two words distinguished only by a capital letter.
> Example: *polish/Polish*

clipping

Cutting off a part of a word to form a new one.
Example: *robot* > *bot*

collocation

Words that are often used together.
Example: *crystal clear*, *commit a crime*

contronym

A word with two opposite meanings.
Example: *to seed* (to plant seeds, to remove seeds)

cranberry morpheme

A particle that distinguishes a word but doesn't have inherent meaning.
Example: **huckleberry**

cutthroat compound

A descriptive word made up of verb + noun.
Example: *turncoat*

demonym

The name for people who live in a particular place.
Example: *Seattleite*

eponym

A word based on someone's name.
Example: **diesel** *engine*

flat adverb

An adverb without *ly*.
Example: *Drive* **slow**

fossil word

A word that has died out but still exists in stock phrases.
Example: *short* **shrift**

genericization

Turning a brand name into a generic word.
Example: *laundromat, dumpster*

heteronym

Words with the same spelling but different pronunciations and meanings.
Example: *permit* (verb), *permit* (noun)

homonym
A word with multiple different meanings, all pronounced the same way.
Example: *bear* (to carry; the animal)

homophone
Words that sound the same but are spelled differently and have different meanings.
Example: *nun, none*

hypercorrection
Using a word incorrectly in an attempt to sound formal.
Example: ***Whom*** *shall I say is calling?*

hypernym, hyponym
A superclass or subclass.
Example: *mammal < > dog< > German shepherd*

hypocorism
A shortened or pet name.
Example: *Michael > Mike > Mikey, barbeque > barbie*

Infix, tmesis
Inserting an element inside a word.
Example: *brand-**spanking**-new*

libfix
A word particle that has detached from a word and can be used to form new words.
Example: *gate* (for "scandal") from *Watergate*

malapropism
Using a word incorrectly (often in a funny way).
Example: *Just a **pigment** of your imagination*

misle
A word that's misinterpreted by reading it wrong.
Example: *coworker = cow + orker*

mononym
A single name for a famous person.
Example: *Oprah*

mountweazel

A fake term in a dictionary or other reference work that's included to catch copyright violators.

Example: The word *esquivalience* is an invented word that appeared in only one dictionary.

negative polarity item (NPI)

Terms that are normally used only in negative constructions.

Example: *don't care **anymore***

nonce word

A word invented for one-time use.

Example: *pompatous*

numeronym

A word made up from or containing numbers.

Example: *K-9, gr8t*

orphan acronym

A name that was originally based on an acronym, but no longer officially is.

Example: *SAT* is no longer "scholastic aptitude test."

patronym, matronym

A family name based on a father's or mother's name.

Example: *Peterson* = son of Peter

pause filler

A sound used to fill a conversational gap.

Example: *Uh …*

plurale tantum

Words that have only a plural form.

Example: *scissors*

portmanteau word

A word created by blending other words.

Example: *emotion + icon > emoticon*

quotative *like*

Using "like" to introduce a quote.

Example: *He was, **like**, "Ew!"*

rebracketing
A change to a word based on reinterpreting its boundaries.
Example: *a napron* > *an apron*

reduplication
Repeating a word (sometimes with variation).
Example: *bye-bye, flim-flam, bagel-schmagel*

retronym
A term that has a qualifier that it did not need earlier.
Example: *acoustic guitar* (vs electric guitar)

semantic bleaching
When a word loses force.
Example: *That sucks*

semantic broadening, semantic narrowing
When a word develops a broader or narrower meaning over time.
Example: *barn* originally referred only to a place to store barley; *deer* originally meant "animal"

singular *they*
Using *they* to refer to a singular person.
Example: *Everyone should bring their own lunch*

skunked term
A term that people avoid because its usage is controversial or often confused.
Example: *bi-monthly*

syllable acronym
An acronym made from syllables instead of just letters.
Example: *sci-fi* from *science fiction*

toponym
The name for a geographic region, or a word based on a geographical name.
Example: *Seattle* (named for the chief of a local indigenous tribe); *tuxedo* (named for Tuxedo Park, NY)

unpaired word
A word that seems like it should have an opposite but doesn't.
Example: *ruthless*

Sentences and phrases

aposiopesis
> An interruption to express emotion.
> Example: *I can't even.*

attachment ambiguity
> Ambiguity based on syntax.
> Example: *I shot an elephant in my pajamas.*

biscuit conditional
> An *if* statement where the *then* clause doesn't depend on the truth of the *if* clause.
> Example: *If you're just joining us, my guest is ...*

conversational deletion
> Leaving out words at the beginning of a sentence.
> Example: *Mind if I join you?*

crash blossom
> An ambiguous headline.
> Example: *Squad Helps Dog Bite Victim*

double genitive
> An expression that contains both *of* and a possessive.
> Example: *He's a friend **of my mother's**.*

double modal
> Using two helping verbs together.
> Example: *I **might could** go.*

garden-path sentence
> A sentence that can lead readers astray due to initial ambiguity.
> Example: *Fat people eat accumulates.*

malaphor
> An idiom mashup.
> Example: *It's not rocket surgery!*

noun pile
> A noun preceded by an unwieldy number of nouns that modify it.
> Example: *Airbag malfunction safety recall follow-up notice*

personal dative
> A pronoun that looks like an indirect object but actually refers to the subject of the sentence.
> Example: *She ate **her** some lunch.*

pleonasm
> A redundant expression.
> Example: *free gift*

redundant acronym phrase
> An expression that contains an acronym plus one of the abbreviated words in the acronym.
> Example: *PIN number*

snowclone
> An expression based on the pattern of another familiar expression.
> Example: *Yes, Virginia, there is life after retirement.*

squinting modifier
> A modifier that might apply either to the word that precedes it or the one that follows.
> Example: *The man we talked to **recently** won a contest.*

tag question
> A rhetorical question at the end of a statement.
> Example: *It sure is cold, **isn't it?***

Sounds

epenthesis
> Inserting sounds to make pronunciation easier.
> Example: Example: *ath-**uh**-lete*

glottal stop
> A sound made by closing the throat.
> Example: The sound between parts of *Uh-oh!*

haplology
> Dropping a syllable that's similar to a neighboring syllable.
> Example: *authori**ta**tive > authoritive*

liquid dissimilation

Not pronouncing the letters *r* or *l* when they appear near other instances of those letters.

Example: *library* > *liberry*

metathesis

Swapping sounds in a word.

Example: *asterisk* > *asteriks*

phonesthemics

Correspondence between sound and meaning.

Example: ***bl****ast,* ***bl****izzard,* ***bl****ow,* ***bl****usters*

phonotactics

Rules about how sounds can and can't be combined in a language.

Example: In English words, a syllable can't start with the sound *pt*.

rebracketing

A change to a word based on reinterpreting its boundaries.

Example: ***a** napron* > ***an** apron*

rhotic/non-rhotic accent

Pronouncing/not pronouncing *r* as written.

Example: *car park*/*cah pahk*

syncope

Leaving out sounds (contracting).

Example: *camera* > *camra*

umlaut

a) Two dots over a letter.

b) A certain kind of vowel in German and other languages.

c) A sound change in certain words.

Examples:

a) *naïve, Blue Öyster Cult*

b) *über* (German)

c) *goose* > *geese*

uptalk

A way of saying a sentence so that it sounds like a question.

Example: *So I went to the movies yesterday? With my friends?*

Punctuation and spelling

avoidance character
Characters used to avoid offensive language.
Example: *Oh, sh**!*

bounding asterisks
Characters around a word to show it's not speech.
Example: **sigh*, [cough]*

grawlix, obscenicon
Characters used to represent strong language in comics.
Example: *#@$%*!*

greengrocer's apostrophe
An apostrophe used to mark the plural of a noun.
Example: *apple's and orange's*

heteronym
Words with the same spelling but different pronunciations and meanings.
Example: *permit* (verb), *permit* (noun)

homonym
A word with multiple different meanings, all pronounced the same way.
Example: *bear* (to carry; the animal)

homophone
Words that sound the same but are spelled differently and have different meanings.
Example: *nun; none*

International Phonetic Alphabet (IPA)
An alphabet that has exactly one symbol for each possible sound in language.
Example: *ælfəbɛt*

numeronym
A word made from or containing numbers.
Example: *K-9, gr8t*

spelling alphabet
Words that are used to sound out letters.
Example: *Alfa Bravo Charlie*

umlaut
a) Two dots over a letter.
b) A certain kind of vowel in German and other languages.
c) A sound change in certain words.

Examples:
a) *naïve, Blue Öyster Cult*
b) *über* (German)
c) *goose > geese*

Ideas

antedating
Finding a cite for a word earlier than the earliest known example.
Example: The honorific *Ms.* was in use much earlier than the 1970s.

corpus
A language database.
Example: The Corpus of Contemporary American English
(https://www.english-corpora.org/coca/)

descriptivism
Language studies that focus on analyzing and describing how native speakers use the language.
Example: Applying usage data to the question of how people understand the phrase *beg the question.*

eggcorn
A mistake that produces a similar (and often reasonable) interpretation of an expression.
Example: *Alzheimer's disease > old-timer's disease*

etymological fallacy
The idea that a word's origin dictates its meaning.
Example: "*Decimate* can only mean 'reduce by one-tenth.'"

etymythology
A false word history.
Example: "*Posh* comes from 'port outward, starboard home.'"

familect
The private slang in a family.
Example: Your family's word for the TV remote or for a favorite meal.

folk etymology
Adapting an unfamiliar or foreign term into something more English-like.
Example: *crevisse* (French) > *crayfish*

hapax legomenon
A word that appears only once in a language or a text.
Example: The word *snowcrie* appears only one time in all Old English texts.

hypercorrection
Using a word or pronunciation incorrectly in an attempt to sound formal.
Example: ***Whom** shall I say is calling?*

minced oath
A euphemism for a swear.
Example: *goddamn > goll durn*

mondegreen
Misheard song lyrics.
Example: *'Scuse me while I kiss this guy*

Muphry's Law
The proposition that any language correction will itself contain mistakes.
Example: Writing a tweet that has a typo while mocking someone's grammar.

onomastics
The study of proper names.
Example: Studying the changing popularity of baby names.

pedant's veto
An objection to usage that's so strident that people avoid that usage.
Example: People object so much to *comprised of* that some style guides recommended avoiding *comprise* altogether.

pejoration
When a term that once was neutral becomes taboo.
Example: *toilet*

phatic communication
Communication for social purposes.
Example: *'sup?*

polysemy
The notion that words can have multiple meanings.
Example: *mole* (an animal; a spy)

prescriptivism
> Language studies that focus on recommending effective usage.
> Example: "Is it better to write *eat healthy* or *eat healthily*?"

recency illusion
> The idea that a word or usage originated recently when it didn't.
> Example: Claiming that people only recently started using *can* to mean permission instead of *may*. (*Can I go out tonight?*)

Scunthorpe problem
> Incorrectly filtering offensive language out of names, email addresses, URLs, etc.
> Example: AOL thought it detected profanity in the town name *Scunthorpe*.

semantic bleaching
> When a word loses force.
> Example: *that **sucks***

semantic broadening, semantic narrowing
> When a word develops a broader or narrower meaning over time.
> Example: *barn* (originally referred only to a place to store barley); *deer* (originally just meant "animal")

shibboleth
> A pronunciation or usage that marks someone as in or out of a group.
> Example: People who mispronounce the city name *Puyallup* mark themselves as not from Washington state.

skunked term
> A term writers avoid because its usage is controversial or often confused.
> Example: *bi-monthly*

word aversion
> An irrational distaste for certain words.
> Example: Aversion to the word *moist*.

zombie rule
> A grammar "rule" that isn't real but seems to be impossible to kill.
> Example: "Don't end a sentence with a preposition."

Good resources

Congratulations for getting through all those words. I hope I've piqued your interest in language and in words to describe it. (Or if I wanted to use an eggcorn, that I "peaked" your interest.)

In this section I'm providing a roundup of the language-y places I visit regularly and, frankly, from which I've learned most of what you've read here. These are all for general readers, with one or two exceptions as noted.

- *Arnold Zwicky's blog* (https://arnoldzwicky.org/), "A blog mostly about language." Over a very long career in linguistics, Arnold Zwicky has been interested in, and written about, a vast range of language-related phenomena. He blogs prolifically, although do note the word *mostly* in "A blog mostly about language"—he also writes about other topics, including some that are *definitely* only for adults.
- *Arrant Pedantry* (https://www.arrantpedantry.com/). A blog by the editor and linguist Jonathon Owen. He doesn't update it frequently, but the posts are deep dives into linguistics-informed usage questions.
- *Atlas Obscura* (https://www.atlasobscura.com/), especially the language-related articles by Dan Nosowitz.
- *Fritinancy* (https://nancyfriedman.typepad.com/away_with_words/). Nancy Friedman is a specialist in product naming, but she also writes about a wide variety of language topics.
- *Grammar Girl: Quick and Dirty Tips* (https://www.quickanddirtytips.com/grammar-girl). A blog and podcast by the writer and editor Mignon Fogarty (known as Grammar Girl) with regular features about usage. Many of the contributions are by linguistically minded usage experts.
- *Language Log* (http://languagelog.ldc.upenn.edu/). The premier blog of the linguistics community, with frequent contributions from over a dozen senior linguists. The entries can get technical, but that's offset by the number and variety of topics—if one thing doesn't interest you, something else might. This is also a

blog where the discussion in the comments is usually worth following.

- *Literal-Minded* (https://literalminded.wordpress.com/). In this blog, the linguist Neal Whitman uses personal experiences (for example, things his kids have said) to explore language.
- *Mental Floss* (https://www.mentalfloss.com/). I particularly like the pieces by Arika Orent.
- *Online Etymology Dictionary* (https://www.etymonline.com/). A concise way to look into the history of English words.
- *Sentence first* (https://stancarey.wordpress.com/). A blog by the extremely level-headed editor Stan Carey, about "usage, grammar, styles, literature, history, and quirks."
- *Strong Language*, "A sweary blog about swearing." (https://stronglang.wordpress.com/) When they say strong language, they are not f*cking around.
- *World Wide Words* (http://worldwidewords.org/). This site by Michael Quinion is an outstanding resource for the history of words and expressions. Quinion has retired, but the site is still a rich source of wordy goodness.
- *Yale Grammatical Diversity Project: English in North America* (http://microsyntax.sites.yale.edu/phenomena). This site discusses investigations into nonstandard English such as double modals (*I might could go*), personal dative (*They ate them some lunch*), and others. The site is a bit academic, but the write-ups on individual phenomena are great.

If you like podcasts, I can also recommend these:

- *The Allusionist* (https://www.theallusionist.org/). Helen Zaltzman explores what words mean and where they came from.
- *Because Language* (https://becauselanguage.com/). Highly entertaining and accessible discussions about a wide-ranging set of language topics.
- *The History of English Podcast* (https://historyofenglishpodcast.com/). Kevin Stroud does a deep dive on the many twists and turns that our language has gone through.

- *Lingthusiasm* (https://lingthusiasm.com/). Gretchen McCulloch and Lauren Gawne explain linguistic phenomena. They are not kidding about the *thusiasm* part. McCulloch is also the author of the book *Because Internet*, a keenly insightful examination of how language works in the 21st century.

- *Word Matters* (https://digital.nepr.net/podcasthub/word-matters/). In this podcast, three editors from Merriam-Webster talk about the meaning and history of words.

There are *tons* more sites as well. There are dozens more blogs and podcasts. And I'm not including paywalled content, like Ben Zimmer's *Word on the Street* language columns in the *Wall Street Journal*.

I also learn a lot by following "linguist Twitter." This includes a lot of people; you can start by looking for the #linguistics hashtag and going from there.

Acknowledgments

Over the years I've been inspired by and gotten help from a lot of people in my efforts to write about language. You'll find some of these names cited in this book, sometimes more than once. Here's a list of folks who've been particularly inspirational to me:

- Nancy Friedman, whom I "met" through blogging (and eventually in real life), from whom I've learned a great deal about naming and about words generally.
- Ben Zimmer, Jedi-level word person. Many years ago Ben pulled me into the world of people who write about words.
- Arnold Zwicky, a linguist who for decades has generously shared his vast and deep knowledge of language, and who has a knack for coming up with great word terms.
- Gretchen McCulloch, internet linguist and ling-thusiast, from whom I've learned many things, including that the story comes first.
- Tim Stewart, fellow word enthusiast, with whom I had some great discussions about a number of these entries.
- Professor Joe Voyles, from whom I took classes at the University of Washington in subjects like Germanic dialects and Gothic (the language). If anyone could make you interested in the seven classes of Germanic strong verbs, it was Professor Voyles.
- Professor Charles Smith, from whom I took English literature and who gave me my introduction to linguistics at Colorado State University. It's been more than 40 years, but I remember a funny discussion about epenthesis in one of his classes ("Math-*e*-matics. Wait, no").

Several people helped me while I was drafting this book. Tom Dykstra, Karen Burns, Emma Pinti, and Stan McKenzie read early versions and gave me great feedback. I'm particularly grateful to Nancy Friedman for her thorough read and sharp eye. Danielle Dalton, Tim Stewart, and Handan Selamoglu all provided feedback on bits and pieces that I asked them about. ("Here, read this and tell me what you think!")

Acknowledgments

Many thanks to Ryan North for letting me use some of his awesome Dinosaur Comics (www.qwantz.com) for this book! (In the entries for eggcorn and minced oath.)

Even though I'm an editor (or maybe *especially* because I'm an editor), I'm particularly grateful to my editor, Ruth Owen, who went way beyond my expectations with her edits, questions, and comments. Any issues you find in the book are probably because I didn't listen to her enough.

And finally there's my wife, Sarah, who lived with this work for years, who supported it enthusiastically, who attentively sat through readings of it, who sat across from me at many pubs and coffee shops while we both worked on our respective projects, and who kept encouraging me through all phases of its creation. This book wouldn't exist if she hadn't helped me make it happen.

About me

You might be wondering what makes me qualified to be writing about all this language stuff, anyway. A fair question!

I'm not a professional linguist. As I note a few times in the book, I'm an editor who lives in the Seattle area. I've worked as a technical writer and technical editor in the software industry for more than 35 years. That experience has given me broad exposure to language and usage issues. Back when I was in school, I studied Germanics (as they called it), which included taking classes in German, of course, and in various antique languages like Old English/Anglo Saxon, Middle English, Middle High German, and Gothic. Fun times. While I was doing that, I also took classes in linguistics. After I got out of school, I studied Spanish for some years, and I've dabbled in Latin.

But really, such expertise as I have is a result of having a keen interest in language, both in my professional life and as an amateur (from Latin *amātor*, "lover"). As you can probably tell from the people I cite in the book, I read about language enthusiastically. For many years I've also written about words on my blog (https://mikepopewords.com/), and this book is an extension of that.

I hope you've found this information as useful and entertaining as I have!

Got feedback?

If you spot errors, have questions, disagree with my assertions, or just want to comment, you can contact me at mike@mikepope.com.